UNNATURAL SELECTION

50 Years of England Test Teams

Trevor Woolley

First published in Great Britain by
VON KRUMM PUBLISHING
21 Sackville Rd
Hove BN3 3WA
www.vonkrummpublishing.co.uk

Copyright 2015 Trevor Woolley

All rights reserved. No part of this publication may be reproduced, stored in a retrieval system, or transmitted, in any form or by any means without the prior written permission of the publisher, nor be otherwise circulated in any form of binding or cover other than that in which it is published and without a similar condition being imposed on the subsequent purchaser.

The right of Trevor Woolley to be identified as the Author of the Work has been asserted by him in accordance with the Copyright, Designs and Patents Act 1998.

A CIP record of this book is available from the British Library.

Cover and all interior graphic design by Lottie Warren

Printed and Bound in Great Britain by
CPI Group (UK) Croydon

ISBN 978-0-9567321-4-9

Contents

Introduction

Making Decisions					1

The Captains					37

Striking a Balance					89

Scoring Runs: 1962-1995				121

Scoring Runs: 1989-2014				155

Taking the Wickets – The Quicks			183

Taking the Wickets – Tweakers			215

Appendices

England Test Series 1962/3-2014
England Test Batting Averages 1962/3-2014
England Test Bowling Averages 1962/3-2014
England Players in ICC Top 20 1962-2014
Acknowledgements / Bibliography

INTRODUCTION

IN the 1960s, the Sunday announcement of the England Test side for the following Thursday's game was part of the ritual of the summer. The news bulletins on Radio 4 (and before that the BBC Home Service), usually concluded with the England twelve (and in those days it was almost always twelve) for the match beginning four days later. Waiting with eager anticipation were not only cricket followers but also prospective Test players themselves. Newspaper cricket correspondents had picked their own choice of team in articles for the Saturday and Sunday press and now they could return to their typewriters to comment on the actual selection for the Monday 'papers.

In the years since, the proliferation of media outlets has altered the formality of the announcement, the timing has become more flexible not least because Test matches no longer inevitably begin on Thursdays, and those selected (and dropped) receive the courtesy of prior knowledge through a call from the chairman of selectors. But the interest among cricket followers is no less. The press and online comment in advance of the selection, and in its wake, is probably more voluminous now than ever before. And the interest of the readership is evidenced by the amount of blogging, comment and conversation which attends the articles which appear on the web. Every cricket follower has an opinion as to who should be in the national team, and no issue generates more discussion among cricketers in pubs, clubs and cyberspace.

These debates are fuelled by the amount of data available on which to draw. Cricket is a game surrounded by statistics, but statistics from which many different conclusions can be drawn. What weight is to be placed on current runs in county cricket against previous runs in Test cricket? When is a lean spell in Test performance evidence of the inevitable temporary troughs which all players suffer, or of terminal decline? For how long does it make sense to persevere with a youngster with potential before concluding that he is not ready for cricket at the international level? Everyone can have a view, and with no 'counterfactual' available, everyone can be right. At the start of the period covered by this book, J F Kennedy was the President of the United States, Krushchev led the Soviet Union, and Harold Macmillan was the British Prime Minister. The Cuban Missile Crisis was recent history, the frontiers of Space were being probed and Britain was granting independence to its still numerous colonies. British society had not yet become permissive. It remained in the shadow of the experience of the Second World War – still deeply conscious of class, respectful of respectability and virtually monocultural.

The world of cricket, unsurprisingly, reflected the norms of the era. In England, the last 'Gentlemen' versus 'Players' fixture took place in 1962, but while the distinction between amateurs and professionals was formally abolished, the culture underlying it withered slowly. First-class cricket was governed by a private members' club – Marylebone Cricket Club – whose attitudes were traditional and conservative. Suspicious of the concept of professionalism in sport, MCC sought, at the very least, to draw its leaders, including the England captain, from the officer classes.

Cricket, in England and more generally, was much less cosmopolitan than it was to become. Only a tiny handful of cricketers not England-qualified played in the County Championship, which remained the centrepiece of the summer. There were, of course, overseas tourists each summer. But while South Africa, West Indies and of course Australia provided very serious opposition to England, New Zealand, India and Pakistan did not begin to do so until the 1970s. The entry of Sri Lanka, Bangladesh (which in any case did not exist as a separate country) and Zimbabwe to the club of Test-playing countries lay even further into the future. England did not tour overseas every winter, but when they did so, it was for several months, the tours comprising numerous provincial and 'up country' games (to show the flag) as well as Test matches.

All this meant that selectors operated in a very different environment in the 1960s. Leading players were excused from overseas tours to the less strong Test-playing countries, many finding more financially-rewarding or enjoyable ways of spending their winters. Even in England, the selectors indulged in a degree of experimentation in selecting sides against New Zealand, India and Pakistan. One-day internationals, which were to become a principal vehicle for assessing the readiness of young players for exposure at the highest level of the game, did not hit cricket until the 1970s.

The history of the Test selection process over the past 50 years has been one of increasing professionalisation. In the 1960s, while the objective was of course to pick sides which would be most likely to win matches (though for overseas tours, sometimes other criteria were involved), there was much less sense of the Test team being an elite, a level in the hierarchy above county cricketers. It was, paradoxically, more democratic. Barriers to entry were lower, as were barriers to exit. While there was, of course, at any one time a core of outstanding players in the side, anything between perhaps two and five spots might be regarded as up for grabs each time the selectors met. And even the outstanding players were not assured a place: as we shall see, at various times each of Fred Trueman, Colin Cowdrey, Ken Barrington, Geoff Boycott and John Snow were dropped on the basis of quite flimsy evidence. Virtually all of the staffs of the then 17 counties were regarded as in the frame for selection, and exceptional one-off performances, especially if in the chance presence of a selector, could propel a player into the England side. Occasionally, as with Bob Barber in 1964, such left-field decisions could prove shrewd, but more usually they did not. Thus the regime encouraged turbulence. Class players could find themselves supplanted by lesser ones, while players like Keith Fletcher and Dennis Amiss, who went on to become very successful, had their early careers undermined by being repeatedly selected then dropped without being able to establish themselves.

In general, selection became more stable as the 70s went on. But between 1970 and 2001, there were 11 home seasons when more than 20 players appeared in a series for England – five of them in the six summers when the great West Indies teams of 1976-95 were the visitors, another three in the four summers when the great Australian teams from 1989 were touring. The selectors found it irresistible to react to the defeats to which

England was repeatedly subject by making changes to the side, even though the real problem was not the choice of the particular 11 who had lost, but that there were not at the time 11 England-qualified players good enough consistently to overcome such formidable opponents. The relative paucity of talent with which the selectors have had to work is indicated by looking at the top 30 Test-career batting and top 20 Test-career bowling averages of players from all countries who played in the period under analysis (and at least 25 Tests in total). English players are represented among the batsmen only by Ken Barrington, and the bowlers only by Fred Trueman. No England player since 1968 features. By contrast, Australia have eight batting and three bowling entries, and the West Indies five batting and six bowling entries. Averages are not everything, but the reality is that over the last 50 years, England have had very few truly outstanding players. In looking at the shape of the selectors' bricks, we should be mindful of the quality of their straw.

That is not to say that striving to improve the composition of the team was pointless. Occasionally players became mentally spent in the face of repeated failure, and young players on the county circuit regularly emerged as potential Test players. But it was asking a lot of a player to make his debut in these circumstances. In those eight summers against West Indies and Australia, 32 players made their debuts, of whom only Peter Such (1993), Graham Thorpe (1993) and Dominic Cork (1995) made a real impact in their first series – though another five (Mike Selvey, Chris Broad, Robin Smith, Angus Fraser and Richard Ellison) made respectable contributions. The other 24 were failures in terms of the series in which they were picked, and only seven went on to have substantial Test careers.

The innovation of 'A' Team tours in the 1990s, and central contracts from 2000, has made Test selection more structured. They have served to narrow the field in which the selectors have looked for players, and to some extent have de-risked new selections because successful 'A' team graduates have demonstrated their abilities at representative level. Of course, not all of those who have done well on 'A' Tours have reproduced that success at Test level, but it has been a much more accurate indicator of international potential than simple county form. Of some 25 players picked for England in the last two decades without 'A' Tour experience, only Matthew Hoggard, Paul Collingwood (whose Test selection came on the back of extensive one-day international experience) and, to a lesser extent, Geraint Jones have gone on to become fixtures in the England team.

Thus selectors in recent years have felt more confident in being less fickle, and that has almost certainly led to better choices. But it has not eliminated selectors becoming hyper-active when the England team has been under the cosh. Against Australia in 2001, for example, England chose 19 players over the course of five Tests, and made a total of 11 changes (though four were injury-driven). In Australia in 2013/4, 18 players were picked, more than in any away series ever. Once the selectors had recoiled from the shock of the loss of three key players (Jonathan Trott, Graeme Swann and Kevin Pietersen – the latter, of course, a self-imposed shock) they regained their cool, and just 14 players represented England in the seven Tests of the summer of 2014.

And yet, for all that has changed over 50 years, the principles of picking a cricket team have remained the same. There is a need for a captain to lead the team – perhaps drawn from among the best available 11 players, perhaps from beyond. The team needs to be balanced – ideally five batsmen, four bowlers, an all-rounder and a wicket-keeper. But throughout this half-century the problem which dominated was the absence for more than half the time of a Tony Greig, an Ian Botham or an Andrew Flintoff. This left the number-six position to be filled by a specialist batsman, taking risk on the fifth bowler, or by someone with both batting and bowling skills but below Test-class in both – the 'bits and pieces' player. Perennially, the trade-off between a wicket-keeper's glovework and batting needed to be considered. And among the bowlers, how many spinners were required? In the 1960s in England, with pitches exposed to the rain after the match had started, selectors were more inclined to pick two spinners, even in a four-man bowling attack. With changes in the ground-covering regulations in the 70s, that balance became much rarer.

The composition and balance of the team is important but without genuinely top-class players it is always a matter of seeking to punch above weight. The perception that a team cannot be great without a genuine all-rounder is simply a fallacy. Neither of the great sides of recent years had one – they would have been even better with one, but Viv Richards and Steve Waugh were lucky enough to lead a group of players, particularly bowlers, of such exceptional abilities that the normal balance was unnecessary.

This book seeks to tell the story of how the England Test side has been picked over the last 50 years. It does not attempt, primarily, to mark the selectors' cards – though it is impossible to avoid personal views, both positive and negative, about some of the decisions which have been made. Rather, it seeks to explain why the choices were as they were: what was the rationale for the selections made, and the context which gave rise to them. Of course, it is only at the margins of the team (or touring party) that decisions are contentious. What is, to me, most interesting about such decisions is the multiplicity of factors which in different cases have come into play; and the logic chains which have led to the preference of one player over another.

The book begins by looking at the decision-making process for selection, and the structures in place to assist those decisions. Subsequent chapters trace the history over the last 50 years of the selection of captains, all-rounders (including wicket-keepers), batsmen, faster bowlers and slow bowlers. Like all history, categorisation in this way is an attempt to place order on chaos: in reality, many selection decisions in one category were influenced or determined by those made in others. The very complexity of selection is at the heart of its fascination.

All the data in this book is current as at the end of 2014.

CHAPTER ONE

MAKING DECISIONS

Panels, Committees and Managers

UNUSUALLY for an international sports team, the responsibility for the selection of England Test teams has always been vested in a committee, rather than an individual. Partly, this reflects the absence, until the late 1980s, of the appointment of team manager – although even with the creation of such a role, decision making has continued to be collective. Partly it reflects the fact that until 1969, the governing body for English cricket was a private members club, the Marylebone Cricket Club (MCC), run on traditional committee lines. For most of the last 50 years, there has been a Test Selection Panel, typically comprising a chairman, up to three other selectors, the captain (once he had been chosen) and, from 1987, the team manager. At the start of our period, the Selection Panel was appointed by MCC and for home Tests, the Selection Panel appointed the captain. In 1968, MCC surrendered its role as England cricket's governing body. A 'Cricket Council' (initially called the 'MCC Council') was established to oversee all cricket, with a 'Test and County Cricket Board' (TCCB) created to supervise first-class cricket. Although many of the MCC's officers transferred to roles on the Council and the TCCB, the moves represented a shift in influence from MCC to the counties. As far as Test selection was concerned, the counties were now responsible for electing the selectors including the chairman, though for some years they went along with the proposals of the executive.

The writ of the Selection Panel, however, was constrained when it came to the selection of squads for tours overseas. Until 1977/8 England toured under the title of MCC, only adopting the name 'England' for the Tests themselves, despite the creation of the TCCB a decade earlier. In a quasi-colonial throwback, MCC continued to see the role of its touring parties as in a significant degree ambassadorial, and consequently required, particularly in the captain, qualities which were not necessarily

Making Decisions

needed for an England captain in England. *The Times'* cricket correspondent, commenting on the candidates passed over for the captaincy for the 1964/5 tour to South Africa, hinted at this thinking in writing somewhat condescendingly '[Brian] Close, one of the best tactical captains among the counties, might have found the burden of leading a side on tour rather much'. In governance terms, the consequence was that MCC appointed a tour sub-committee to choose the touring captain, and then, with the addition of the captain, subsequently the touring party. The sub-committee typically comprised the home selectors, the tour manager, and a senior member of MCC – often the *eminence grise* of MCC in the 50s, 60s and 70s, Gubby Allen. And the decisions of the sub-committee were subject to endorsement by the full MCC Committee. The different sources of authority for choosing England sides at home and overseas had the potential to create absurdity, and it created a crisis most obviously over the selection of Colin Cowdrey ahead of Brian Close to lead England in the West Indies in 1967/8, when MCC overruled the home selectors. Even when power formally passed to the TCCB, officials from MCC committees would augment the selectors in picking touring parties. Gubby Allen was on the committee which picked the 1974/5 touring party, for example; and Ray Illingworth believes that in his role as a leading member of the Cricket Council, Allen was influential in persuading the home selectors to appoint Mike Denness to replace him as England captain for the tour to the West Indies in 1973/4. The pattern continued through the 1980s, with the chair of the Cricket Council and the chair of the TCCB's Cricket Committee, as well as the tour manager, typically attending or being represented at tour-selection meetings.

Perhaps paradoxically, when it came to the selection of sides from the touring party for individual Test matches overseas, power was more concentrated. Although tour committees would be appointed – comprising manager, captain, vice-captain and perhaps two other senior players – to oversee a variety of matters, selection decisions effectively rested with the captain (or, later, the captain and team manager jointly). The arrangement was not considered to be controversial until 2006/7.

Nevertheless, the chairman of selectors has been the single figure of greatest importance to the selection of the England cricket team for most of the last 50 years, and at times his appointment has generated as much debate as that of the players themselves. Normally a former Test player, and a graduate of the Panel, there have been nine such appointments

Unnatural Selection

since 1962. Walter Robins, a former leg spinner, who played 19 Tests for England between 1929 and 1937, was chairman of selectors from 1962 to 1964. Described by Ted Dexter as 'a man of strange moods and unintelligible behaviour', he was a proselytiser of 'brighter cricket'. 'Play aggressively at all times or you will not be selected for England' was his ultimatum to first-class cricketers when he was appointed. An example of his thinking was evident when, as tour manager of the England team in the West Indies in 1959/60, he pressed for England to set their opponents a sporting target in the last innings of the final Test. England were 1-0 up in the series, and unsurprisingly their captain, Cowdrey (standing in for Peter May, who had returned home ill), was not prepared to risk defeat on the last day when England had little prospect of bowling West Indies out. Robins was unimpressed, and admonished Cowdrey in front of the team. Writing in *The Cricketer* in 1967, Cowdrey said 'I was not to realise that this show of strength on my part that day was to rebound on me in the years to come'. For it was Cowdrey's misfortune that Robins was chairman when England were looking for a successor as captain to May in 1962. Robins explained that '...we do not want someone who might wait for victory to come but a leader who will take positive steps to achieve that victory. We will tell the captain that his object is to win every match as soon as possible'. Robins did not see Cowdrey as such a person. In 1964, he pressed unsuccessfully for the inclusion of the 22-year-old leg spinner, Robin Hobbs, in the England side – more, one suspects, because he was a leg spinner and therefore by definition an attacking bowler, than because of any evidence that he would be successful. No doubt he was at the forefront of the selection of Bob Barber later that summer, which was indeed to prove a resounding success.

Robins was succeeded by Doug Insole, who had played nine Tests for England in the 50s. Just 39, he was a different generation from Robins, and less mercurial. But he and his panel remained committed to the brighter cricket theme, dropping Ken Barrington and then Geoff Boycott for slow scoring. His four years as chairman will for ever be associated with the controversy over the choice of England captain for the tour to the West Indies in 1967/8, where he publicly disassociated himself from the appointment of Cowdrey; and the 'D'Oliveira Affair', on which he has kept his account of the fateful meeting to select the touring party to South Africa on the evening of 27 August 1968 resolutely private. Insole remained influential in England selection decisions for many years to

Making Decisions

come, as a cricket administrator, and as a manager on overseas tours.

The first chairman of selectors under the new TCCB was a break from tradition with the appointment of a former professional, rather than amateur, but nonetheless traditionalist, Alec Bedser. Bedser had been a selector since 1962, and was to be chairman through to the end of the 1981 season; even then he served a further four years under the chairmanship of his successor. Arguably no single individual in the last 50 years has had such an influence on England selection.

From 1982 to 1988, the chairmanship was filled by May. An outstanding Test captain from 1955 to 1961, and a selector from 1965 to 1968, he was well qualified for the role. But he struggled to establish a rapport with both the players, and an increasingly intrusive media which, during the 1980s, developed an interest in players' off field activities. This culminated in the stories that precipitated Mike Gatting's downfall as captain in 1988, followed by the farcical selection of four different skippers in one series. May quit at a very low point in selectorial history.

The mechanics of the selection process underwent a significant change for the start of the 1989 season. The selection committee was replaced by a new 'England' committee, with wider responsibilities than just Test selection. These were to include all matters involving national teams, down to age-group level. The England committee was responsible for appointing the captain, and thereafter a sub-committee, comprising just the chairman, the team manager and the captain, would be responsible for the selection of the England side for both home and overseas Tests. The TCCB, however, empowered the chairman of its Cricket Committee (a member of the England committee but not the selection sub-committee), at the time Ossie Wheatley, with a right of veto in England committee decisions. As we shall see, the veto was used at just about the first opportunity. From now on, in theory at least, the England captain was appointed by a broader, or different, body from the selection committee. Authority lay with the England Committee, and it met in 1993 to appoint Mike Atherton as Graham Gooch's successor. In 1997 and 1999, the chairman of the new England and Wales Cricket Board and the chairman of selectors jointly interviewed two candidates. The mid-series resignation of Nasser Hussain in 2003 left little opportunity for formal interviews, and in any case there was only one candidate – Michael Vaughan: the decision was taken by the chairman and coach. By

2006, the responsibility for appointing England captains seems to have returned at least in practice to the selection committee.

The post of team manager was derived from the position of assistant manager on overseas tours which Barrington and Norman Gifford had filled variously from the late 1970s. The duties of the assistant manager fell substantially short of that of coach, the role into which it eventually evolved, involving, as they did, relieving the manager of some administrative duties and helping the captain with the organisation of practices. David Gower's perceived deficiencies in this latter respect, and laissez-faire attitude towards his team, were regarded as significant contributors to England's disastrous 5-0 defeat in the West Indies in 1985/6. Hence for the 1986/7 tour to Australia, led by Gatting, Micky Stewart undertook the enhanced role of team manager, 'giving emphasis to players' fitness, practice facilities and day-to-day discipline'. Stewart was also appointed as a selector on the tour. England won the Ashes, and the new arrangements were judged to be an improvement. Thus, in 1987, Stewart was appointed 'England Team Manager', with responsibilities no longer confined to overseas tours, as 'a way of building on the success achieved in Australia during the winter and of achieving continuity'. He and his successors joined the Selection Panel for home Tests too.

The first chairman to be appointed under this dispensation was Dexter. In many ways, as a former England captain and outstanding batsman, and from the public school and Cambridge University stables, Dexter was a clone of his predecessor, though he was altogether more flamboyant and unconventional as an individual. His appointment was one which fell to the full TCCB, but it leaked out before the TCCB chairman, Raman Subba Row, had had time formally to consult the Board. While there is no reason to imagine that the Board would not have supported Dexter, there is evidence to believe that some county chairmen resented being taken for granted about this, and this was to manifest itself a few years later. First, in 1992, Dennis Amiss was appointed by the TCCB to the panel of selectors in a first move towards restoring the status quo ante. Secondly, at the end of 1993, the TCCB agreed to re-establish the old-style selection committee, to comprise chairman, manager, two other selectors, and the captain – the first four to be elected by the members of the Board. And thirdly, when it came to elect a new chairman, the Board plumped not for the executive's

Making Decisions

preference, Mike (M J K) Smith, but for the man who stood against him, Ray Illingworth. Illingworth's choices for the other two selectors, Brian Bolus and Fred Titmus, were also elected.

Dexter's resignation in 1993 followed a familiar run of England defeats (nine in the 10 previous matches) which had also done for Gooch as captain. It was not until 1994 that the vote took place on Dexter's successor, by when England had also gone down 3-1 in the West Indies. Smith, as tour manager in the West Indies, was now tainted by failure too, and perhaps his amateur status when a player was too similar to the two previous chairmen whose reigns had not been marked by conspicuous success to recommend him to the TCCB. Illingworth was certainly the antithesis of May, Dexter and Smith: although a former (and very successful) England captain, he was a northerner from a working-class background, who had had his run-ins with the MCC establishment during his time as a player. But while the decision partly reflected a demand for a change of style, it also represented a revolt by the counties against an executive which appeared to have been diminishing their influence.

England performed respectably in 1994, but lost the Ashes again the following winter. The arrangements for managing the England team once again came under scrutiny. There was no single point of accountability: Illingworth was ultimately responsible for selecting the party which had gone to Australia, but had no authority in Australia. This rested with tour manager M J K Smith, team manager Keith Fletcher, who had succeeded Stewart, and the captain – Atherton. Although selection decisions as such had not been a big issue in Australia, Illingworth argued strongly that the responsibilities for selection and team management were inseparable. In a sense, this was a view that was ahead of its time, but in 1995 the TCCB had effectively to decide whether to stick with Illingworth or Fletcher, and they went with Illingworth, contracting him for a year in the combined role of chairman of selectors, team manager and – for the tour to South Africa, and the World Cup which followed, in 1995/6 – tour manager too.

There was much to be said, in governance terms, for an arrangement in which a single individual would (in the words of the TCCB statement announcing Illingworth's role) act as 'chairman of selectors, take on full responsibility for the England team and be accountable for its performance'. The issue was whether Illingworth, especially at 63, was the right man for the job. There were indications, not least in his very public falling out with Devon Malcolm in South Africa, of an inability to bridge the generation gap in man management. In March 1996, it seemed as if Illingworth would face an election to continue as chairman of selectors from David Graveney, the former Gloucestershire and Durham bowler. At the time Graveney was chief executive of the Professional Cricketers Association (PCA), and had been elected to the selection committee in 1995. In the end, Graveney concluded that to exercise the role of both chairman of selectors and chief executive of the PCA would give rise to insoluble conflicts of interest, and he stood down. But it was a shot across Illingworth's bows, and he stood down as team manager, citing the need for a younger man (he was replaced in this capacity by David Lloyd); and his resignation as chairman of selectors followed at the end of the 1996 season.

Illingworth's successor as chairman was Graveney (he continued to be chief executive of the PCA until 2003, presumably now taking a different view of the potential for conflicts of interest), appointed by the England Management Advisory Committee of the new England and Wales Cricket Board (ECB) which had replaced the Cricket Council and the TCCB in 1997. The new structure was designed deliberately to shift power away from the counties and focus very unapologetically on the England cricket team. Thus in 2000 'central contracts' were introduced, through which the England team manager could nominate England players to be contracted with the ECB rather than their counties, thereby enabling him to decide when they should play for their counties. Since 2000, the appearance of centrally-contracted players for their counties has become increasingly rare: even when not on international duty, players are frequently prohibited from playing for their counties in order to rest them and/or avoid the risk of injury. From 2006 a 'Development Squad' was introduced, which evolved into a 'Performance Squad' from 2007, and the 'England Performance Programme' in 2011; the ECB reserved the right to withdraw members of these squads from county games even though they were not centrally contracted. In 2008 'increment contracts' were introduced, through which the ECB made one-off payments to the players concerned in addition to their salaries from their counties. And in 2011 'potential Performance Programme' players were nominated. Meanwhile, in 2001 a National Academy was created, initially in Australia, but later at Loughborough, for the development of young players.

8 Making Decisions

The selection regime under Graveney initially matched that of Illingworth, with a committee comprising the chairman, coach, captain and two others. Duncan Fletcher, appointed England coach in 1999, represented a significant departure from his three predecessors – Stewart, Fletcher and Lloyd. A Zimbabwean, he had not played for England and was not steeped in county cricket. He brought a single mindedness to the management of the England team which did not fit comfortably with a committee approach to selection. He had an uneasy relationship with Graveney, and at times an explosive one with Rod Marsh, the former Australian wicket-keeper who, as director of the England Academy, for a time sat on the selection committee. Generally, Fletcher's view prevailed in selection, though not always. For example, Andrew Flintoff was not included in the party to tour India in 2001/2 against Fletcher's wishes, but Fletcher managed subsequently to summon him from the Academy in Australia to join the squad. In 2003 the captain ceased formally to be a member of the selection committee, though it is clear that Vaughan, Kevin Pietersen and Andrew Strauss continued to exercise influence through the coach, especially overseas, when the only member of the committee present, and involved in selection decisions, was the coach.

This was an issue on which the Schofield Report, set up to review the future of England cricket after the 5-0 defeat by Australia in the Ashes in 2006/7, focussed. Ken Schofield was critical of the team selected for the first Test of the series: England

> 'fielded a five-man bowling attack in Hoggard, Harmison, Flintoff, Anderson and Giles that had collectively bowled less overs in the immediate build-up than perhaps any in history. Giles and Anderson (save for some 11 overs in the final County Championship match) had been unable to bowl at all during the English season, whilst Flintoff had also battled serious injury following the first Sri Lanka match at Lord's. Harmison had also bowled little due to niggles leaving Matthew Hoggard as the only bowler to arrive and appear "battle-hardened"....
> The selection for the opening two Test Matches in Australia suggested those empowered – including Captain and Coach – felt a policy of sticking with those available Players who had achieved success in England some 15 months earlier – regardless it appeared of form or indeed match fitness.

> The selections of Messrs Anderson, Giles and Geraint Jones, the wicket keeper would clearly fall into this category with much being asked of them after serious injury and/or loss of form... many still feel it difficult to understand the sudden demotion of Messrs Read, Panesar and Mahmood whose efforts had appeared capable from the Team which had achieved home success against Pakistan [in the summer of 2006].'

Schofield considered that this demonstrated a weakness in governance relating to:

> 'the confusing accountability for the selection of the England team, and the variances between home and away series. The position and authority of Chairman of Selectors has been allowed to be diluted, particularly during the winter. The indifferent relationship between the current Chairman [Graveney] and the former Head Coach [Fletcher] cannot be repeated. Why is a selector not in attendance at every game England plays?'

Schofield recommended the appointment of a full time 'national selector', who would chair a panel which at home would comprise the coach – now called 'team director' – and one other selector, while overseas selection would fall to the national selector and team director, with 'executive authority for selection in case of disagreement' vested in the national selector. The team director and captain would be responsible for deciding who to omit on the day from a squad of 12 or 13 picked for a particular match; in the event of disagreement, the national selector would rule.

The ECB broadly accepted these recommendations, albeit deciding to appoint two selectors, rather than one, to sit on the new panel in addition to the national selector and team director. It invited applications for the new post of national selector, and while Graveney put his name forward, the ECB chose Geoff Miller, who took office early in 2008. Miller had played Test cricket for England in the late 70s and early 80s, and served as a selector alongside Graveney since 2001. He remained the national selector until the end of 2013, when he was replaced by James Whitaker, a former Leicestershire player with one England cap who, like Miller, graduated to his position from membership of the selection committee. Fletcher stood down as England coach in 2007, to be succeeded by Peter Moores. Moores lost his position in 2009 in the wake of Pietersen's removal from the captaincy and was replaced by Andy Flower.

Flower, another Zimbabwean, presided over England's historic run of three successive Ashes triumphs between 2009 and 2013, along with a brief occupation of the number one spot among Test-playing countries in 2011. But like Fletcher seven years before, he could not survive a 5-0 whitewash in Australia in the winter of 2013/4, and he resigned after the tour. In a development mirroring the role of the England captain, Flower had earlier stood down as England's one-day and T20 coach, on the grounds that the demands of being present at every England international outing were unsustainable – and might itself prompt his early resignation. Thus, in 2013, the job was split, with Ashley Giles, the former England spin bowler and then Warwickshire coach, taking on the role for limited-overs games. This arrangement proved controversial. Some argued that with Flower less immediately concerned about England's one-day performance, he was more inclined to insist on resting those of England's Test players who were also in the one-day squad, thus weakening the team available for Giles. Certainly the indifferent performance of England in limited-overs cricket under this regime (ODIs: won 10, lost 14; T20: won 6 lost 11) gave rise to second thoughts about its efficacy, and the split role was dispensed with 18 months after its introduction. England's performance also did little to help Giles's chances of succeeding Flower, though he remained the favourite until England's humiliating defeat by the Netherlands in the World T20 in Bangladesh in March 2014. The timing could not have been more unfortunate for Giles, as it was England's last game before the decision on Flower's successor was due to be made. In the circumstances, it would have been a brave appointments committee to have chosen Giles, even had they previously been minded to do so. So it was that Peter Moores, his nemesis Pietersen now departed from the international stage, came to be appointed to replace both Flower and Giles.

As this book went to print, further changes in the governance of the England team were being mooted in the light of the dismissal of Paul Downton as the ECB's Managing Director, England Cricket. The post, it has been announced, will be abolished, to be replaced by that of 'Director of England Cricket' – a role apparently more significantly different from that it replaces than the subtle alteration in title might suggest. It seems that the new director will be more focussed on the Test side, and more personally accountable for its performance on the Illingworth model of 1995-6. But unlike Illingworth, the director will work alongside both a coach and chairman of selectors, as well as a captain. It will be interesting to see how this arrangement manages to avoid diffusing accountability: there is a risk of ribs being bruised by elbows in the jostling of a confined space.

It is of interest to compare the records of the various chairmen in terms of the performance of the teams they selected – though it would be facile, when so many other variables were at play, to regard this as measures of their own performance as selectors:

Chairman	Tests	Won	Lost	Drawn	% Won	% Lost
Robins	33	10	5	18	30	15
Insole	38	12	6	20	32	16
Bedser	127	42	28	57	33	22
May	72	15	28	29	21	39
Dexter	45	10	21	14	22	47
Illingworth	33	8	9	16	24	27
Graveney	136	54	46	36	40	34
Miller	75	33	20	22	44	27
Whitaker	7	3	2	2	42	28

(The five Tests against the West Indies in 1993/4 are attributed to none of the chairmen as the touring party was chosen when the post was vacant.)

Balance of Power

The balance of power within the selection panel has shifted to and fro over the decades. Until 1976, the convention was that in the event of disagreement, the captain, rather than the chair of selectors, had the last word. It is remarkable, reading Cowdrey's account of the events of 1968 how, as captain, he was personally involved not merely in selection judgements, but in the mechanics of selection – phoning players to establish their fitness, and making the call to Basil D'Oliveira to report to the Oval for the final Test match despite having had no opportunity to consult the chairman. On the other hand, Denness was unsuccessful in securing the selection of John Snow for either the 1973/4 or 1974/5 tours in the face of opposition from the other selectors. Denness has written that in 1973/4 he secured 'about 85%' of the players he wanted – so maybe 13 or 14 players out of 16. But since 11 or 12 of the party were shoe-ins, it seems he had his way in only about half of the places up for debate. By contrast, Close was recalled in 1976 at Tony Greig's insistence, and in the face of opposition from the chairman – a decision which, it seems, precipitated a change in the committee's voting rules give the chairman the casting vote. Although the other selectors were not appointed by the chairman, it is likely that most of them on most issues would be more likely to go with the chairman rather than the captain – though any committee would be cautious about presenting an established captain with a team about whose composition the captain had serious reservations. But Mark Butcher, standing in for the injured Nasser Hussain in 1999, had no say in the selectors' decision to play two spinners in a home Test – a judgement about the balance of the attack which he did not share. He was consequently forced to choose to bat on winning the toss on a green wicket and remains bitter about both the undermining of his authority and the lack of support he received from the selectors after the game.

    The balance shifted back to the captain with the reduction in the selection panel to chairman, team manager and captain in 1989. Even when, in that season, the captain (David Gower) and team manager (Stewart) were not close, Gower has recorded that in selection matters he had his own way ('more or less'). And in an interview in 1989, Dexter said 'I'm not sure what, if any, veto powers I have' – a rather surprising uncertainty on his part. Thereafter, the Gooch/Stewart axis became the predominant influence on the three-man committee, and there is little evidence of Dexter imposing his views. Certainly, the repeated controversial omissions of Gower from 1989/90 to 1992/3 (see Chapter 4) appear to reflect the strong views of Stewart and Gooch, although there is no evidence that Dexter argued against them. Indeed, Gooch has suggested that Dexter directed Gower's omission from the 1989/90 squad to tour the Caribbean in order to move away from the 'champagne set' image with which Gower, Ian Botham and Allan Lamb were associated; but if this is true it is difficult not to believe that it was a view encouraged by Stewart, whose relations with Gower were famously poor. Even when the young Atherton succeeded Gooch, his was the voice which counted: for the 1993/4 tour to the West Indies – 'I had almost complete control over the selection of the squad...I got exactly the tour party I wanted'. In this instance, however, there was an interregnum between Dexter and Illingworth as chairman, and the team manager, Keith Fletcher, had only relatively recently taken over from Stewart, so no one was in a strong institutional position to gainsay the captain.

All changed with the appointment of Illingworth. The reversion to a traditional selection committee was a conscious decision of the TCCB to enhance the position of chairman, and Illingworth made it a condition of taking the job that he be given a right of veto over individual decisions. He chose not to exercise it in 1994, when Atherton argued for John Crawley ahead of Graham Thorpe, who was Illingworth's preference. But he overrode the captain in insisting on the selection of Martin McCague ahead of Angus Fraser and – depending on which of Atherton's and Illingworth's accounts you accept – of Gatting for the tour to Australia in 1994/5.

In two important areas, there was a fundamental difference of approach between Illingworth and Atherton. First, Atherton wrote that

> 'he was firmly of the opinion that it was time to plan for the future. We should draw a line under what had gone before, put an end to the selectorial merry-go-round and pick a group of young players with attitude, in whom we had faith, and move boldly forward. Keith Fletcher needed little persuading.'

Thus, for example, neither Gower nor Gatting was included in the 1993/4 tour party. The three oldest players were 30, the rest were in their 20s. Illingworth, by contrast, was more impressed by form in the County Championship than by potential. As England captain he had presided over what was probably England's oldest side of the last half century for the third Test against Australia in 1972: he and D'Oliveira were over the age of 40, M J K Smith was 39, and only two players were in their 20s: the average age was 33. The previous year, he had recalled fast bowler John Price, who had played only a handful of Tests in his prime, and was approaching his 34th birthday. As chairman of selectors, not only did he

Making Decisions

recall Gatting, but he also gave debuts to three county stalwarts at the age of 33: opening bowler Joey Benjamin, batsman Alan Wells and off spinner Mike Watkinson. Very evidently these were not choices for the future, and indeed the first two played singleton Tests, and the third just four.

The other difference was over the balance of the side. Illingworth was a strong believer in five-man bowling attacks, which had served him well as captain: in his 31 Tests as captain, he had five front-line bowlers on 28 occasions – albeit in an era when England were blessed with better all-rounders than they were in the 90s. Atherton was more inclined to the four-bowler attack, including a single spinner, which Gooch had favoured as captain. In the 11 Tests of 1993 and 1993/4 which preceded Illingworth's appointment, England fielded five bowlers on only two occasions. During Illingworth's 33 Tests as chairman, five bowlers were fielded 24 times.

Even before Illingworth's departure, the balance of power began to pass from chairman to captain. Illingworth's surrender of his supremo position (*One-Man Committee* as he titled his book of this period) with the appointment of Lloyd as team manager reduced his own authority from 1996, while his successor, Graveney, was a much more consensual figure. The criticism of him levelled by, among others, Hussain, is that he was too weak as chairman – too ready to consult and be influenced, lacking the courage of his convictions and inclined to sit on the fence. It is not difficult to conclude that the appointment of a strong-minded captain in Hussain and coach in Duncan Fletcher in 1999 created the dominant power base in the selection committee, though it took a while for this to become established. The selection of the touring party to South Africa in 1999/2000 was very much a compromise between different approaches by the captain and the other selectors. Paradoxically, perhaps, it was the selectors who pressed for root-and-branch change, while Hussain and Fletcher argued for the need to retain the established players. When Hussain ceased to be a selector in 2003, Fletcher's position became even stronger, and remained so after Vaughan took over from Hussain as captain. Fletcher's personal selection decisions on the 2006/7 tour to Australia, dropping Chris Read and Monty Panesar whom the selection committee had concluded were the right players to fill the wicket-keeping and spin-bowling positions respectively in the

Tests immediately preceding the tour, reflected the power the coach was now able to exercise in selection matters. But because England lost 5-0, precipitating the Schofield review, the exercise of that power now became regarded as part of the problem. The Schofield Report recommended, as we have seen, a rebalance of power on the selection committee. Because there is little evidence that Miller, Flower and Strauss, or Whitaker, Moores and Cook, do or have differed over selection issues, it is difficult to assess where the predominant influence in selection currently lies.

Evidence and Grounds for Selection

On what, then, do selectors base their judgements? Apart, clearly, from the performances of players in Tests, the main evidence base available to the selectors is performance in first-class cricket, principally the County Championship. Fifty years ago, this provided a mass of information from which to reach decisions. In 1963, for example, the County Championship ran to 28 matches per county. Batsmen typically had 50 first-class innings in a season (the maximum in 1963 was 60). Eight bowlers bowled more than 1000 overs in 1963 – Derek Shackleton, the Hampshire medium pacer, bowled an extraordinary 1387. Clearly the volume of first-class cricket has diminished over the years – just 16 County Championship matches per county in 2014, albeit of four rather than three days, but even in 1990 Phil Tufnell had the opportunity to bowl more than 1000 first-class overs.

The volume of first-class cricket meant that the first-class averages were statistically significant. And there was a strong correlation between performance in Test matches, and performance in county matches – especially for batsman. Of course, there have been exceptions. Graeme Hick and Mark Ramprakash were never able to repeat their outstanding county records in Tests, and Gatting was able to do so only over a small part of his career. By contrast, Gower, and to some extent Atherton, generally performed much better in Tests than in county matches once they had established themselves. For faster bowlers in particular, the correlation was a good deal less strong. Snow very consciously saved himself for Test matches, to the extent of being dropped by his county, Sussex, in his prime. So too did Bob Willis and Botham.

While County Championship performance could be an important indicator of an individual's potential to perform at Test level, the data it produced needed to be handled with care. It more obviously offered a measure of form, rather than class. It demonstrated who was scoring runs and taking wickets, but in itself offered nothing about the quality of the attack against which the runs had been scored, or the quality of the pitches on which the wickets had been taken. Both could be highly variable. And of course it said nothing about the ability of an individual who, successful in benign conditions in front of a crowd of hundreds, would react when confronted in a Test match by some of the best players in the world in the full glare of media attention.

The amount of county cricket until relatively recently made it harder for selectors to resist the temptation to tinker with the Test side. When an individual (especially one not well established) failed, or the Test team lost, there was always someone who had just scored a couple of hundreds or taken a hatful of wickets for whom a case could be made for inclusion. There was also a widely held expectation that those who performed well in the Championship somehow had a right to a Test place. It is striking in the newspaper articles speculating on whom the Test selectors might choose how often the phrase that so and so 'deserves a chance' crops up. It is as if the selectors had an obligation to reward county cricketers, rather than an obligation to select the best England side. Frequently cricket correspondents expressed pleasure at the recognition of a solid county stalwart in the Test team. It is unlikely that the selectors were themselves immune to this way of thinking and occasionally such a selection was (usually for a short period) an unmitigated success, such as in the cases of Ken Higgs, David Steele and Clive Radley.

Another danger for the selectors was the scope the championship provided for anecdotal evidence to support a selection. The presence of a selector at a particular match provided an opportunity for an individual to impress sometimes impressionable observers. For example, for the first Test match against Australia in 1964, it had been expected that 26-year-old Price would be chosen as Fred Trueman's opening bowling partner. Price had toured India the previous winter, and had taken a five-for in the third Test of that series. He had been selected to play for MCC against the Australians before the first Test, and had taken four of the only seven Australian wickets to fall in the match. But 35-year-old Jack Flavell was preferred to him – partly because of his better early-season form in the Championship, but principally, it seems, because of Dexter's own experience playing for Sussex against Flavell's Worcestershire the day before the Test side was selected. Flavell dismissed both Sussex openers and had Dexter dropped at the wicket off his first ball. Flavell played in two of the first three Tests of the summer with limited success before being replaced by Price.

An individual performance on a number of other occasions served to force the entry into the Test team of someone who had not previously been in the selectors' eye. As we shall see, Barber's century for Warwickshire against the Australians in August 1964 catapulted him into the England side for the final Test of the series. In 1976, Close's 88 and 40 for Somerset against the West Indies led to his recall to the Test team at the age of 46. That he had not been considered to be in the frame before this match is evidenced by the fact that he scored these runs while a formal 'Test trial' was being played, to which he had not been invited.

In the 1980s, performances in the end-of-season domestic 60-over competition final could influence decisions. In 1980, Botham, England captain and Man of the Match adjudicator, described the 50 not out scored by Roland Butcher for Middlesex against Surrey as 'one of the most exciting Gillette Cup innings I have seen'. Butcher had played a one-day international against the West Indies, and made 52, a fortnight before, but he was not regarded as a strong England prospect, having had an unspectacular season in county cricket. His selection for the winter tour to the West Indies which followed appears to have been determined by these two one-day performances at the end of the season. For the final Test of 1981, Wayne Larkins replaced Gooch in the England side with a place as third opener (behind Boycott and Gooch) on the winter tour to India at stake. Larkins made 34 and 24. As chance would have it, Larkins was opening the batting with Geoff Cook for Northamptonshire in the final of the season's NatWest Trophy (NatWest had replaced Gillette as sponsor) a few days later. Cook made 111, Larkins 51. Three days later, England's side for the tour to India was chosen, and Cook was picked ahead of Larkins. True, Mike Brearley, England's captain in the summer of 1981 would have been involved in selecting the team for the sixth Test, and Fletcher, England's captain for the winter, would have been a party to the selection of the touring team to India. But all that had changed to promote Cook ahead of Larkins as the next opening batsman cab on the rank was their respective performances in the NatWest final. Christopher Cowdrey's 58 in a losing cause for Kent in the 1984 final is likely to have helped his cause when the touring party to India for the following winter was picked, though in this case there is no reason to believe that it was decisive.

Recognising the limitations of the County Championship as an indicator of Test ability, the selectors looked for other opportunities to trial candidates for national recognition in more demanding circumstances. Until 1985, a mix of actual and potential Test players was selected to play for MCC against the tourists in May, a week or so prior to the selection of the side for the first Test of the summer. Success or failure in this fixture was not decisive in Test selection, but it could be influential at the margins. In 1966, for example, M J K Smith's 140 against the West Indies assured him of his place for the first Test – although this was to be his last as captain. Wicket-keeper John Murray also scored a century, and whilst it did not precipitate an immediate recall, it probably influenced his return to the Test side at the end of the summer. Colin Milburn's aggressive 64 helped to secure his debut for the first Test, especially as a rival, John Edrich, who had been in the Test side during the winter of 1965/6, made two low scores. In 1975, the young Gooch made a belligerent 75 for MCC against Australia, and made his England debut at the age of 20 for the first Test which followed: it is doubtful that the selectors would have chosen someone so young to face up to Lillee and Thomson without collateral of this sort. In 1985, cricketer at the opposite end of his career was selected to play for MCC against Australia – Derek Underwood, by then 40 years old. Banned from playing for England from 1982 until 1985 because of his participation in the rebel South Africa tour of 1982, he continued to be arguably the best slow bowler in county cricket. A strong performance against Australia could have led to an England recall, but his match figures were 1-96, and he did not play for England again.

In 1973, 1974 and 1976 England staged formal 'Test trials' between sides ostensibly representing the best 22 players in England. The 1973 fixture was interesting as the England captaincy was at stake – Tony Lewis captaining the MCC Tour Xl (to India and Pakistan the previous winter) against the Rest captained by Illingworth (England's captain in 1972). The 1974 match was significant for the runs scored by Edrich, 106 and

Unnatural Selection

95, which resulted in his recall after two years outside the England side; and for what the 1975 *Wisden* described as 'the shocking opening from Snow and [John] Lever in which the shine was lost with Boycott and Amiss hardly needing to lay bat on the ball'. Snow had been dropped controversially from the side which toured the West Indies in 1973/4, and this was a missed opportunity to prove his critics wrong. The 1976 fixture was significant because of the selection of someone (Close) for the first Test who had not made it into the 22 for the trial. This rather undermined the rationale for the match, and, perhaps for this reason, it was not repeated.

In the absence of a Test trial, one option was to trial players in Tests themselves. The 1962 series against a weak Pakistan side was considered by the selectors to be an extended trial for the winter's tour to Australia (including of the potential captains). All 17 of those who went on to tour the Antipodes played at least one Test in 1962. So uncompetitive was the Pakistan side, however, that it is doubtful whether the selectors learned much of value.

In the late 1970s and into the 1980s, the selectors frequently experimented by choosing a candidate for the winter touring party to play in the last Test of the series, particularly when England had already won the series (a strictly limiting criterion). Selection in these circumstances was frequently a poisoned chalice. In 1979, for example, both Alan Butcher and David Bairstow were selected for the last Test of the series against India. Bairstow went on to be selected for the 1979/80 tour; Butcher made 14 and 20, was passed over in favour of Larkins (who had not previously played Test cricket) and never played another Test. Larkins, the beneficiary in 1979, was, as we have seen, the loser in 1981, when in similar circumstances he played in the final Test but was omitted in favour of Cook for the winter tour. Paul Parker was also picked for the final Test of the 1981 series, scoring 0 and 13, but never played again. Neil Williams was brought in as an opening bowler for his debut for the final Test in 1990, took 2-148, and that was his Test career. Martin Bicknell, who had not played Test cricket, was preferred to him for the 1990/1 tour. Others, of course, who made their debuts in the final Test of a series as an 'experiment' did go on the overseas tour which followed: John Emburey in 1978; Graeme Fowler and Vic Marks in 1980. In 1988 the selectors used the singleton England v Sri Lanka Test as a Test trial, and gave debuts to Kim Barnett, Dave Lawrence, Phil

Making Decisions

Newport and Jack Russell – all of whom were selected for the tour to India the following winter which was subsequently cancelled.

It is difficult to understand the logic of this approach. One Test was surely insufficient evidence on which to reach a conclusion as to the relative merit of two candidates for one place – especially if the other was not playing. Selecting Butcher *and* Larkins in 1979, or Larkins *and* Cook in 1981, or Williams *and* Bicknell in 1990 might just have been interesting – although had that happened the selectors would virtually have committed themselves to selecting the one of the two to have performed better in a single match. But to select one, as being the next best of their type available, and then reverse that call on the basis of the performance of just one of the candidates in a single match, seems arbitrary. As for Parker, there was never going to be a position for him as a middle-order batsman on the tour to India which followed (Fletcher was captain, and Gower, Gatting and Chris Tavare, all established in 1981, would fill the other three places), so his selection for the final Test of the series seems particularly pointless. There was perhaps more of a case for using a Test match which did not need to be won to give experience to a player who had not played Test cricket but was assured of a place on the tour to follow – but that is a different matter.

If all this sounds like something out of a different historical era, it is worth recalling that England arguably returned to experimentation with the team for the final Test against Australia in 2013, the series already having been won. The selection decisions for this match were precipitated by an injury to Tim Bresnan, who had been included as part of a four-man bowling attack, alongside James Anderson, Stuart Broad, and Graeme Swann, in each of the previous three Tests. The conventional choice would have been to have replaced Bresnan with another quick bowler – with Chris Tremlett regarded as the next in line, and indeed included in the squad for the Oval. But England were keen to play Simon Kerrigan, the uncapped slow left armer: partly because they thought the Oval pitch might justify a second spinner (though England had last played two specialist spinners in a home Test in 2009 – and that had not proved to be a success); but partly, it seems, to try out Kerrigan with the position of reserve spinner for the back-to-back tour to Australia vacant given the demise of Monty Panesar. Because, however, England could not contemplate going into a Test match without a third seamer (especially in view of Kerrigan's unproven abilities), it was necessary to drop a batsman (Jonny Bairstow) to include a fifth bowler. And while Tremlett was the next best third seamer, because he (and Kerrigan) were limited batsmen, they chose the Warwickshire all-rounder Chris Woakes to fill this role. It is difficult, at least in retrospect, not to think that both England's batting and bowling attack would have been stronger had Tremlett simply replaced Bresnan, and just one spinner played; and that had the series been at stake, that would indeed have been the selection.

A variation on the theme of experimentation occurred in 2012 when, with England 2-0 up in the three-Test series against the West Indies, England 'rested' their two opening bowlers – Jimmy Anderson and Stuart Broad. There were those who took the view that with the advent of central contracts, international cricketers played far less than their predecessors anyway, and that England should pick their strongest team at all times. A secondary reason was to compare the three players competing for the third seamer spot in the side – Tim Bresnan, Steven Finn and Graham Onions – in, as it were, controlled conditions. The value of the experiment was constrained by the weather, which limited the match to two days. Though none of the three produced outstanding results, the consensus of most observers was that Onions had bowled best of the three. It did not, however, lead to his selection in the three Tests which followed.

From the 1970s, a new source of evidence on which the selectors could draw in assessing players for Test cricket emerged in the form of the one-day international. Over the decades, the extent to which one-day teams have mirrored the Test team, and the extent to which they have been filled by one-day specialists, has ebbed and flowed. Generally, players who have played a substantial number of Tests have played a substantial number of one-day games, and vice versa. In the era of one-day internationals, only Mark Butcher has played more than 10 Tests (in fact 71) without playing in a one-day international. Plenty of one-day international players have not played Test cricket, of whom the most notable are Vikram Solanki (51 ODIs), Luke Wright (50) and Craig Kieswetter (46). It was Solanki's misfortune to be competing for a Test opening position in the era of Atherton, Marcus Trescothick, Vaughan and Strauss. Kieswetter was matched against Matt Prior (a mystery of the last five years is why Prior has been unable to replicate successfully his explosive batting in Tests in the one-day form of the game). As for

Wright, he is the classic one day 'bits and pieces' cricketer, whom the selectors judged insufficiently good as a batsman or bowler for Test cricket (though he toured South Africa and then Bangladesh as part of the Test squad in 2009/10). Many one-day internationals who did not play Test cricket were of this type, and not credible contenders for Test cricket. But there were a few specialist batsmen, bowlers and wicket-keepers who might have been given Test opportunities had they not failed to impress in their one-day performances: examples are Geoff Humpage (wicket-keeper), Monty Lynch (batsman), Mal Loye (batsman), Ed Joyce (opening batsman) and Joe Denly (opening batsman). Two other one-day specialists, Neil Fairbrother (75 ODIs) and Nick Knight (100) played in just a handful of Tests. Interestingly, Knight developed into a one-day specialist even though his Test debut preceded his one-day debut by a year.

Many players played Test cricket before they played one-day internationals, and many made their debut in both forms of the game in the same summer or tour. In these cases, clearly, performance in the limited-over matches was not an influence on Test selection. Others progressed to the Test team on the back of impressing in one-day internationals. Examples of this were Ben Hollioake in 1997, Trescothick in 2000, Strauss in 2004, and – most strikingly – Pietersen in 2005, all of whose Test debuts followed closely on the back of their one-day debuts. In the last three of these cases, it is likely that the players would have made their Test debuts around the time they did regardless of their one-day performances, but the evidence derived from the one-day games probably accelerated their advancement. Hollioake, who at 19 was England's youngest debutant since Brian Close in 1949, was picked on the basis of a single ODI innings – 63 in 48 balls – in his only ODI match. In some ways, the selection was reminiscent of Barber's in 1964, though in Hollioake's case, England played four Tests between his eye-catching innings and his Test appearance (and, alas, the innings was less portentous). In 2014, Jos Buttler did not start the season as Prior's obvious heir apparent in the Test team, but his 121 off 102 balls against Sri Lanka in a one-day international at the start of the season was probably the crucial factor in seeing off potential rivals when the wicket-keeping spot fell vacant.

Graeme Swann forced his way into the Test team on the back of a rather more sustained run of success in 14 one-day matches over the previous year. In other cases, the selectors took longer to conclude that one-day performance merited Test selection. Shaun Udal went 11 years between his one-day debut in 1994, and his Test debut in 2005. Paul Collingwood played in 42 ODIs before being selected for two Tests, and another 38 before his third Test. He is a rare example of a player establishing a Test career on the back of a one-day one. The jury is out, but probably close to reaching a verdict, on whether Eoin Morgan will provide another. He was picked for Tests after 41 ODIs, by when he was averaging 39 – comparable to England's best ODI batsmen. But he was unable to replicate this form in 19 Tests and as others have established themselves ahead of him, and his own one-day form has deteriorated, it seems highly unlikely that he will force his way back into the Test side.

From 1989/90, England institutionalised the 'A' team winter tour. Tours by potential England players had taken place on an irregular basis for many years. Mike Brearley had led an MCC under-25 side to Pakistan back in 1966/7, and 'B' team tours had taken place spasmodically earlier in the 80s. But from 1989/90, they occurred every winter. They were always principally development sides of young players – never more so than when integrated with the new ECB Academy in 2001/2. From 2004/5, they have evolved more into a broader second England squad, albeit with an emphasis on younger players. From 2007/8, they adopted the sobriquet 'England Lions'.

Since 1991, around three-quarters of England's debutants have been graduates of 'A' tours. Of England's most successful Test players who made their debut in this period, only Matthew Hoggard and Collingwood failed to tread this path. Both were relatively late developers. Even Collingwood's one-day international debut was not until the age of 25 (though it remains a little surprising that he had not been picked up for an 'A' tour prior to this). Hoggard was only 23 on debut, but he had done little in previous seasons to suggest that he was Test material, and his selection was something of a flyer. Of course, the talent evident in the players chosen for 'A' tours in the first place would have ensured that they were on the selectors' radar even had no 'A' tours taken place. And success on the 'A' tour did not always trump performance in the County Championship. For example, Dean Headley was the successful fast bowler on the 1995/6 'A' Tour to Pakistan, but he was passed over in favour of Simon Brown and Alan Mullally when Test places became available in 1996, and then in favour of Chris Silverwood for the 1996/7 winter tours: Brown and Mullally (though not Silverwood) had better county seasons than Headley in 1996. Michael Vaughan did well in Zimbabwe and South Africa in 1998/9, but Aftab Habib was chosen ahead of him for the vacant middle-order position which became available in 1999 on the basis of superior county performances that season. The 21-year-old Richard Dawson was chosen ahead of Swann for the 2001/2 winter tours despite Swann's success in the West Indies on the 'A' tour there earlier in 2001. Dawson's county form in 2001 was superior, and neither Duncan Fletcher nor Hussain were fans of Swann after some incidents when he toured South Africa with the senior team in 1999/2000. But in the last decade, 'A' team performance has normally been regarded by the selectors as a better guide than county form.

Occasionally, however, outstanding performances on 'A' tours did allow players to leapfrog their rivals. Mark Lathwell's successes in Australia in 1992/3 (including 175 against Tasmania in the presence of chairman Dexter) undoubtedly facilitated his entry into the England side the following summer, when his county form was unexceptional. The 1994 *Wisden* wrote of his tour that 'not since David Gower emerged had a youngster quickened the pulse like Lathwell'. Alas, the pulse quickly returned to normal as Lathwell's Test career was limited to the two he played in 1993 at the age of 21. Crawley's outstanding tour of South Africa in 1993/4 helped to lead to his Test debut the next summer – though his county form in 1994 might have been sufficient on its own. Jonathan Trott's success in New Zealand in 2008/9 placed him in the selectors' eye and assisted his Test selection in 2009. Sam Robson's selection for England in 2014 was principally enabled by his successful Lions' tour of Sri Lanka the previous winter (though the equally successful James Taylor was unable to secure a vacant middle-order position).

'A' Tours have unquestionably had benefits for the development of England cricketers. For the selectors, they have provided an additional indicator of a player's Test potential, and from time to time, one which has proved critical to a selection decision. Generally, however, the selectors have regarded the evidence of 'A' team performance as something to be weighed alongside other indicators, especially county form, and to some extent ODI performance, when seeking to refresh the Test side.

The rationale of the MCC versus tourists matches was revived in 2006 with England 'A'/Lions fixtures against one or both of the summer's tourists. In some cases these sides included current Test players as well as those on the fringes. On a number of occasions, performances in these matches could be decisive in determining subsequent Test selection. Jon Lewis's match return of 9-90 against Sri Lanka in 2006 led to his inclusion in the side for the third Test match for his only Test at the age of 30. England were diminished by injuries, but Lewis's performance ensured that he was preferred, for the moment, to the young Stuart Broad, who also played in that match but with less success. Later in the season, Chris Read's 150 not out for England 'A' against Pakistan was key to his replacing Geraint Jones as wicket-keeper in the Test series which followed. Michael Carberry's 108 for the Lions against New Zealand in 2008 no doubt helped his cause when England were looking for an opening batsman after Strauss was rested for the tour to Bangladesh in 2009/10. Carberry had not played in the Lions game against West Indies in 2009, but neither of the openers who did distinguished himself. Morgan's 193 for the Lions against Sri Lanka in 2011 resulted in him, rather than Ravi Bopara, replacing the retired Collingwood as England's number six in the series which followed. And James Taylor's century for the Lions against the West Indies in 2012 eventually led to his selection for England – though Jonny Bairstow, who had played in the same game and scored a fifty, was preferred in the first instance.

Central Contracts and the Search for Consistency

Selection has been made even more structured, however, through the introduction of central contracts. For the last decade or so, central contracts have served to identify a group of players as the core of the Test side. It has radically altered the terms of trade of selection by creating an elite group of cricketers, with an expectation that in normal circumstances, they will be picked for England ahead of county cricketers without central contracts. Generally around a dozen central contracts have been awarded each season since 2000, with additional 'increment' contracts from 2008. It has been unusual for a centrally-contracted player to be dropped in favour of a non-contracted player. In the first year, the selectors awarded a bizarre central contract to the uncapped Chris Schofield, who played just two Tests, and also to Ramprakash and Hick, both of whom were omitted during the course of the summer of

2000. Thereafter, however, the selectors have only rarely substituted a non-contracted player for a contracted player: Read (briefly) supplanted Jones in 2006; Strauss was temporarily dropped (for Bopara) for the 2007/8 tour to Sri Lanka; Broad and Anderson ousted Steve Harmison and Hoggard in New Zealand in 2007/8; Swann was preferred to Panesar in the West Indies in 2008/9, when Owais Shah, and then Bopara, also replaced Bell; Bresnan was preferred to Finn in Australia in 2010/1 and again in 2011; Morgan was dropped for Samit Patel in Sri Lanka in 2011/2, and then for Bairstow, Bopara and Taylor, in 2012; both Bresnan and Finn were awarded central contracts in October 2013, but both had been left out by the end of the tour to Australia which followed, effectively (and initially) for Tremlett and Boyd Rankin respectively. Pietersen was also dropped in 2012, and again in 2014, but that is another story. Of course, injuries to centrally-contracted players have given opportunities to others, and on occasions they have missed out when the balance of the side has changed so as not to require them. In 2007, 2008 and 2009 England awarded no central contract to a wicket-keeper, thus requiring at least one place in the side to be filled by a player without one.

Central contracts have been significant more than just as a regulator of cricketers' employment: they have introduced a bias towards the selection of a defined and relatively small number of players. Thus in the 15 home summers since their introduction, the average number of players selected has been just under 16. This compares with 19 in the 90s, 20.5 in the 80s, 17 in the 70s, and 20 from 1963 to 1969. And since 2000, there have typically been seven Tests a summer, whereas before then there were only five or six (and four in the four summers when England hosted the World Cup). Central contracts, then, have had the effect of significantly changing selection policy: by creating a presumption that fishing will be restricted to a small pool, and the larger ocean only exploited when the small pool is unable to deliver.

Naturally, there were, as we shall see, plenty of Test players between 1963 and 2000 who were automatic, or virtually automatic, selections for the duration of all or much of their careers. In that sense they were part of an informal elite. But at any one time they were fewer in number. For example, between 1963 and 1999 on average 5.7 England places were occupied by players who had played, or were to play, more than 50 Tests for England; the figure for the period since 2000 is 7.4 – and of course this is understated as in due course a number of players who

Unnatural Selection

played in recent years who have not yet reached 50 caps will do so. Even taking account of the increasing frequency of Test matches, and hence the greater likelihood of a player making 50 appearances, this is a significant difference. Before 2000, therefore, the selectors acquired a substantial proportion of their catch from the ocean rather than the pool. Partly, this may be because there were genuinely fewer outstanding players in previous eras; and/or that the relative success of England in Test cricket in the last decade compared with previous periods has had the consequence of greater selection stability. More fundamentally, however, there was less sense in earlier eras that a gulf separated the standards of Test and county cricket. Selectors were thus far more inclined to select on the basis of current form rather than potential or proven Test class.

This manifested itself in a number of ways. First, the selectors were more willing to drop established players going through relatively poor runs of form. Thus, among batsmen, for example, Barrington was dropped in 1968 after seven Tests without a century, Boycott in 1966 after 12 Tests without a century, Cowdrey in 1966 after 10, Edrich in 1966 after five, Amiss in 1977 after seven, Gower in 1980 after eight, Derek Randall in 1984 after four, Thorpe in 1994 after seven. Since then, the selectors have been more willing to persevere with established batsmen. Alec Stewart went 18 Tests without a century between 1992 and 1993/4, Thorpe 19 between 1994/5 and 1996/7, Pietersen 17 between 2009/10 and 2010/11, Cook 15 between 2007/8 and 2008/9, and a further 17 since 2013: in no cases was one dropped. The only exception to this pattern was the dropping of Ian Bell in 2008/9 after just six Tests without a century. We shall also see the selectors of the 60s and 70s willing to discard Trueman and Snow on particularly flimsy evidence of poor form.

Secondly, there have been fewer debutants since the introduction of central contracts. Since 2000, England have played 186 Tests and given debuts to 65 players – an average of one debutant nearly every three Tests. Between 1962/3 and 1999/00, England played 379 Tests and gave debuts to 185 players – an average of one debutant every two Tests. And the selectors of previous times were generally more impatient of players who failed to make an immediate impact. For example, before central contracts, only 11% of debutants had a run of five Tests or more; since central contracts, the proportion has increased to 25%.

Making Decisions

Thirdly, by being readier to select form county players, the selectors before 1997 (when Graveney replaced Illingworth as chairman) were more inclined to pick players for the first time at a later stage in their careers. Thirty England players have made their debut over the age of 30 since 1962/3 – 25 in the 342 Tests before the end of 1996 (an average of one every 14 Tests), five in the 223 Tests since (one every 45 Tests). Generally, the average age of debutants has reduced from 27 in the 1970s, to less than 25 in the last decade, reflecting the greater emphasis on looking to pick players with potential to command a Test place for an extended period, rather than players who happened to be the most successful in county cricket at the time. Hence, for example, in 2012, when the selectors were seeking new middle-order batsmen to replace Morgan, who had had a poor series the previous winter, and latterly Pietersen, they turned to two 22-year-olds, Bairstow and Taylor, rather than the most successful England-qualified batsman in county cricket, 29-year-old Nick Compton. Admittedly that policy was reversed in India later in the year, when Compton was preferred as Strauss's replacement to the 21-year-old Joe Root. But Compton's England career was short – though not, in all likelihood, as short as that of the other 29-year-old debutant of recent years – Boyd Rankin, who looks set to join the club of one-Test wonders.

Of course, the shift over the years has been one of emphasis. The selectors had some spectacular successes in the 1960s and 1970s in spotting talent at an early age: Snow was first picked at 23, Underwood at 21, Alan Knott at 21, Willis at 21, Gooch at 20, Botham at 21, and Gower at 21 – even if not all made an immediate impact. Other than Jeff Jones and Alan Ward, whose careers were cut short by injury, only Pat Pocock among 21-year-old debutants in the 60s and 70s failed to establish himself as a regular Test player. By contrast, in more recent times, the selectors may have been guilty of a degree of impulsiveness in inclining to select on potential, insufficiently supported by wider evidence. While four of the nine 21-year-olds and below picked since 2000 have been impressively successful (Anderson, Cook, Broad and Root) another two (Schofield and Dawson) spectacularly failed to fulfil their perceived potential, while a third, James Foster, failed to establish a Test place. Steve Finn's initial success was not sustained, but he seems likely to return to the Test side at some stage; while Liam Plunkett, after making no initial impact, unexpectedly forced his way back into the Test

Unnatural Selection

side in 2014.

On the other hand, the selectors in recent years have been astute in spotting older players who have had extended Test careers. Thus Strauss made his debut at 27, Trott at 28, and Swann at 29, and played 100, 49 (so far) and 60 Tests respectively. From the last century, only four such mature debutants have had similarly extended careers: D'Oliveira (debut at 34, 44 Tests); Brearley (34, 39); Bob Taylor (29, 57); and Lamb (27, 79). But D'Oliveira and Lamb would have been picked at younger ages had they been eligible, Brearley would have played many fewer Tests had he not been captain, and Taylor's pedigree had been long established but he was competing for a single place against Knott. County stalwarts picked for the first time at these sorts of ages have occasionally made a very positive impact for a short period (Higgs, chosen at 28; Brian Luckhurst, at 31; Steele at 33; John Lever at 27; Radley at 33), but until Strauss, the vast majority of players picked for the first time at 27 or over have failed to justify their selection. That is not to say that the selection was in all cases misguided (though it seems to have been so in many): in some instances, for whatever reason, the younger options may have been unattractive. But it does suggest that if a player has not indicated sufficient potential for selection in his early or mid-20s, it requires a very significant weight of evidence to justify his making his debut in his late 20s.

While central contracts, performance squads and Lions tours have introduced structure into selection which has led to greater stability, structures can crumble when confronted by exceptional events. When England toured Australia in 2013/4, on the back of a successful Ashes series in 2013, they had a side which looked unusually stable by historic standards. Eight of the side in the first Test had played 48 Tests or more, and only two places were a matter for debate. By the end of the series, however, three players' Test careers appeared to have come to a close: Trott, Swann and Pietersen. The reasons for these unexpected terminations are examined elsewhere. But England's loss of 213 Tests' worth of experience in the course of a single series was unprecedented, and sent selection into a spin. In seven Tests between the last of the summer of 2013 and the first of the summer of 2014, nine players made their debut. During the five-Test Ashes series in Australia, no less than 18 players represented England. This was more like selection in the late

80s and early 90s.

Selection is not exclusively about concrete evidence – at any rate as manifested in performance data. From time to time, the selectors made some choices which were unashamedly not based on evidence – but were hunches. The hunch principle owes much to Frank Tyson, who as a relatively inexperienced fast bowler (one Test, and 105 first-class wickets spread over three seasons) blew away the Australians in 1954/5 with raw pace. Ever since, the selectors have, on occasions, sought to pick young players on the basis of perceived talent even when this has yet to be manifested in solid figures. In particular, they have looked for bowlers with pace. Commenting on his (successful) efforts to persuade the selectors to include the young Harmison and Simon Jones in the first England Academy intake for 2001/2, Duncan Fletcher has written 'I think fast bowlers can progress almost overnight. Batsmen take time, and spinners take even longer, but the quickies can suddenly discover that they can intimidate the batsmen and they are away'. The selections of Ward (1969), Willis (1970/1), Graham Dilley (1979/80), Norman Cowans (1982/3), Greg Thomas (1985/6), Silverwood (1996/7), Alex Tudor (1998/9), Hoggard (2000), and Plunkett (2005/6) are all examples of this thinking. Some have been more successful than others. With the advent of the 'A' tours, a more structured progression to the senior side has meant that generally the hunch has led to selection for the junior side, while the selectors have sought evidence of talent in this forum before awarding a Test cap. Apart from Plunkett (debut at 20), England's youngest debutants of the last decade – Anderson (20), Cook (21), Broad (21), Finn (20), Root (21) – all had prior 'A' team experience.

Character and Personality

Then there have been the unquantifiable qualities of 'character' and 'personality'. 'Character', in this context, can be defined as the mental strength which enables an individual to perform well under pressure – better, perhaps, than his innate talent would suggest. Hussain has written 'while I consider myself to be a good judge of character I'm not so good at judging players' and explains that he was happy to give up being a selector 'as long as I could have my say in selection on the character of players'. Thus Hussain identifies Vaughan and Trescothick as players 'who had an aura about them from the start, the right personality to succeed at the highest level... they took to Test cricket like ducks to water' despite unexceptional performances in county cricket. Similarly Strauss impressed both Duncan Fletcher and Vaughan, who wrote '...I could see right away that this was the kind of character I wanted in my team. He had been around the one-dayers in Sri Lanka and his whole demeanour just confirmed what we had first thought, that he possessed the right credentials to be a Test player of stature'. If one man exemplifies character-based selection, it is Close, whose call ups in 1963, 1966 and 1976 – in each case against the West Indies – were all a reflection of his perceived mental strength. John Woodcock of *The Times* wrote of him after his selection in 1976 'he is absolutely fearless, the sort of man to have won a Victoria Cross had he ever gone into battle'.

Others, however much talent they had, seemed to lack character. The most obvious chasm between county and Test performance over the last fifty years was probably that of Ramprakash, and most commentators have concluded that this was attributable to mental weakness. But others, too, failed to pass the character test. For example, Vaughan has written of Read that he was 'a decent keeper and a nice lad for sure, who on occasions could be particularly good fun around the bar; but I just felt that he struggled with the pressure of playing for England'. Thus Vaughan was instrumental in Read's replacement by Jones in 2003/4, and argued unsuccessfully for Foster, rather than Read, being the reserve keeper for the 2004/5 tour to South Africa.

'Personality' is about how individuals in the team relate to each other. It is the essence of the conundrum that cricket is a team game comprised of individual performances. Team spirit, a unified dressing room, is an important ingredient of success. But are these essential characteristics, or merely highly desirable ones? To what extent is an inability or unwillingness to embrace the team ethos a disqualification for selection, regardless of the talents of the individuals concerned?

These issues have recurred over the last half century, and influenced the composition of Test teams. Boycott, famously obsessed with his own performance to the exclusion of all else, could infuriate his team mates to the extent that Botham once deliberately ran him out when they were batting together because he was scoring too slowly. The selectors, however, always wanted to pick him – at any rate after 1967. The problem was his refusal to play Test cricket after being passed over for the England captaincy (in favour of Denness), from 1974 to 1977. The view was that Boycott's idiosyncrasies could be accommodated, though it is doubtful if that would have been the case much beyond 1982. Willis describes how on the 1981/2 tour, Boycott 'plainly could not cope with the Indian environment, neither enjoying the country nor getting on with the food or the people. Once he had achieved his objective of breaking the all-time record for aggregate Test runs, his appetite for cricket, and especially for the tour, appeared to wane day by day.' It culminated in Boycott leaving the field in what proved to be his final Test, apparently because of illness, only to play golf instead. He flew home, and thereafter joined the rebel tour to South Africa.

Snow was regarded as someone difficult to manage. He believed in preserving his energies for Test matches, and was dropped by his county for not trying and accused of doing the same in some MCC matches on tour. Undoubtedly this was held against him when it came to selecting the tour parties for 1973/4 and 1974/5, though in a curious way he was anticipating the introduction of central contracts with their objective of preserving the bodies of fast bowlers by limiting their workload.

Philippe Edmonds, the slow left-arm bowler who delivered successive bouncers at Richard Hadlee in protest at being bowled at (in his view) the wrong time, and who during the Perth Test match of 1978/9 had said to his captain, chest to chest 'get off my fucking back Brearley, or I'll fucking fix you', was not to everyone's taste. His biographer, Simon Barnes, has described his relationship with Brearley as a 'cosmic mismatch', and Botham and Willis avoided picking him as much as possible. Brearley himself is on record as disagreeing with this:

> 'in my opinion the England selectors were wrong to leave Edmonds out of the tour parties to Australia in 1982/3 and to New Zealand and Pakistan in 1983/4. He can indeed be hard to handle; but it is the job of captain and managers to do just that, and not to select four spinners inferior in ability to Edmonds to avoid such problems, particularly when he had successful seasons at home in 1982 and 1983'.

Gower and then Gatting seemed to be up for the challenge, and he played 28 of his 51 Tests after Gower was appointed captain in 1984 and after the age of 33.

One cannot imagine Gower threatening to punch his captain's

teeth down his throat, but his personality too proved to be incompatible with the regime at the turn of the 80s. Essentially, however, Gower's falling out with Stewart and Gooch from 1989/90 to 1992/3 represented a fundamental difference of approach about how to run the England team. Gower believed strongly that people who had reached Test level – especially those, such as himself, who were established Test players – ought to be personally responsible for their match preparation, be that in terms of fitness, practice, or indeed, on tour, social activities. It was a laissez-faire attitude, but one based on an assumption that Test players were mature and responsible individuals. Stewart and Gooch regarded players less as individuals and more as members of a team, with an obligation to conform to collective norms. For Gower, this was regimentation. For Stewart and Gooch, it was professionalism – a way of raising standards. The difference in ethos has been portrayed as Cavaliers v Roundheads. In retrospect, it remains extraordinary that the selectors regarded Gower's unwillingness to show enthusiasm for the management's ethos as sufficiently detrimental to the team as to exclude him, and his outstanding talent, from it. Equally, however, it was Gower who was behind the times. Although their approach was arguably unnecessarily intolerant, Stewart and Gooch were the precursors of Fletcher and Flower in creating what became known as 'Team England' by transforming what was essentially a regime in which a group of county cricketers occasionally got together to play international cricket, to one in which first-class cricket's purpose was to serve the requirements of Test cricket.

Until very recently, Gower's exclusion from the England team for 'personality', rather than cricket, reasons appeared antediluvian, the product of an age which had passed into history. But in 2012, and then again in 2014, England's best player was once again dropped for reasons relating to his relationship with the rest of the team, and its management.

It is difficult to imagine two more different personalities than Gower and Pietersen – the one insouciant, self-deprecating, dry and relaxed; the other driven, self-unaware, prickly and sensitive. The nature of Pietersen's break down with his managers and captains bears little comparison with Gower's with Stewart and Gooch. But the consequence was the same. It is too soon to reach definitive judgements about the Pietersen saga. While Pietersen has told his side of the story in a ghost-written autobiography, the other *dramatis personae* have been more constrained. What seems clear, however, is that the England coaches who followed Duncan Fletcher found Pietersen difficult, and at times impossible, to manage; and that a significant element of the dressing room regarded Pietersen as unable to conform to team ethics and, because of his overt pursuit of an obviously personal agenda (for example in his strange interview after the second Test against South Africa in 2012 when he proclaimed that the saddest thing about his being forced out of the Test side would be 'that the spectators just love watching me play'), isolated and perhaps ridiculed him.

When Pietersen was first dropped in 2012, it was following an impressive century against South Africa and after the principal source of dispute between him and the ECB that summer – Pietersen's demand to play T20 but not ODI matches for England – had been resolved by Pietersen's total capitulation on the issue (albeit communicated to his employers by the rather unconventional method of a staged You Tube interview). The England management could have declared victory and moved on, but instead chose to regard the incident in which Pieteresen sent text messages to members of the South African team – the contents of which have never been disclosed – to dispense with his services.

The dilemma for the selectors was of the extent to which an individual's outstanding talent outweighed the collateral damage he was perceived to inflict on the collective effort of the team. In 2012, there was no doubt as to the magnitude of that talent, and the ECB, somewhat hesitantly, made efforts, in the rather curious language adopted by Giles Clarke, the ECB chairman to 'reintegrate' Pietersen into the England side following his (unspecified) 'transgressions'. For the following twelve months, England won Test series against both India and Australia (and drew a series with New Zealand) with Pietersen in the side, and he scored two centuries in the twelve tests he played: the equation seemed to favour the talent over the collateral damage. When, however, England were humiliated in Australia in 2013/4, with Pietersen failing to stand out among the other England batsmen who failed, the balance of advantage was regarded as having fundamentally changed.

What was curious, and probably unique, was that the England selectors decided not merely to drop Pietersen, but to end his international career. The selection which gave rise to this was the announcement of the squads for England's ODI series in the Caribbean in February 2014, to be followed by the World T20 in Bangladesh the following month. It would have been possible to have omitted Pietersen without commenting on his future beyond then. He had not, for example, played in the ODI series in Australia which followed the Ashes in January 2014 because of injury. Concerns about his fitness could legitimately have been cited, and his selection for Tests in the summer of 2014 could have been made dependent on early-season form in the County Championship, where Pietersen would have been disadvantaged anyway because of his IPL commitments in April and early May. Instead, Paul Downton, England's new Managing Director of England Cricket, said of his omission 'everyone was aware that there was a need to begin the long-term planning after the Australia tour. Therefore we have decided the time is right to look to the future and start to rebuild not only the team but also team ethic and philosophy'. It was made clear that, unprecedentedly, regardless of his future form, Pietersen would never be picked for England again: because form was not the issue. If there was any wriggle room in the ECB's decision of early 2014, Pietersen's decision to publish a book later in the year highly critical of both the management of the England side and of many of his former team mates appeared to have removed it — and incidentally offered a more persuasive rationale for dispensing with him than the ECB had managed at the time. It was therefore one of the most extraordinary developments in the history of Test selection over the last 50 years when the chairman-designate of the ECB, Colin Graves, indicated in March 2015 that there might be a way back for Pietersen, as a consequence of which Pietersen committed himself to playing county cricket for Surrey in the forthcoming season. It is a bizarre sub-plot to an Ashes summer.

This recent development is all the more curious because the success of Gary Ballance and Root as successors to Pietersen (and Trott) in the Tests of the summer of 2014 suggested that his absence was missed less than his supporters may have hoped. England's humiliating failure to qualify for the quarter-finals of the 2015 World Cup, however, seemed in part at least to reflect a selection policy for ODIs (beyond the scope of this book) that was averse to flare and non-conformity and failed to recognise how the techniques of T20 were key to success in the 50-over game. It seems at least possible that new levels of batting aggression will become the norm in Test cricket too, and selectors will need to place greater emphasis on exuberance and self-expression, and find different ways of managing the personality issues to which this may, in some cases, give rise.

CHAPTER TWO

THE CAPTAINS

THE role of captain in a cricket team is unique in sport. Two components are common to captaincy in other sports. The captain must be a leader – able to motivate those in his side to perform to their best, and to make the whole greater than the sum of the parts. And he must undertake representational duties – the speech at formal events, and, for the national captain (though not exclusively among team members these days), the post-match media interview. The cricket captain, however, is in addition responsible for the tactical direction of the game on the field of play. The choice of whether to bat or field on winning the toss, the placing of the field, and the changing of the bowling, are decisions which may determine the outcome of the game. The selection of the England cricket captain has therefore been regarded as a variable almost independent of the rest of the choice of the side. Unlike the practice in Australia until relatively recently, England captains have been chosen ahead of the other 10 members of the team, and have subsequently, until recently, participated in their selection.

Only since 1998, however, have captains been appointed for indefinite periods – that is, until they resign or are sacked. Prior to then, the practice was to appoint captains for a defined term. For overseas series, the duration was clearly for the period of the tour, but for home series, captains were frequently appointed for as little as one Test at a time, and seldom for a complete rubber. Of course, all other members of the side were, and continue to be, chosen for one Test at a time but in making no distinction in regards to the captaincy, the selectors failed to recognise the strategic role a captain plays, or ought to play, in the development of a Test team and in the planning of a campaign rather than simply of particular battles. And by varying the lengths of the tenure they granted captains, they sent very clear messages about the confidence they had in their selection. Hence, for example, Mike Gatting was appointed for the entire series against Pakistan in 1987, but only for the first Test against the West Indies in 1988. By making such short-duration appointments, it was implicit that the selectors regarded the captain as being on trial, which might not induce the best mind set. Although there were exceptions, the life expectancy of captains appointed for a singleton Test at the start of a series was short – Mike Smith 1966, Mike Denness 1975, Ian Botham 1981, David Gower 1986 and Gatting 1988.

Amateurs versus Professionals

England entered the 1960s in a period of unusual stability as far as the captaincy was concerned. Peter May had led since 1955, during which time England had continued to be the strongest of the Test-playing nations – until the Ashes were lost to Australia in 1958/59. Nevertheless, aged just 30, still England's premier batsman, and with a record of 18 wins and just nine defeats from 35 Tests in charge, there seemed no reason why May should not continue to captain England for many years to come. He fell ill, however, during the tour to the West Indies at the start of 1960 and missed the last two Tests. While he returned to captain England for the last three Tests of the 1961 Ashes series, which England lost 2-1, his heart was no longer in it. At the end of the season, he retired from international cricket.

May had an heir apparent in Colin Cowdrey. Ticking all the same boxes as May (public school and Oxbridge, an amateur in the days before the 'Gentleman' and 'Player' distinction was formally abolished, a longstanding county captain, and one of the country's premier batsmen), he had been May's vice-captain on both the 1958/9 and 1959/60 tours, and had stood in for May when he was injured in 1959, and when absent ill in 1960. At the time of May's retirement, Cowdrey had already captained England on 11 occasions.

Had Cowdrey been available for the 1961/2 tour to India and Pakistan, he would unquestionably have been appointed captain, and might have held that position for as many Tests as May. But he chose to have the winter off (as did other senior players from the 1961 side such as Fred Trueman and Brian Statham), and the next cab in the rank of those with the same sort of CV as May's and Cowdrey's, Ted Dexter, got the job. Selection to captain MCC on a tour to the Indian sub-continent in the 1960s was not, however, regarded as necessarily of enduring significance. There was an element in these tours of 'showing the flag', and there was little pressure put on players who preferred to absent

Unnatural Selection

themselves. The big looming issue for the selectors was who should lead England to Australia in 1962/3 in the attempt to regain the Ashes. Dexter was now in the frame, but he was not automatically the front runner. The selectors decided to use the series against a weak Pakistan side in England in 1962 to stage an unofficial competition between Dexter and Cowdrey: Dexter was to captain the first two Tests; Cowdrey the third and also the 'Gentlemen' in the 'Gentlemen v Players' match which followed it and which was regarded as a Test trial. In the event, Cowdrey was ill and the captaincy of the Gentlemen reverted to Dexter. England won the first three Tests against Pakistan very easily, so they offered the selectors no useful evidence with which to discriminate between the candidates.

Unexpectedly, a third candidate entered the ring during 1962. The mercurial chairman of selectors, Walter Robins, encouraged The Reverend David Sheppard to take a sabbatical from pastoral duties, and to return to play county cricket (at Sussex – under Dexter's captaincy) with a view to leading England in Australia the following winter. Sheppard had captained England in two Tests in 1954 after a two-year break from Test cricket when Hutton was ill, but he had not played Test cricket since 1957, and only very little county cricket.

No attempt was made by Robins to disguise from the press that there were three candidates fighting it out for the captaincy during the summer of 1962, and unsurprisingly the contest attracted intense media interest. The climax was the Gentlemen v Players match which immediately preceded the meeting which would decide the victor. Sheppard's century for the Gentlemen seemed to demonstrate that he had lost none of his talent during his period away from the game. Many contemporary commentators believed that he would get the nod, though it would surely have been extraordinary to have preferred him ahead of Dexter or Cowdrey. In the end, however, the sub-committee appointed by MCC and chaired by Robins voted unanimously for Dexter.

Dexter was 27 when he was appointed for the 1962/3 tour, and at the height of his powers. His selection might have been expected to settle the England captaincy for a generation but Dexter's interests were many and wide ranging, and among his ambitions was to sit as a Conservative MP in the House of Commons. It is difficult to imagine any of his successors harbouring such aspirations – Andrew Strauss firmly denied rumours that he might follow suit. He was chosen to fight the safe Labour seat of Cardiff South East held by James Callaghan. The timing of the next General Election was uncertain, but the autumn of 1963, four years into the Parliament, was a strong possibility. If that were to be the case, Dexter could hardly commit himself to an overseas tour the following winter without admitting that he had no chance of winning the seat. Accordingly, he was unavailable for the trip to India in 1963/4.

Unsurprisingly, Cowdrey, who had once again been vice-captain in Dexter's 1962/3 party, a role he played no less than five times, was selected to lead the tour to India. But Cowdrey had famously broken his arm in the Lord's Test against the West Indies in the summer of 1963, and as the India tour approached, his injury healed more slowly than expected. He was forced to withdraw from the party, though he was to join it half way through after illness deprived the tourists of Ken Barrington and Micky Stewart, the man who had been nominated as his vice-captain, Mike ('M J K') Smith, took over.

Smith had not been an automatic selection for the tour. He had played the last of his 22 Tests to date on Dexter's tour to the sub-continent two years before, since when he had not been a serious challenger for a Test place. His Test average was a modest 32, but he was a very successful county batsman, scoring 2000 runs in every season between 1957 and 1962 (including over 3000 in 1961), and had topped the first-class batting averages in 1963. He was also regarded as a particularly good player of spin bowling, though he had actually had a disappointing tour to India and Pakistan in 1961/2. Without scoring a century, he was to have a respectable tour of India in 1963/4 as a batsman. All five Tests were drawn in a series notable both for the slow tempo of play and the variety of illnesses and injuries to which the tourists succumbed. The England team for one Test was determined by the 11 members of the party who were fit, with journalist Henry Blofeld the next in line to be picked! Smith was judged to have handled these vexations well. His manager wrote of him in his post-tour report 'under conditions where leadership is a first essential, he could not be faulted. When conditions were difficult he was completely unflappable.' But he added 'one wonders whether his ideas as a captain were a little rigid and whether a little more experimentation might have paid dividends.'

The selectors seemed genuinely uncertain at the start of the 1964 season whether to plump for Dexter or Smith. There were real doubts about Dexter as captain. His aggression as a batsman seemed not to have inspired his captaincy in Australia in 1962/3 when, for example, needing to win the final Test to regain the Ashes, England had scored at a rate of only 34 runs per 100 balls. He had presided over a 3-1 defeat by the West Indies in 1963, and with the General Election now set for October 1964, he would be unable to commit to leading England in their winter tour to South Africa for exactly the reasons which had prevented him captaining in India. Both were chosen to play for MCC against the Australian tourists before the series started, with Smith as captain. Although this one match failed to provide conclusive evidence (MCC lost by nine wickets; Dexter scored 60 in two innings, Smith 39), it is likely that the selectors decided that they had to be able to pick their strongest side against Australia, and they could not be confident that Smith would be in it. So it transpired: Dexter was appointed captain, and Smith made it only as far as 12th man for one Test.

It is interesting to speculate whether Dexter would have kept the captaincy had his political ambitions not decided the matter. He led England to defeat against Australia in 1964, and attracted a lot of criticism, not necessarily fairly, for his decision in the one match of the rubber which was not drawn for his decision to take the new ball at a time when the England spinners were on top. In reply to England's 268, Australia recovered from 178-7 to reach 389 and set up a seven-wicket victory. MCC's report to its members on the 1964 series referred to disappointment at the lack of a positive approach by both the Australian and England teams in the Test matches – a fairly explicit criticism of the captains involved. Whatever, there was never any serious prospect of Dexter being handed back the reins after the 1964/5 tour as he had after 1963/4. *The Times*' (in those days anonymous) cricket correspondent declared at the start of the 1965 season: 'everyone hopes that Dexter will make himself available for Australia [the 1965/6 tour] – as a player rather than as a reporter or anything as incongruous as that. But his term as captain was a failure.'

So Smith captained England in South Africa in 1964/5 – no consideration appears to have been given to Cowdrey's credentials – starting an unbroken run of 20 Tests, the longest period of stability in the England captaincy during the 1960s. There were few complaints about his leadership. Once again, he received rave reviews from his tour manager in South Africa, Donald Carr, who wrote of the 'magnificent example and leadership of the captain M J K Smith, who managed to get the best out of each player on all occasions. He cannot be commended too highly in this respect and I have heard many leading South African administrators envying MCC in their fortune to have such a captain available.'

Wisden's correspondent on the 1965/6 tour, E M Wellings, wrote in the 1967 almanack that Smith's 'great virtue lay in his ability as a tour leader to take the players along with him. He had no tricks of leadership – in the modern idiom no gimmicks. He was in fact somewhat self-effacing. Yet he had a flair for leading and binding a team together'. But after a century in the third Test in South Africa, he went 17 more with only a single fifty, a run which would not have been tolerated in any other specialist batsman. And ultimately the selectors were forced to conclude that they could not carry as a captain a man who was failing to deliver as a player. Smith survived to captain England in the first Test against the West Indies in 1966 on the back of a century against the tourists for MCC in the traditional May fixture. But he was dropped after England were defeated by West Indies by an innings – a match in which he failed to reach double figures.

After the demise of Smith, the selectors turned to Cowdrey as captain. For five years circumstance had conspired to deny him the role for which he seemed predestined, but the prize was his for just three Tests. In the first two, England failed to drive home the advantages they commanded at certain stages over the West Indies. At Lord's, West Indies in their second innings were five wickets down with a lead of only 11 before recovering to set England 284 to win: the match was drawn. At Trent Bridge, England secured a first innings lead of 90 but lost by 139 runs. In the fourth Test, England collapsed in a heap to lose by an innings and 55 runs. *The Times*' correspondent thundered 'I have reported well over 100 Test matches in these columns, but never one in which England were so thoroughly outplayed, or in which they played so poorly. Any of the other Test match sides, including New Zealand, India and Pakistan, could have expected to produce a better showing.'

This was one of those all too familiar moments in the history of England Test cricket over the last 50 years where the public's and – whether because of it or despite it – the selectors' mood was to demand change for change's sake. Cowdrey was replaced as captain by Brian Close, who had played his last Test for England in 1963. In that series, and especially in the second innings of the Lord's Test, when he had allowed himself to be struck on the body by Wes Hall and Charlie Griffith rather than risk his wicket by playing the lifting delivery with his bat, Close had created a reputation for fearless determination which offered a stark contrast to England's performances in 1966. He had a powerful self-belief, and was well thought of as a tactician. The change was all the more radical because Close was a professional – only the second to captain England after Len Hutton. Hutton's had been a controversial appointment, and one which some senior figures in MCC regretted because they considered him to lack the ambassadorial qualities which they regarded as essential to leading England overseas. Close's selection might be thought to represent a transition to a more modern era, although by choosing someone who had not merited inclusion as a player, the selectors had once again put their faith in the concept of a specialist captain; and it was perhaps significant that England had no tour the following winter. In announcing Close's appointment, Billy Griffith, the secretary of MCC, said, perhaps contradicting himself, that 'the selectors in no way attribute the defeats that England have suffered to the captaincy that has gone before: but they do feel that a change of approach may result in a change of fortune'.

It was not just a new tactical approach which Close brought. The side that was selected for the Oval showed six changes from that which played in the fourth Test. England's team then had been Geoff Boycott, Bob Barber, Colin Milburn, Tom Graveney, Cowdrey, Basil D'Oliveira, Jim Parks, Fred Titmus, Ken Higgs, Derek Underwood and John Snow. For the fifth Test, it was Boycott, Barber, John Edrich, Graveney, Dennis Amiss, D'Oliveira, Close, Ray Illingworth, John Murray, Higgs and Snow. Most of the changes were to a large extent presentational. Thus Milburn was dropped, despite scoring 94 in the first Test and 126 in the second, to raise the standard of fielding; Illingworth replaced Titmus because he played for Close at Yorkshire; Murray was selected to increase the proportion of the team untainted by failure. In circumstances not dissimilar from those which would obtain following the disastrous defeats England, captained by David Gower, suffered at the hands of Australia in 1989, the previous captain was dropped principally because of his identification with failure. There was no question that Cowdrey, then aged 33, did not remain one of England's premier batsmen, any more than there was in the case of Gower when he was dropped in 1989.

On the face of it, the selectors' night of the long knives was a success. England beat West Indies in the Oval Test by an innings. The match was won for England by two remarkable lower-wicket partnerships. After West Indies had been bowled out for 268, England were reduced to 166-7. Graveney and Murray then proceeded to add 217 for the eighth wicket, both scoring centuries; and after that Higgs and Snow put on 128 for the last wicket. If Close can take no credit for the performance of his batsmen, he nonetheless received praise for his handling of the side in the field. The editor of *Wisden* wrote

> 'he had proved his ability as a leader for Yorkshire and he led England in the same positive way; his bowling changes were successful, notably the early introduction of Barber [an occasional leg spinner], and his personal example close to the batsman at short-leg made an aggressive set of fielders who took all the catches offered.'

But he added 'perhaps, luck did go his way for once'.

However, the changes, made in the heat of the perceived crisis, soon began to unravel. When England next played West Indies, 18 months later, the side contained just four of those who played in the fifth Test (Boycott, Edrich, Graveney, D'Oliveira), but six of those who played in the fourth (Boycott, Cowdrey, Graveney, D'Oliveira, Parks and Titmus). Thus the shake-up proved to be tactical rather than strategic, and the shape of the defeated side in 1966 proved to be more enduring than the victorious one.

The most obvious change not to endure was that of Close himself, whose tenure as England captain was to prove shorter than might have been expected in the aftermath of his Oval triumph. He led England to victory over India and Pakistan in five of the six Tests in the summer of 1967 (the other was drawn). His demise was to come not as a result of any failings in his performances in Test matches. Rather it was, at least ostensibly, the consequence of the County Championship match between Warwickshire and Yorkshire on 18 August 1967. Warwickshire needed to score 142 to win in the last 100 minutes of the game. In an incident which led directly to the rule which set a minimum number of overs to be bowled in the last hour of a match, Close's Yorkshire side contrived to bowl just 24 overs in the innings – perhaps six fewer than might have been expected at the tempo cricket was played in the 60s.

The timing could not have been worse for Close, as the MCC Tour Selection Committee (Doug Insole, Alec Bedser, Don Kenyon, Peter May – the four England home selectors – Les Ames, the tour manager for the West Indies, and David Clark) met the day after the conclusion of the controversial county game. It had earlier met on 28 July and 'agreed that the choice of captain lay between Mr D B Close and Mr M J K Smith, with the former as the most likely selection', but a final decision was deferred until after the second Test match of the series then in progress against Pakistan. It is surprising that Smith was still considered credible, though he was not for much longer as a few weeks later he announced his retirement from first-class cricket. It is, however, evidence of the unease of some members of MCC at the prospect of Close leading an overseas tour. In the MCC archive there is an anonymous letter sent on 28 June to the Secretary, Billy Griffith, from an 'Old West Indian Cricketer' from Trinidad. In it the author argues somewhat colourfully against MCC allowing '3rd or 4th class types of men to lead their cricket teams both at home and abroad'. He suggests 'ill mannered men', such as Tony Lock and Trueman, would not behave as they did had they been captained by amateurs. 'Why not go back to your policy of appointing university graduates as captains?' Intriguingly, Griffith, rather than filing it with those from the green ink brigade, marked this letter 'DBC [Donald Carr – the assistant secretary – rather than D B Close!] we must keep this letter as it clearly represents my views.' There is no explanation mark at the end to imply this comment was sarcastic.

Griffith was not alone. May, at the meeting on 28 July, and Ames at the meeting on 19 August, both argued that the team should be selected first, and the captain chosen from among it. This was a radical proposal from not obviously radical sources. It is difficult not to see in it a plot to reinstate Cowdrey. May was a close friend of Cowdrey and Ames was secretary-manager at Kent where Cowdrey was captain. While Cowdrey was almost certain of a place as a player, Close was not, as Ames pointed out. Insole successfully persuaded the Committee to resist this suggestion at both meetings. He summed up that 'in the opinion of the majority of the Board of Cricket Selectors, Mr D B Close was the best man for the job. Other candidates had been fully considered;

and taking everything into consideration, the Committee felt bound to recommend Mr D B Close.' However, it was also agreed that no decision should be made until the Executive Committee of the Advisory County Cricket Committee (ACCC) had completed its consideration of the umpires' reports on the Yorkshire v Warwickshire game.

The Committee met again on 23 August, with the President of MCC, Arthur Gilligan, who had earlier chaired the meeting of the Executive Committee of the ACCC, also present. A statement released by MCC had said that the Executive Committee had concluded that Yorkshire's 'tactics constituted unfair play and were against the best interests of the game. Furthermore the Committee held the captain, Brian Close, entirely responsible for these tactics. They have therefore severely censured him.' Insole

> 'suggested that the [Selection] Committee should consider whether or not, in light of the Executive Committee's decision, they wished to withdraw their previous recommendation, and, in any case he believed an alternative to Close should be put forward, in case the MCC Committee were not prepared to accept him. The desirability of choosing the team before the captain should also be considered'

The minutes go on to record that:

> 'three members considered that, in view of the Executive Committee's decision, it would be most undesirable to appoint Close. They believed there would be a most unfavourable public reaction, particularly in the West Indies [the 'Old West Indies Cricketer'?] to such an appointment. The remaining members considered that the original recommendation should stand, since they believed him to be the best candidate. They also found it difficult to find a suitable alternative.'

It seems that Insole, Bedser, and Kenyon supported Close, and May, Ames and Clark did not. At the time, it was reported that all four home selectors had supported Close. But the minutes record the chairman as saying the Committee were 'evenly divided regarding the appointment of Close'. In that event one of Insole, Bedser, Kenyon and May must have

Unnatural Selection

voted against Close, and May seems the most likely. As for the alternative, three votes went to Cowdrey, one to Titmus, and one to Parks. Titmus and Parks at the time captained Middlesex and Sussex respectively, and while the former was a plausible candidate, the latter, as both a wicket-keeper and someone not in the current Test side, was an impossible suggestion. The decision was passed on to the main MCC Committee, and they went for Cowdrey. Close did not make the touring party.

So, for the third time in the 60s, Cowdrey took over the reins of the England captaincy, this time for a period of three series and 12 Tests. He secured a rare triumph in winning a series against West Indies in 1967/8 (albeit assisted by a surprisingly generous declaration by Sobers in the one Test to achieve a positive result), and drew the subsequent Ashes rubber in England. On Sunday, 25 May 1969, however, Cowdrey tore an achilles tendon playing for Kent against Glamorgan. It was clear that he would not be fit again much before the end of the season, and a new England captain would need to be found. Graveney had been Cowdrey's vice-captain from when Titmus had suffered the boating accident which deprived him of four toes on the West Indies tour, and had captained England for one Test against Australia in 1968 when Cowdrey was injured. But there were doubts about Graveney's talents as a captain (*Wisden's* correspondent said in the 1969 edition that he was 'a sad disappointment' as vice-captain on the 1968/9 tour to Pakistan). It seems that the Northamptonshire captain, Roger Prideaux, was in the running, as he was chosen to lead MCC against the West Indian tourists the weekend after Cowdrey's injury. Prideaux had opened England's batting in two of England's Tests against Pakistan, but without success, and though it was not apparent at the time, his brief Test career was over.

  The man the selectors turned to was Illingworth, who had moved from Yorkshire to captain Leicestershire at the start of the 1969 season. Illingworth had been unavailable for the winter tour to Pakistan, but, at the age of 36, and with Titmus assumed to be no longer fit to play Test cricket, he had established himself as England's premier off spinner the previous summer. He had a high reputation as a tactician, which he enhanced during his time as England captain. Thus, unusually, the selectors were able to appoint someone who was both the best available captain, and able to command his place in the side as a player. In fact, after he became captain, Illingworth developed into a genuine Test all-rounder. At the end of 1968, he had played in 30 Tests with a solitary 50 and a batting average of only 16. During his 31 Tests as captain, however, he scored two centuries and four fifties, and averaged 28.6.

Illingworth continued as England captain in 1970 despite Cowdrey's return from injury. This was against the Rest of the World, a series which replaced the South Africa tour which had been abandoned at short notice, and for some years was regarded as having full Test status. While England were comprehensively beaten 4-1, Illingworth scored six fifties and was by a margin England's highest run scorer. But it was far from certain that he would be considered suitable to lead England on an overseas tour, to Australia in 1970/1. Just as three years' previously, there continued to be those in the MCC hierarchy who would have preferred a former amateur as captain. Illingworth and Cowdrey represented opposite poles in the English cricket of the day – the one an astute and determined but slightly prickly northerner from a working-class background, the other a highly-talented public school-educated gentleman of Kent. Illingworth believes that the chairman of selectors, Alec Bedser, voted for Cowdrey. Certainly, there seems to have been some sort of compromise, for, unprecedentedly, Cowdrey was invited to be vice-captain at the same time as Illingworth was appointed captain, and uniquely for a vice-captain was on the committee which selected the touring party. Illingworth himself would have preferred Boycott as vice-captain. It was as if there was a deliberate effort to enhance the status of the vice-captaincy because of doubts about Illingworth's credentials for some aspects of the captaincy.

By regaining the Ashes in 1970/1, Illingworth's position as England captain was secure for another couple of years. But it had been a controversial tour. Illingworth had a poor relationship with the tour manager, David Clark, and a major row broke out when, after the Melbourne Test had been abandoned without a ball being bowled, Clark, along with Gubby Allen, but without consulting Illingworth, arranged with the Australian authorities for an additional seventh Test at the end of the tour. Even in a more deferential age, this was high-handed behaviour by the management, and Illingworth encouraged the players to demand an increase in their tour remuneration. Later, in the final Test, Illingworth unilaterally led his side from the field after beer cans had been hurled at Snow fielding on the boundary, and a spectator had

Unnatural Selection

grabbed his shirt. This action also led to a row between the captain and manager.

Illingworth's unbroken run of 25 Tests was the longest between May in the 1950s and Brearley in the late 1970s. The issue was how long he could continue, especially once he passed 40 in the summer of 1972; and whether he would be regarded as suitable to lead England on another overseas tour following the controversies in Australia. There was no winter tour in 1971/2, and he chose not to tour India and Pakistan in 1972/3. This appeared to force the issue of the succession. Two of the potentially most credible candidates from among the England team of that summer, Boycott and Edrich, had, however, also made themselves unavailable for the tour. Among county captains, Denness, Norman Gifford, Close, Brian Bolus and A C Smith had Test experience, but Bolus and Smith were no longer plausible candidates for Test cricket, while Close, who had an outstanding county season in 1972, was 41 and hardly a long-term successor to Illingworth. The selectors passed over Gifford for the captaincy (though he made the touring party), made Denness vice-captain and gave the captaincy to Tony Lewis of Glamorgan.

The nearest that Lewis had come to playing Test cricket was when he had been twelfth man for the Oval Test of 1966. Aged 34 at the end of the 1972 season, he would normally have expected to need an exceptional run of form to be considered a candidate for the Test side. But in 1972 he had finished 66th in the first-class batting averages. He was the last amateur to be appointed to the England captaincy and the last to make his Test debut as captain. It is difficult not to see in his appointment the final throw of England cricket's *ancien regime*. The contemporary arguments for his selection certainly seem a little dated now. In *The Times*, John Woodcock wrote:

> 'Lewis has much to recommend him. He is, in the first place, a good player, if not quite as outstandingly good as he looked like becoming when he first came into first class cricket at the tender age of 17. He is also a good enough captain to have led Glamorgan to the County Championship in 1969 and a good enough journalist to have a regular job writing and broadcasting mostly on rugby football. This should help, him in dealing with the press. All who know him like him and they do so for the best

reasons. He is a friendly, honest and straightforward cricketer, who loves the game and is the same person to all people.'

For someone apparently chosen to play for England on the grounds of his friendliness and journalistic skills, Lewis did not acquit himself at all badly. He scored a century in one of the Tests against India, and returned with a respectable Test average of 38. At the start of the 1973 season, he was pitched head-to-head against Illingworth as each captained a side in a formal 'Test trial'. The fact that Illingworth's side won, and that Lewis scored 0 and 8 not out, may have been what tipped the balance Illingworth's way. Illingworth regained the captaincy, Lewis was selected for the first Test against New Zealand and failed twice, was injured for the second and never again played for England.

During 1973, Illingworth's position became increasingly less secure. At 41, he was under some pressure to demonstrate that he remained a Test-class player. In the first half of the summer, England's quicker bowlers easily accounted for New Zealand in two of the Tests, and Illingworth had little occasion to bowl. But West Indies proved to be a much more formidable proposition and Illingworth made little impression as a bowler. Had England won or squared the series, Illingworth would probably have been retained. But they lost 2-0, by a massive innings and 226 runs in the third Test.

A New Order

At least with the benefit of hindsight, it is an indictment of the selectors that they had no succession plan for Illingworth. It was hardly to be expected that he would be a candidate to lead England in the 1974/5 Ashes series even had he had more success than he did in 1973. For various reasons, however, there were difficulties with all the established Test players. Boycott, England's premier batsman, and, at 32, in his prime, was not, with some justification, regarded as a team player who would command the support of the dressing room. His decision in 1974 to make himself unavailable for Test cricket was perhaps the most telling of a number of pieces of evidence for this. Edrich, through a combination of his absence from the India/Pakistan tour and of an uncharacteristically lean season in county cricket the following summer, was no longer in the side. Keith Fletcher, who had established himself the previous winter, and who at

Unnatural Selection

29 was a good age to take over the captaincy, was apparently disqualified from consideration by his lack of experience as a county captain. Tony Greig, who had taken over as captain of Sussex that summer, did not suffer from such a disqualification, but does not appear, at this stage, to have been regarded as a serious candidate. Indeed, bizarrely, the man regarded by John Woodcock in *The Times* as the 'obvious alternative' to the man selected was Cowdrey, who was only a few months' Illingworth's junior, and who had not played Test cricket for over two years.

The captaincy fell to Denness, who had recently succeeded Cowdrey as captain of Kent. He had played nine previous Tests, eight against India and Pakistan in 1972/3, where he had been Lewis's vice-captain. But he had not been selected in 1973. His respectable but unspectacular record the previous winter was not enough to command a place – and maybe Illingworth, perceiving a rival, encouraged the selectors to look elsewhere. E W Swanton wrote in *The Cricketer* 'the obvious criticism of the selectors – and an acceptable explanation has not been offered – is that Denness should have been given the opportunity to carry on this summer where he left off as vice-captain in the East. A successful Test season at home would have left the succession clear'.

Denness was to prove himself to be a highly effective player of bowling below the top class. Against India in the summer of 1974, he averaged 96; against New Zealand in the winter of 1974/5 he scored 181 and 59 not out. In the sixth Test against Australia immediately before, when Australia were without Jeff Thomson and Dennis Lillee injured himself after six overs, he made 188. But against the West Indies in 1973/4, Pakistan in 1974 and against the full fury of Lillee and Thomson in 1974/5, he did not perform at the required level. The 1974/5 series was a humiliation for England. They lost an Ashes series for the first time since 1964, and by the devastating margin of 4-1. England's one victory was in that final Test: before this, England had failed to reach 300 in 10 attempts, and Greig alone had scored a century. No England batsman distinguished himself against Lillee and Thomson, which makes Denness's decision to drop himself after the third Test all the more extraordinary. He had, it is true, scored only 65 runs in six innings but the man his omission accommodated was Fletcher, who had managed just 40 in four innings before being dropped himself for the third Test. The third and fourth Tests were separated only by a one-day international, in which Fletcher's score of 31 hardly represented a compelling case for reinstatement ahead of his captain. The decision was Denness's alone – it was not discussed by the tour selection committee – and comes across as desperate and impulsive. Edrich captained in the fourth Test in Denness's absence and sustained a fractured rib from a ball from Lillee which rendered him unfit for the fifth Test thus necessitating Denness's return.

Denness could hardly have been held personally responsible for the inability of his batsmen to cope with Australia's fast bowlers. But his captaincy had provoked some criticism – it was alleged that he was not entirely in control of field changes, and Wisden's correspondent, John Thicknesse, in the 1976 edition, attacked his failure to use Underwood and Titmus in tandem in the fifth Test at Adelaide when the ball was turning. The decision to drop himself appeared to be a case of refusing to engage with the enemy – for which traditionally there was only one sentence. But the fact that he returned from the Antipodes with 428 runs to his name from his last three Test innings, albeit against weaker bowling, saved him from the firing squad.

Thus Denness captained England in the first World Cup at the start of the summer where England lost to Australia in the semi-final, and retained the captaincy for the first Test of the 1975 series – again against Australia. He stood down during the first Test. In a statement, he said:

> 'I had spoken to the chairman of the selectors on the second day of the match at Edgbaston and put the point that I felt a change in the captaincy would be the answer, irrespective of the outcome of the match. The reason I did was purely personal and private and in my view in the best interests of English cricket.'

That second day of the Edgbaston Test had been a dire one for England. Australia had been bowled out for 359 just after lunch, and after one over of the England innings, the ground was deluged by a thunder storm. When England resumed, it was on a wet, uncovered, pitch which was ruthlessly exploited by Lillee and Max Walker. By close of play, England were 83-7, with Denness one of the seven – out for three. The impact of the weather might have been regarded as bad luck were it not for the fact that Denness had won the toss and put Australia in when rain was

Unnatural Selection

forecast. There was at least the suspicion that the decision had been negatively influenced by a fear of England's batsmen collapsing on the first day of the match to Australia's fast bowlers, thus giving them an initiative that they might retain for the series. As it turned out, England lost by an innings and 85 runs, with Denness failing in the second innings.

Denness says that he resigned even before play began on the second day, and that the reason was a leak which appeared in the morning's papers saying that the selectors did not support Denness's decision to insert Australia. In view of its source, he regarded this as undermining his position. While the leak was reprehensible, and what it said about the selectors' confidence in Denness unsettling, in itself it was a curious reason to precipitate a resignation, and the decision once again seems impulsive. But if Denness's fate was not inevitable at the moment he resigned, it was a few hours later when play finished on the second day. It is hardly likely that the selectors would have retained him as captain for the next Test.

Denness's resignation was announced the day after England's defeat, and with it the appointment of Greig as his successor. He had been Denness's vice-captain in the West Indies in 1973/4 (though Edrich had filled this role the following winter on his return to the Test team). He was the outstanding player in a mediocre England side, by now 28 but a veteran of 39 Tests and into his third season of captaining Sussex. His self-confident, not to say brash, personality offered the sort of contrast with his predecessor's more introspective approach for which the needs of the hour appeared to call. It was arguably one of the selectors' easier decisions about the captaincy in the 60s and 70s.

Greig's appointment precipitated a more significant set of changes to the England team than had immediately followed the series defeat in Australia. Between the first and fourth Tests of 1975, Amiss, Fletcher, Denness, Graham Gooch, and Geoff Arnold had been replaced by Barry Wood, David Steele, Graham Roope, Bob Woolmer and Philippe Edmonds. The following year, against a strong and successful West Indies side, the influence of Greig was evident in the recall of Close, as well as the introduction of another five debutants – Mike Brearley, Mike Selvey, Chris Balderstone, Peter Willey and Geoff Miller. By the end of the 1976 series, only four of those who had played in the first Test against Australia in 1975 remained. Another 11 players had been called on at various times during the intervening eight Tests, but none survived to the final Test. While the changes in 1975 had a positive effect in that England drew the next three Tests, they had no impact on England's fortunes against the West Indies the following summer. The imperative to make changes in response to defeats, however, remained.

It might have been expected that Greig would have had an extended period as England captain. His place in the side was absolutely secure – he was not dropped from the moment he was first selected for the Test side until the time he ceased to be available: an unbroken sequence of 58 matches. His record as captain was respectable. True, he led England when they were blown away by the West Indies side in 1976. But he won the series in India in 1976/7, the first of only three such series victories by England in India in the last 50 years.

In 1977, however, Test cricket suffered its greatest-ever upheaval. It was during the Centenary Test between Australia and England in March that Kerry Packer approached Greig with his plans for World Series Cricket. Packer's agenda was to secure exclusive television rights to Test cricket in Australia for his own Channel 9 station. Cricket in Australia had always been covered by the Australian Broadcasting Commission, who had an extant contract with the Australian Cricket Board until the start of the 1979/80 season. It was Packer's plan to recruit the world's leading Test players, with the offer of contracts and fees far in excess of those available to them from their domestic cricket boards, and to set up a rival one-day competition, World Series Cricket, to be covered by Channel 9, to challenge traditional Test cricket. Contracting these players would be an extremely powerful card to play in negotiating with the Australian Cricket Board for television rights to Test cricket; and if this were unsuccessful, Packer hoped that by involving the best players in the world, World Series Cricket would replace, at least in Australia, Test cricket as the principal focus for the cricketing public's interest.

Between March and May 1977, Packer, with Greig his principal recruiting sergeant, signed up the nucleus of the some 50 players who were to play World Series Cricket. These included 18 Australians, among them 12 of the 1977 Australian touring party in England, and 15 West Indians. The England side was to be less affected. Apart from Greig, initially only Snow, Underwood and Alan Knott joined World Series Cricket, though Amiss and later Woolmer did so during the course of the summer.

Negotiations between the cricket authorities and Packer continued until August. But as early as 13 May, Greig was dismissed as England captain. A statement by Freddie Brown, Chairman of the Cricket Council, said that Greig's

> 'action has inevitably impaired the trust which existed between the cricket authorities and the captain of the England side. The captaincy of the England team involves close liaison with the selectors in the management, selection and development of England players for the future and clearly Greig is unlikely to be able to do this as his stated intention is to be contracted to be elsewhere during the next three winters.'

Greig, and the other Packer rebels, continued to be available for the 1977 Ashes series. When, however, negotiations with Packer finally broke down in August, the International Cricket Conference agreed that no player who had made himself available to play in any match previously 'disapproved of by the Conference' (ie a World Series Cricket match) would be eligible to play in any Test match without the express consent of the Conference. The extension of this ban by England's Test and County Cricket Board to county cricket was successfully challenged in the Courts by Packer on grounds of restraint of trade. But Packer players were no longer selected for Test cricket, except in the case of the West Indies, who included Packer players in their teams for the 1977/8 tour by Australia, but not thereafter until the exclusion was lifted.

Early in 1979, the Australian Broadcasting Commission's contract with the Australian Cricket Board came up for renewal. The Board awarded exclusive television rights to its matches, for a period of 10 years, to Channel 9. Henceforth, World Series Cricket, in the form initially of the Benson and Hedges Cup, with its various innovations such as day/night games, coloured clothing and 30-yard circles, would be undertaken under the Board's auspices. Packer ceased to employ the players he had recruited, and the ban was lifted. West Indies and Pakistan selected their Packer players for the 1979 World Cup in England, but it was not until the following winter that England and Australia considered them for selection.

The Captains

Man Management and the Art of Captaincy

Greig's successor as England captain was Mike Brearley. It was an uncontroversial choice because Brearley had been Greig's vice-captain in India the previous winter, and had been regarded as a potential England captain from the time he had skippered Cambridge University in 1964. He had led an MCC Under-25 team to Pakistan in 1966/7, and was mentioned as an alternative to Lewis as captain for the 1972/3 tour. He was also a highly-regarded county captain who had led Middlesex to the County Championship in 1976. His Test experience was both limited and modest. He had made his debut only the previous summer, at the age of 34, and had been dropped after two undistinguished performances. He was therefore in some ways fortunate to be selected to go to India at all, although his county form had been as good as any other contender. In India, although he scored a double-hundred against West Zone at the start of the tour, he did not shine. At the start of the 1977 series, after eight matches, his Test average was only 24. But with the Packer players precluded, there was no other credible candidate for the captaincy among the Test team.

Because he was captain, Brearley retained his Test place for another 31 matches, when otherwise he would undoubtedly have been dropped. In other circumstances, he would have been a more obvious candidate than Amiss to be left out to accommodate Boycott's return from exile for the third Test in 1977, although Amiss had displayed his peculiar fallibility to Australian bowling, and signing for Packer did not count in his favour. Similarly, had he not been captain, Brearley would almost certainly have gone when Gooch emerged as an England opening batsman in 1978. As it was, Brearley moved down the order, displacing Roope who was having a good run in Tests.

In 39 Tests, Brearley averaged less than 23, and never scored a century. No England batsman has ever played so many Tests for so low an average and without scoring a century. In only one series did he average over 30. Brearley, more than any other England captain of the last 50 years, with the brief exception of Christopher Cowdrey, was selected because of his contribution to the team as a captain.

That contribution was not insignificant. His record as captain was won 18, lost four, drew nine. Few doubt that he was both a very astute tactician and had an extraordinary ability to get others to give of their best. Lillee famously described him as having a degree in people. The dramatic improvement in Ian Botham's performance once Brearley took over the captaincy in the famous 1981 series against Australia remains the most famous example.

Brearley also enjoyed the quality Napoleon rated most highly in his generals: luck. He never had to captain England against West Indies at a time when they were the number one Test side in the world, and in his four series against Australia, in one Australia had been depleted by the absence of Packer players, in a second Denis Lillee was absent, and in a third Greg Chappell was unavailable. The one series that Brearley captained when both Lillee and Chappell were in the Australian side England lost 3-0.

Finally, Brearley was fortunate to have at his disposal probably the most formidable bowling attack that England possessed until the last decade. Botham and Bob Willis, England's leading and third leading wicket takers of all time, were at their peak; in support were Chris Old, Mike Hendrick, and John Lever – any two of whom made for a significant second echelon of attack. And in 1977, Derek Underwood, England's greatest spin bowler of the last 50 years, was still around. Most England captains of the last half century would have given their right arm for such a combination.

Brearley announced early in 1980 that he would not be available to tour the West Indies the following winter. This did not automatically preclude him from captaining England for the preceding series in the summer but there were quite strong arguments for making a change. England had just lost a series in Australia, Brearley's batting continued to disappoint, and he was now 38 and could not be expected to get any better.

There were a number of possible successors. Boycott had captained England for four Tests on the 1977/8 tours when Brearley was injured, but was not generally considered to have been a success. On Brearley's next two tours his vice-captain had been Willis, but there were reservations about placing the responsibilities of captaincy on the shoulders of England's principal strike bowler. And then there was Botham. He, and to a much lesser extent Gooch and Bob Taylor, alone returned from the winter of 1979/80 with his reputation enhanced. His all-round performance in the Test in Bombay was phenomenal: he took

13 wickets and scored a century. It was perhaps natural that people doubted whether there was anything he was incapable of. He was the biggest cricketing personality of the day – rather as Andrew Flintoff was 25 years later – and the people's favourite. But he was a gamble: the selectors were setting aside their rule that an England captain needed to have proved himself first as a county captain, and at the age of 24, Botham was England's youngest skipper since the Hon Ivo Bligh in 1882.

John Woodcock, in *The Times*, saw the issues thus:

> 'Botham wants the job. He is as ambitious as he is irrepressible. Just how resilient he might be under the constant pressure, both on and off the field, which attends the England captaincy, remains to be seen. Although maturing fast, he is still impulsive and still only fairly responsible. Who else in the cricket world would have risked life and limb, and the chance of a fortune, playing fourth division football for Scunthorpe United upon returning from Bombay in February? It seemed like madness at the time – yet he got away with it and it would be a pity to discourage such eagerness for the challenge.'

Woodcock added presciently, however, that 'Botham, being the all-round cricketer he is, already has his hands full. The risk of his own game being undermined is obvious to all.'

Just as Brearley possessed an abundance of the qualities required of a good captain, including a substantial dollop of good fortune, so Botham's inherent limitations as a skipper were exacerbated by misfortune. Of his 12 Tests as England captain, nine were against the West Indies. In 1980, England were more successful against West Indies than in any home series against them between 1969 and 1991. They lost the series 1-0, and in the one decisive result had a vital catch been held, West Indies' two-wicket victory might have been turned into an England win. True, in a less wet summer England might not have secured four draws, but they showed more resilience than they had in 1976, or were to in 1984 or 1988. The subsequent tour to the Caribbean was ill-fated. Willis was forced to return home early due to injury. The Robin Jackman affair (the unhappiness of some of the islands' governments about his having played cricket in South Africa) led to the disruption of the tour and the cancellation of the Guyana Test. And Ken Barrington, the much-

Unnatural Selection

loved tour manager, died in Barbados. In the circumstances, England's 2-0 defeat in the series was understandable.

What did for Botham, however, was what John Woodcock had feared at the time he was appointed: the impact of the captaincy on his own form. Before becoming England captain, in 25 Tests Botham had scored 1336 runs at an average of 40 and taken 139 wickets at an average of 18. In 12 Tests as captain, he scored 276 runs at an average of 13 and took 35 wickets at an average of 32. It was his form, rather than England's results, which led Botham and the selectors to conclude that a change in leadership was needed after the first two Tests of the 1981 series against Australia. England lost the first by four wickets. But it was during the rain affected, but evenly contested, second Test, in which he bagged a pair, that the decision to replace Botham was made. There seems to have been little debate about Botham's successor. Brearley was duly appointed, and there followed an extraordinary three Tests in which England achieved unlikely victories with Botham excelling in a famous trio of performances. At Headingley, Botham came in during England's second innings with the score still 140 behind Australia's first innings total, and hit 149 to leave Australia a target of 130 for victory; Willis took 8-43, and England won by 18 runs. At Edgbaston, Australia, needing just 151 for victory, were bowled out in their second innings for 121, Botham taking 5-11. Then at Old Trafford, England were 205 ahead of Australia in their second innings when Botham came to the crease to score 118 in 102 balls to help set Australia a fourth innings target of 506, which was well beyond them. It had been an extraordinary reversal of collective and personal fortune.

Brearley was unavailable for the winter tour to India in 1981/2. It was perhaps unsurprising that the selectors should have sought as close to a like-for-like replacement as they could find: that is to say someone with a proven record as a county captain, even if that meant casting the net wider than those who were in contention for a Test place simply as a player. Thus it was that Fletcher came to be appointed captain. He was regarded as a shrewd captain of Essex, and, at 37, continued to be a heavy scorer in the County Championship. He had not played Test cricket since the Centenary Test in Melbourne in 1977. Then, as in 1974/5, he had been unable to cope with Australia's pace attack, but he still enjoyed a reputation as a good player of spin bowling, reflecting his outstanding tour of India and Pakistan in 1972/3 – though success had eluded him when he returned to India four years later.

But England lost the six Test series against India 1-0. The rubber was characterised by slow scoring and slow over rates. Fletcher seemed unable to show the flair as England captain which he had exhibited when leading Essex. He was also criticized for appearing to show dissent at an umpire's decision against him by hitting the stumps with his bat as he returned to the pavilion. His own form as a batsman was modest with a top score in the Tests of 69, and sixth place in the Test batting averages.

It was, however, by no means a foregone conclusion that Fletcher would lose the England captaincy after the India tour. Perhaps things would have been different had the 1982 season not seen a new chairman of selectors – May, who took over from Bedser. May, of course, had not been party to the decision to appoint Fletcher, and probably felt less constraint in looking elsewhere for his England captain than might have Bedser. He decided to go for someone whose place in the team on merit was not in doubt. In this context, as he explained in an interview at the end of his tenure as chairman, he was mindful of the availability of the newly eligible Allan Lamb from the start of the 1982 season, thus stiffening the competition for middle-order places (though Lamb, Gower and Fletcher at three, four and five would have been a respectable solution – as it was, Fletcher was effectively replaced by the recalled Derek Randall).

But May's options were narrower than they might have been, for during the winter of 1981/2, the South African cricket authorities had secretly recruited fifteen England cricketers for a 'rebel' tour of the country in March 1982. Sponsored by South African Breweries, the rebels were offered big financial rewards for an enterprise which only the most naïve among them could have failed to realize would jeopardise their Test careers. Those involved were Boycott, Gooch, Amiss, Wayne Larkins, Woolmer, Willey, Knott, Geoff Humpage, John Emburey, Underwood, Old, Hendrick, Lever, Arnie Sidebottom and Les Taylor. Eleven of the fifteen had played for England in the previous twelve months, and five had toured India. Gooch, although without county captaincy experience at that stage, might otherwise have been a contender for the England captaincy (he was appointed captain of the rebel team).

As it was, May appointed Bob Willis, who had been England's vice-captain on each overseas tour since 1978/9, and who had been captain of Warwickshire since 1980. In some ways, Willis was an obvious choice. But there were concerns. John Woodcock, in *The Times*, summed up his strengths and weaknesses:

> 'There is no doubting his courage, his determination, or his humour, and he is uncompromisingly opposed to the shabbier aspects of the game. For all that, it is difficult not to have reservations about his appointment. Though currently fit, his record in this respect is not good. He also gets so 'psyched up' on big occasions that he may have trouble applying himself to the team and the tactical requirements of a changing situation. When for two days he captained England in Auckland in 1978, he badly under-bowled himself.'

In what looks like a rare example, for that era, of succession planning, the selectors appointed as Willis's vice-captain David Gower. As England's premier batsman, he was an obvious candidate to groom, and when Willis fell ill in Pakistan in 1984, Gower took over the captaincy and retained it when Willis was briefly fit again in 1984. Aged 26 when he took over, he had the prospect of being in charge for a long period. Inevitably England were hammered by the West Indies in 1984, but a rare series win in India in 1984/5, followed by a thumping Ashes series win in 1985, appeared to secure Gower a prolonged tenure.

Gower, Gatting and Gooch

The wheels became severely detached in the Caribbean in 1985/6. England's batting was completely demolished. Their average first innings total in five Tests was just 207, and in 10 attempts only twice did they reach 250. Gower alone averaged more than 30, but his laid-back style of captaincy came under a lot of criticism. He chose to rest himself for the opening first-class fixture, and went sailing on the second day rather than watch his side in action. Despite the poor results, he appeared to show little interest in net practices – though, as he was at pains subsequently to point out, the quality of the net facilities on offer were such as to make them of dubious value. He also had difficulty handling Botham, who was out of form and less fit than he had been, while another senior player, Gooch, spent much of the tour in a sulk as he found himself subject to local criticism for his prominent role in the 1982 South African Breweries tour. It is impossible to know whether in practice a more ostentatiously assertive captaincy would have raised England's performances in that series. But by leading in the style he did, when the side's performances were so poor, Gower exposed himself to criticism.

There was a case for relieving Gower of the captaincy after the Caribbean tour, but with an indecisiveness which was to be repeated frequently over the next few years, the selectors appointed him for the two start-of-season one-day internationals and the first of the three Tests against India only. Surely they had enough evidence at the start of the 1986 summer to know whether Gower was, or was not, the man they wanted as England captain? Effectively, the arrangement took the longer-term decision out of their hands and placed it in the outcome of the first Test. A mediocre India side won this by five wickets, and Gower's departure became inevitable.

The succession to Gower was again straightforward. Mike Gatting had taken over from Gower as vice-captain when the latter was elevated, had finally established himself as a middle-order batsman and become an automatic selection and had, since 1983, captained his county, Middlesex. Like Gower three years before, he appeared to have the prospect of a long period in charge.

England touring sides progressively developed a 'laager' mentality when faced with the challenges of playing abroad in the 1980s. Partly this was due to the increasing presence of tabloid-press reporters seeking salacious off-the-field stories This had been a particular problem on the 1983/4 tour to New Zealand and the 1985/6 tour to the West Indies. In some cases, the players had legitimate security concerns, such as when the British High Commissioner in India was assassinated the morning after entertaining the England tourists in Delhi in November 1984. Perhaps, too, the players began to be affected by the growing xenophobia of the English popular press in the 80s. All these factors contributed to a predisposition on the part of England cricketers to place the worst construction on the vexations of playing cricket overseas, and to react accordingly.

Pakistan had long been England cricketers' least favourite country to tour. Ian Botham had once famously described it as a good place to send your mother-in-law. England tourists were always sceptical of the impartiality of the home umpires, and during the 1980s mistrust on this score both grew and was reciprocated. Imran Khan had criticized umpire David Constant in the series in England in 1982, and prior to the 1987 tour, Pakistan had asked that both Constant and Ken Palmer be removed from the Test-match panel. The Test and County Cricket Board explicitly rejected this request, although they had acceded to such representations in respect of Constant from the touring Indians in 1982; subsequently there was public criticism of both umpires by the Pakistan manager. It was an unhappy prelude to England's tour to Pakistan in the winter of 1987/8.

It was unsurprising that, the TCCB not having agreed to Pakistan's request in regard to Constant in 1987, the Pakistani cricket authorities should have rejected a similar England request in relation to umpire Shakeel Khan for the first Test of the 1987/8 series. During this Test, Chris Broad refused to accept a caught-behind decision given against him by Shakeel, and almost a minute passed before his partner, Gooch, persuaded him to leave the field. In his autobiography, Gooch described what happened thus:

> 'I was at the other end and there was certainly a noise of some sort as the ball beat the bat. Chris stood there and said 'I didn't hit it, I'm not going', and he started to exchange heated words with the close fielders. 'I am not going', he said, 'you can like it or lump it, I'm staying'. It wasn't just fleeting. He stood there for ages. In the end, I came down the wicket and told him he just had to go. He still refused. Eventually I persuaded him to see sense.'

Whatever the quality of Shakeel's decision, and others in the match (and there is evidence to suggest that they left much to be desired: team manager Micky Stewart considered nine out of England's 20 wickets to fall in the match were down to umpiring error) the judgement of the tour manager, Peter Lush, in merely reprimanding Broad, came not far short of condoning his ostentatious dissent. And Gatting's position after the match was uncompromising, saying that 'we knew roughly what to expect but never expected it to be quite so blatant. They [Pakistan] were desperate to win a Test match, but if I was them I wouldn't be very happy about the way they did it'. This was virtually a declaration of war.

For the second Test, in Faisalabad, one of the umpires was Shakoor Rana. He had been involved in controversy in 1984 when he had turned down an appeal for a catch behind the wicket against Javed Miandad, causing the opposing New Zealand captain, Jeremy Coney, to take his team off the field in protest. He was hardly a man to inspire confidence in the England team three years later. The incident which almost brought the tour to an end was not, however, one involving the adjudication of an appeal. Rather, bizarrely, it was the result of Shakoor accusing Gatting of sharp practice by allegedly moving a fielder without informing the batsman. Gatting vigorously denied the charge, and quickly became involved in an exchange of finger wagging and, it would seem, abuse. Shakoor refused to take the field the next day unless Gatting apologised, and Gatting refused to apologise unless Shakoor reciprocated. No play took place that day while negotiations took place between the two countries' cricketing authorities. Ultimately the TCCB, contrary to the wishes of not only Gatting but also of Lush, instructed Gatting to apologise unilaterally. In a hand written note, Gatting wrote 'Dear Shakoor Rana, I apologise for the bad language used during the 2nd day of the Test match at Fisalabad (sic). Mike Gatting, 11th Dec 1987.'

The incident undoubtedly influenced the decision to remove Gatting from the England captaincy six months later, although the proximate causes were different ones. Whether Gatting's conduct on the field, or his refusal immediately to defuse the situation with an apology, were in themselves sufficient reason to sack him, if not at once then at the end of the winter, is debatable. He did, after all, have the broad support of both his tour and team managers for his actions. And the chairman of the TCCB, Raman Subba Row, flew to Pakistan soon after the events and announced the Board's full backing for Gatting. Privately, each player was awarded £1000 as a 'hardship bonus'. It seemed, therefore, that the authorities considered Gatting to be as much sinned against as sinning.

England's troubles did not end when they left Pakistan in December 1987. There followed a tour to New Zealand and Australia, with three Tests in the former and a single Test against Australia as part of that country's bicentennial celebrations. In that Test match Broad, having scored 139, smashed his stumps with his bat after playing on to Steve

Waugh. He was fined £500 by the England management. In the first Test against New Zealand, Graham Dilley was fined £250 for swearing loudly after appeals for a catch were turned down. *Wisden's* correspondent, Alan Lee, reported on the tour in the 1989 edition thus:

> 'the decision to punish had plainly not met with the agreement of the captain, Mike Gatting, whose attitude to overseas umpires appeared not to have altered. Although Gatting indulged in nothing as overtly appalling as his row with Shakoor Rana in Pakistan, his expressions and gestures regularly spoke volumes. There were too many times when he appeared to be leading English dissent against decisions, rather than calming it. It was impossible to pretend that the series was well umpired, but that is hardly the point.'

West Indies were the tourists in 1988. Since the Ashes triumph of two winters before, England had played twelve Tests, lost two and drawn 10 including three against modest New Zealand opposition. Gatting, albeit under provocation, had in Pakistan indulged in behaviour unbecoming an England captain. He had also permitted, and arguably encouraged, an attitude to develop in his side in which challenging foreign umpires' decisions was regarded as legitimate. On the other hand he had been supported by his local management and the chairman of the TCCB, although the Board had subsequently reprimanded Subba Row for his unilateral decision to award the 'hardship' bonus. He clearly enjoyed the confidence of the team manager in New Zealand, Micky Stewart, and he certainly had the team behind him.

Against this background, the selectors hedged their bets. Gatting was reappointed England captain, but only for the three Texaco Trophy one-day internationals and the first two Tests. Although not unusual, there was little logic in such an arrangement, which was symptomatic of the selectors' lack of strategy for the demanding series ahead. Just as when Gower had been appointed in similar circumstances two summers before, it was not as if there was any uncertainty about Gatting's capabilities – after all, he had led England in 22 Tests. Rather, it appeared as a gesture of the selectors' dissatisfaction with the events of the previous winter. As a way of preparing England for the challenges ahead, however, this very public equivocation was hardly helpful.

England won the Texaco Trophy series 3-0, and drew the first Test – the first time that they had not lost to the West Indies in a Test since 1981. But new storms were brewing. First, Gatting became embroiled in a dispute with the TCCB over his autobiography. Under the terms of his contract, Gatting was not permitted to write about recent tours. One of the chapters in Gatting's *Leading from the Front* was about the events the previous winter in Pakistan, and the TCCB asked for it to be withdrawn. Instead, it was rewritten in the third person by Gatting's co-author, a transparent device which led, in August, to Gatting being fined £5000 by the Board. Then on the morning of Wednesday 8 June, the day after the first Test, *The Sun* ran a front-page story accusing three unnamed England players, one of whom was subsequently revealed to be Gatting, of being involved in a 'sex orgy' at the team hotel on the previous Saturday night. In retrospect, the England authorities might have been better advised to dismiss the story as irrelevant, and wait for it to blow over. But at the time, against the background of the events of the winter, it was more difficult to draw a distinction between their proper concern about the behaviour of England players on the field and the arguably less material considerations pertaining to their private lives. As it was, May, the chairman of selectors, ordered an inquiry into the events. Gatting conceded that he had invited a young woman into his hotel room on the night in question, but denied any impropriety. May accepted this, but nonetheless concluded that 'Gatting had behaved irresponsibly during a Test match by inviting female company to his room for a drink in the late evening.' It was noted that 'warnings had previously been issued to all England players concerning the standard of behaviour expected of them at all time, both on and off the field, and these had been ignored.' Gatting was relieved of the captaincy forthwith, and plans were made for the imposition of a curfew during Test matches.

The action of the selectors was controversial. Graeme Wright, the editor of *Wisden*, wrote in the 1989 edition 'I feel they had little option but to pursue the course of action they did if they were to expect certain standards from the England captain and his team.' Certainly the selectors had little alternative but to take action against Gatting once the allegations were found to have some substance, for it was implicit in embarking on the inquiry in the first place that if the accusations were true, Gatting's behaviour was unacceptable. But defining standards in these areas is notoriously difficult, and in attempting to do so, the selectors served only to encourage the intrusive activities of the tabloid press. It is also doubtful whether such standards were relevant. *The Guardian's* Cricket Correspondent, Mathew Engel, took this view:

> 'Cricket has never functioned in this way. Firstly it is impracticable. It may be possible to control footballers totally the night before they play a dozen games a year. Cricketers often play international cricket more than one hundred days a year, never mind all the county and ordinary touring matches. It is absurd to make such strict rules and everyone knows it (we'll see how long the manager's curfew lasts). Nor is it right. Everyone knows how the game's greatest geniuses – Sobers, Miller and Compton to name only the most obvious – have made their own pre-match rules. Cricket is both a team game and an expression of individuality; a cricketer is entitled to be judged on his cricket. If he fails, he should get dropped; it is as simple as that.'

Gatting was succeeded as England captain by John Emburey. It was in one sense a straightforward choice. Emburey had played in all but four of England's Tests since he had become eligible following the completion of his South Africa tour ban in 1985, and had been Gatting's vice-captain on the previous two winter tours. But he was not – or should not have been – a shoe-in for the England team. In the previous 10 Test matches prior to his appointment as captain, he had taken just 12 wickets for 885 runs. He was to preside over two substantial defeats by West Indies. The second, at Old Trafford, was particularly humiliating, for England's two innings combined mustered only 228 runs and lasted just 103 overs. In an atmosphere not unlike that after England's defeat at Headingley in 1966, the pressure for change was irresistible. While Emburey could hardly be blamed for the failure of England's batsmen, his continuing inability to take wickets raised serious questions about his place in the side, and he was dropped.

The choice of his successor also had the whiff of 1966. Exceptionally, Gooch had been appointed vice-captain under Emburey when normally vice-captains are only formally appointed for overseas tours. Gooch was therefore very much next in line to be offered the poisoned chalice. But the selectors bafflingly decided to look outside the Test side for a successful county captain, and turned to Christopher Cowdrey of Kent for the last two Tests of the rubber. The decision seems to have been taken at a meeting which went wider than the selectors and included a number of the TCCB hierarchy. These latter may perhaps have articulated the danger to the winter tour of India if Gooch were to be appointed, in view of the Indian Government's sensitivity to Gooch's prominent role in the rebel South African tour. Certainly the outcome was not unanimous. Stewart would have reinstated Gatting or gone for Gooch. May, Cowdrey's godfather, said 'our performances in the series to date have been very disappointing but we believe Cowdrey's style of leadership is what is now required.' It was an enormous gamble. Cowdrey's credentials were far inferior to Close's in 1966, or Brearley's in 1981. He had previously played five Tests for England in India in 1984/5 when he had been selected as the nearest – but still very distant – thing that could be found to a substitute for Ian Botham, who was unavailable. He had scored 97 runs at an average of 16 and taken five wickets at an average of 86. Nothing in his performances for Kent since then remotely suggested that he might merit a Test place. The gamble was stupendously unsuccessful. England lost the fourth Test by 10 wickets. Cowdrey scored nought and five, and, as one of a four-man attack, bowled just five overs without taking a wicket.

    Cowdrey had been appointed for two Tests. However, in the county game which followed the fourth Test, he suffered a severe bruise on his foot, and withdrew from the squad. There is evidence in Gower's autobiography to suggest that the selectors found this injury not inconvenient and that they encouraged Cowdrey's early withdrawal – though this is denied by Stewart. Allan Lamb, who was also doubtful because of injury, was allowed until the morning of the match to establish whether he would be fit but failed. And while Cowdrey was fit for the sixth Test of the summer, against Sri Lanka, he was neither reappointed captain nor selected at all, despite his successor as England captain having had no more success in the final Test against the West Indies than his predecessors. Cowdrey himself considered his treatment immensely unfair, and got into trouble for disclosing his complaints in *The Sun*. But the error was not the failure to restore the captaincy to him when he was fit again: he should surely never have been appointed in the first place unless he was seen as an England captain for the long term. With the limited resources at England's disposal, and against the immensely powerful West Indies side of the 80s, it was unrealistic to imagine that simply a change in style of leadership would reverse England's fortunes. What was really needed was someone who was assured a place in the team, and could rebuild it over a number of series.

In fact, Cowdrey's successor was such a man – Gooch. Given that the vacancy occurred at 48-hours' notice, effectively limiting the candidates to those already selected, and that David Gower had been dropped, there was no realistic alternative. A veteran of 28 Tests and a former captain of Essex, he ticked most of the boxes. His tenure, however, was limited to two Tests – and in one of these, his first, he dislocated his finger in the fourth innings of the match requiring Derek Pringle to take over as England's fifth captain in the series. England were due to tour India in 1988/9, and Gooch was appointed for the tour despite the chairman of the Test and County Cricket Board, Subba Row, having asked the selectors not to. Following his selection, the Indians duly cancelled the tour.

For the 1989 season, May had retired as chairman of selectors, and Dexter was chosen to chair the new England committee. The other members were Stewart, Alan Smith (chief executive of the TCCB) and Ossie Wheatley (chairman of the TCCB's Cricket Committee). The Board, as a direct consequence of the choice of Gooch for the abortive India tour, empowered Wheatley with a right of veto in England committee decisions. Dexter was no fan of Gooch. In August 1988 he had written of Gooch that 'he has all the charisma of a wet fish'. (Christopher Martin-Jenkins, in *The Cricketer* wrote in similar vein that Gooch 'remains a faithful PC Plod, not an innovative head of CID'.) Dexter was mindful of Gooch's unsuccessful year as Essex captain in 1987, after which he had stood down from the job – though he resumed it in 1989. Stewart's clear preference was for Gatting to be England captain. Stewart had managed the England team which Gatting had led to Australia in 1986/7 and to Australia and New Zealand in 1987/8. They had established a close rapport, and Stewart shared many of Gatting's resentments at the way he had been treated in recent times – although he had, of course, been a party to Gatting's dismissal as captain the previous summer. In an Ashes summer, Gatting possessed the important qualification of having been captain of the England team which had triumphed in their most recent series encounter. It seems that Stewart persuaded Dexter that Gatting was the right man for the job, and he was duly Dexter's recommendation to the full England committee. Gatting, however, was unacceptable to Wheatley. Using the powers with which he had been vested to represent the wider interests of the game, he vetoed Gatting's appointment. Wheatley took the view that his behaviour in Pakistan had been unacceptable, and that the England cricket authorities could not be seen to be condoning it. No doubt he would have considered that Gatting should not have been made England captain at the start of the previous summer. But his having gone for other reasons, Wheatley was not disposed to reinstate him. With Gatting vetoed and Gooch not favoured, the choice of England captain reverted to Gower.

Gower's tenure as captain was to endure only slightly longer than that of his three predecessors. Nineteen eighty-nine was a disastrous summer for England, losing as they did 4-0 to Australia. It was one thing to be thumped by the mighty West Indies, quite another to fail to compete in a series against an Australian side which had previously lost two Ashes rubbers in succession. The series was a selectorial nightmare. No less than 29 players, including five debutants, represented England that summer. A total of 22 changes were made, of which 14 were forced on the selectors. Never before had England been so dogged by injury. Only for the fifth Test were all members of the squad picked at the weekend before the Test still fit on the Thursday morning. Another three changes were forced on the selectors when it emerged during the fourth Test that there was to be another unauthorised tour, led by Gatting, to South Africa the following winter. The other members of the touring party were Kim Barnett, Broad, Tim Robinson, Alan Wells, Bill Athey, Mathew Maynard, Cowdrey, Emburey, David Graveney, Dilley, Neil Foster, Paul Jarvis, Richard Ellison, Greg Thomas and Bruce French. All but Graveney and Wells were former England players, and 12 had played for England in the course of the previous 18 months. They were banned from playing for England for five years, though the ban was lifted, not entirely logically, when South Africa was readmitted to the Test-playing fold at the end of 1992.

These misfortunes visited upon the England side in 1989 were beyond Gower's control. But he had attracted criticism for the lack of conviction in his captaincy and his inability to relate to at least some of the younger players. He had also fallen out completely with the team manager, Stewart. He considered resigning at the end of the series,

Unnatural Selection

but decided to leave the decision to the England committee – in effect to Dexter. Dexter decided that the summer's humiliation necessitated radical change, and Gower was sacked.

The period 1987-9, spanning as it did the tenures of two chairs of selectors, five captains, one team manager, and 37 players, represented the lowest point in the administration of the England cricket team in the last 50 years. It had started well, with England retaining the Ashes in Australia. In the next three years, however, they played 25 Tests, and won only one – the singleton against Sri Lanka at the end of the 1988 series. Of the other 24, 11 were lost, and 13 drawn. Four out of five series were lost. At first the selectors kept their cool: only 16 players were called on in the 1987 series against Pakistan, which was about average for that era. But in 1988 against West Indies and Sri Lanka, 23 players were selected and in 1989, against Australia, an extraordinary 29 – the largest number ever. Over the two summers, 37 different players represented England in Tests. In all, the selectors made 50 changes between the first Test of 1988 and the sixth of 1989. Seventeen were necessitated by injury (or enabled by a return of a player from injury); three were the consequence of players signing up to the rebel tour of South Africa; four can be attributed to decisions to change the balance of the side – especially as between seam and spin bowlers – from one Test to the next; and a couple were the result of the shenanigans about the captaincy in 1988. But a staggering 24 were due to the selectors simply taking a different view as to who was the better player.

Philip DeFreitas was dropped on four separate occasions during these two summers. In part this reflected his strong fitness record: as other quicker bowlers succumbed to injury (as, at various times, did each of Gladstone Small, Jarvis, Dilley, Newport, Foster, Angus Fraser, Devon Malcolm and Botham), DeFreitas was recalled, only to be omitted when the player he replaced, or another, returned from injury. Tim Curtis, Martyn Moxon and Broad were dropped, recalled and dropped again over this period. It is perhaps most remarkable in the case of the batsmen how fickle the selectors were. Gooch opened the batting in 11 of the 12 Tests in this period: his partners were successively Broad, Broad, Moxon, Curtis, Curtis, Curtis, Robinson, Broad, Broad, Curtis, Curtis, and John Stephenson. (The openers on the occasion Gooch did not play were Curtis and Moxon.) Only Broad, in the first Test of 1988, managed a fifty opening with Gooch, and in that sense it might be argued that the selectors had little option but to try alternatives.

What is surprising is that the selectors judged that someone like Broad or Curtis, having failed to convince them during one spell in the side, might convince them in a second. Lower down the order, both Maynard and Rob Bailey were dropped after one Test. Maynard and Bailey made their debuts in the fifth Test against the West Indies in 1988 – Bailey scoring a respectable 43 in the first innings. One had to be left out for the far less demanding Test against Sri Lanka which followed to accommodate the returning Lamb, but it was less clear why the other should be dropped as well to include another debutant, Barnett. The logic, such as it was, was that Barnett had only not played in the fifth Test, ahead of Bailey and Maynard, because of injury, but it is debatable whether that should have trumped the case for continuity. As it was, a staggering seven changes were made to the side between these two Tests. The following year, Chris Tavare was recalled after a five-year absence in place of Gatting, who had suffered a family bereavement. Whether Tavare was a good choice is open to question – his previous Test record had been relatively modest, and he was not having an outstanding summer in county cricket. But if he were the right choice for the third Test, it is difficult to understand why the selectors should have regarded Robinson as the better choice for the fourth Test, when all that had changed in the interim was that Tavare had scored two in his single innings in that third Test.

Why were the selectors so fickle over this period? Partly, they had to cope with a plethora of injuries, which to some extent had consequences beyond simply filling the place of the injured player. But the majority of injuries were to bowlers which does not explain the inconsistent selection of batsmen. Partly it was due to the changes in the chair of selectors, and the captaincy, with each new captain having his own ideas as to who should be in the side. In the first side in which Gooch was involved in the selection, for the singleton Test against Sri Lanka at the end of the 1988 summer, which saw those seven changes, it is easy to see his hand in some of those picked, such as his old mate Emburey.

Overwhelmingly, however, the selectors felt that they needed to react to the poor performances on the field – not least under pressure from the press which wanted to see failure punished by dropping those who had failed, even though they might have been the best available. Fifty changes on from the side fielded at Trent Bridge in 1988, the England side at the Oval in 1989 was not obviously stronger, and would not have been materially improved even had the South Africa rebel tourists not been excluded. Of the 26 players picked over the two summers who were not in that Trent Bridge side, only five – Robin Smith, Jack Russell, Mike Atherton, Fraser and Malcolm – went on to develop substantial subsequent Test careers. Of the other 21, seven were effectively precluded from doing so by touring South Africa, though of those, at most two had much Test-cricket potential left in them. It is difficult not to believe that greater continuity would have yielded better results than such often apparently random change.

Gooch was in most ways the obvious successor to Gower, just as he had been to Cowdrey 12 months before. But it did involve a fairly substantial change of heart on the part of Dexter, who had, effectively, sacked Gooch at the start of the summer. Dexter explained the decision thus:

> 'times have changed. David Gower was appointed to captain what looked a very settled England team [this was hardly the case: 23 players had represented England during the summer of 1988]. But a lot of things have happened, and a lot of players have been lost. We are in a new situation and Graham is very well qualified to handle it.'

The reality was that there was no alternative to Gooch. Apart from Gower and himself, none of the Oval side was a credible England captain, and Dexter was hardly likely to repeat the experiment of bringing in an outsider to lead the team. It was ironic that the tour for which Gooch was now appointed captain should be to the West Indies – where he had been so unhappy in 1985/6. There was a clear risk that, with Gooch as captain, the tour, or parts of it, might be cancelled just as the India tour the winter before had been, but the risk did not materialize.

The touring party picked for the 1989/90 tour to the West Indies which followed represented a determination by the selectors, and especially the new captain, Graham Gooch, to break with the past, and mould a new England team with a greater emphasis on character and professionalism. Most obviously, this manifested itself in the omission of Gower and

Botham. But a different view – presumably Gooch's – was taken of a number of players who had been regarded as the best 11 available players for the sixth Test of 1989. Of these, not only Gower, but also Stephenson, Atherton, Pringle, Nick Cook and Alan Igglesden all failed to make it into the touring squad. In the case of Stephenson, Igglesden (who had been debutants for the sixth Test) and Atherton (who had made his debut one Test earlier), the selectors simply made a different judgement as to whom they regarded as the best young players around. This reversal was most obvious in the selection of Nasser Hussain ahead of his exact contemporary Atherton. The other uncapped batsman was Alec Stewart, which meant that four of the seven specialist batsmen (Larkins and Bailey were the others) had not played in the 1989 series. Of the bowlers, Pringle was judged unlikely to be effective in Caribbean conditions, while the preference for the uncapped slow left armer Keith Medlycott ahead of Cook and the uncapped Ricardo Ellcock ahead of Igglesden again represented a changed assessment of relative talent.

In that England were a more successful side over the next couple of years than they had been over the previous two and a half, the scale of the changes made to draw a line under what had gone before might be judged justified. But of the new selections, only Stewart immediately cemented a place in the side for the long term. Hussain was not picked again for another three and a half years after his first tour, and it was 1996 before he came to command a regular place. Medlycott and Ellcock never made it into a Test side, Bailey was not chosen again after 1989/90, and Larkins played only another three more Tests. In terms, therefore, of building a settled side for the future, the small revolution of 1989/90 must be considered a limited success.

But in another respect, the appointment of Gooch in 1989 marks a watershed. In the 27 years and 270 Tests between 1962/3 and 1989, England had a total of 17 captains (excluding those such as Graveney and Edrich who stood in for one-offs) and changed the captaincy 23 times. In the 25 years and 295 Tests since there have been 9 captains (excluding one-offs such as Lamb and Mark Butcher) and just 11 changes. Before 1989, the selectors had given the captaincy to players who had not played in the Test immediately prior to that in which they assumed the leadership on 12 occasions. On three of these (Dexter 1964, Illingworth 1969 and Illingworth 1973) the new captain had been unavailable for the tour preceding his appointment. On eight of the other nine (Smith

Unnatural Selection 75

1963, Smith 1964, Close 1966, Lewis 1972, Denness 1973, Brearley 1981, Fletcher 1981 and Cowdrey 1988) the new captain had previously failed to make the side on his merits as a player. Gower's selection as captain in 1989 cannot be placed in quite the same category as that of those eight. He had not played in the last two Tests of the 1988 series, but this was due to a loss of form which, in a batsman with 100 Tests behind him and still only 31 might reasonably have been expected to be a temporary disqualification from the England side; and indeed he had been chosen for the abortive 1988/9 tour to India. Of Smith, Close, Lewis, Denness, Brearley, Fletcher and Cowdrey, only Brearley, as it were, died in his bed. Smith, Lewis, Denness, Fletcher and Cowdrey were all dismissed at least in part because they were not considered to be good enough Test cricketers. Lewis alone retained his place in the side after losing the captaincy, but only for one Test. Smith was to have three more Tests but not for six years after he relinquished the captaincy. For Denness, Fletcher and Christopher Cowdrey, their Test career ended once they ceased to be captain. After 1989, the England captain was always chosen from among those already holding down a place as a player in the England side.

Gooch was to captain England in 32 out of their next 37 Tests (missing five due to injury). It was a welcome period of stability, and to begin with England seemed to be making progress from the nadir of 1989. They raised their game against the West Indies in 1989/90, being unlucky to lose 2-1, beat New Zealand and India in 1990, had a disappointing tour of Australia in 1990/1 (but not as bad as 1989), bounced back to square a series against West Indies in 1991 for the first time since 1973/4, beat New Zealand again and reached the World Cup final in 1991/2. Thereafter, things began to deteriorate as England lost to Pakistan 2-1 in 1992 – albeit in a close-fought series. The winter of 1992/3 was a disaster, with England losing 3-0 to India and, for the first time, to Sri Lanka. The summer of 1993 saw England no more competitive against the Australians than they had been in 1989. After four Tests, England were 3-0 down and Australia had retained the Ashes. England had lost eight out of their last nine matches. At this moment, Gooch resigned.

In his autobiography, he described his rationale:

'Before Australia completed an even bigger innings victory at

Headingley, I knew for certain that the time had come for me to stand down. Nobody would talk me out of it this time, although Keith Fletcher tried. I was in a gloomy depression, banging the same old drum, but the players weren't reacting. Nobody was following my tune. It was time for a fresh, younger bandleader with a newer approach and brighter ideas.'

The Modern Approach

The principal candidates for the succession were Stewart, Atherton and, rather surprisingly, Gatting. The odds, at the time of Gooch's resignation, were 6-4, 7-4 and 7-2 respectively. Apparently Hugh Morris, Barnett and Moxon (all inexperienced at Test level and none at the time in the England side) were also considered, but not, one suspects, for long. Stewart was the heir apparent in that he had been Gooch's vice-captain in New Zealand in 1991/2 and the sub-continent in 1992/3 when he had captained England twice in Gooch's absence. These two defeats (one against Sri Lanka) could hardly have helped his cause, but a more substantial issue was whether he could combine captaining with keeping wicket. Generally in his early Tests, Stewart played as a specialist batsman, but in the 1993 series he had been the incumbent wicket-keeper. Atherton was an established batsman and former captain of Cambridge University. Gatting had a track record as captain (which appealed to some but deterred others), but his decision to lead the rebel tour to South Africa in 1988 did him no favours, and he had recently been dropped from the England side.

The decision was taken by the England committee, comprising Dexter, Micky Stewart, Fletcher (Stewart's replacement as team manager), Wheatley and Alan Smith. The decision was unanimous in favour of Atherton, although Micky Stewart put in a word for his son, as Dexter light-heartedly but insensitively disclosed. Announcing the decision, Dexter said that 'our agreed criteria included the need for mental toughness. All six might have brought that to the job but where Michael scored was in the area of tactical awareness and a fresh approach'. At 25, Atherton was England's youngest captain since Botham.

Atherton, like Gooch at the end of the 1989 series, was both instrumental in selecting the side for the tour to the West Indies which followed and determined to build for the future saying, 'we want a clean

Unnatural Selection

break with the past'. The oldest player in the party was 30: Gooch was unavailable, Gatting was overlooked, and Gower was not recalled despite speculation that the new regime might be more favourably disposed towards him. But while it was a younger side, it was hardly a 'clean break': 14 of the 17 in the party had been among the 24 who had appeared against Australia the previous season, and there were no uncapped players. Of the 10 who played in the 1993 series but were not picked for the 1993/4 tour, eight were recalled to the Test side at some point – most in the next couple of years. Only the veteran Foster, and the unfortunate Mark Lathwell, were discarded for good. Once again, the selectors found that those once thought to be the best players did not necessarily cease to be so because the side in which they played lost.

Atherton was permitted an even longer unbroken run as England captain than Gooch – in all, 52 Tests. His record was similar to Gooch's, losing two series to Australia, two to West Indies in the Caribbean but squaring a series in England, squaring and losing series against South Africa, beating New Zealand twice and India once and losing at home to Pakistan. It was a modest set of achievements, but England were a modest side. Atherton's place in the side was never in doubt, he was always available and he did indeed exhibit mental toughness and resilience. His two predecessors had stood down – or had been asked to stand down – at the conclusion of a losing home Ashes series. After England lost again to Australia in 1997, Alan Lee, in *The Times*, wrote 'he [Atherton] is tired, worn down by the burden of four years in one of the toughest jobs in British sport, and, unless a few days of rest and recuperation can reinvigorate his mind, he knows the time has come.' It is perhaps surprising that the selectors did not recognize this. Atherton himself says that he sought to resign as soon as the Ashes were lost after the fifth Test, but agreed to see through the series. He goes on to express regret at not going then, but allowing himself to be persuaded by the then chair of selectors, David Graveney, to carry on. In part he was influenced by England's exciting and unexpected victory over Australia in the sixth Test. It was, however, to be for only one more series. After defeat in the Caribbean in 1997/8, Atherton handed in the seals of office, and this time there was no push back.

It was a two-horse race for the succession. While Alec Stewart had been Atherton's vice-captain on his first three overseas tours, Nasser Hussain had undertaken these duties on his final two. Both were formally interviewed for the job by Lord MacLaurin, chairman of the England and Wales Cricket Board, and David Graveney. Derek Pringle, an Essex man and fan of Hussain, perhaps unfairly wrote in *The Independent* 'neat and freshly peeled at all times, Stewart comes closest to conforming to the image of a captain, as MacLaurin the cricket fan remembers them from the past', adding that 'if Stewart has the image, it is Hussain who has the imagination'. The problem for Stewart, apart from his alleged lack of imagination, was his age, 35, which might suggest a short tenure in the role (although he was famously fit, and younger than Gooch when he was appointed in 1989); and his position as England wicket-keeper. Although on the 1997/8 tour, he had played as a specialist batsman, there was a desire that he should resume the role of all-rounder. So why was he chosen ahead of Hussain? Alan Lee, in *The Times*, wrote:

> 'Hussain has never quite shed the combustibility of his earlier years and such traits have no place within the edicts laid out for the job by Lord MacLaurin of Knebworth, the chairman of the England and Wales Cricket Board. Hussain is also an intense, self-absorbed man, not naturally sensitive to others. His astute cricketing brain may one day make him an outstanding captain, but a sense of inner security must come first'.

Hussain did not have long to wait. While Stewart got off to a good start, with a home series win over South Africa, this was followed by defeat by Sri Lanka in a singleton Test and the customary series defeat by Australia the following winter. It was, however, England's failure to qualify for the 'Super Six' stage in the home 1999 World Cup behind Zimbabwe which finished Stewart's reign. This time the alternative to Hussain was Mark Ramprakash, who was also interviewed. But Ramprakash was even more combustible than Hussain, and a less established England batsman. Since his recall to the England side in 1996, Hussain had been an automatic selection, and his leadership potential had been realized through his captaincy of the England 'A' side and the England vice-captaincy for three successive overseas tours. Like Atherton, he was to be granted an extended period in charge comprising four years and 45 Tests.

Unnatural Selection

Hussain took over against the familiar backdrop of England failures, but what ought to have been a gentle introduction with a home series against New Zealand proved anything but. England's 2-1 defeat represented a new nadir, and, now paired with Duncan Fletcher, the touring party to South Africa in 1999/2000 once again sought to draw new lines under previous debacles. They argued for the retention of experienced players such as Atherton, Stewart and Graeme Thorpe for the South Africa tour against pressure from the other selectors (in particular, it seems, Brian Bolus) for wholesale change. Nevertheless, it was a new look party, with four uncapped players – Chris Adams, Gavin Hamilton, Graeme Swann and Michael Vaughan – along with two others (Darren Gough and Andrew Flintoff) who had missed the 1999 series through injury. Fletcher has written 'it concerned me that the tour was being seen as something of a trial. So many players were being tried out that it had the look of a development trip rather than a full-blown test tour.' It was a familiar story of the selectors over-reacting to failure.

England's fortunes improved from 2000, with unlikely series wins in Sri Lanka and Pakistan, and, at last, against the West Indies. England captains, however, find it hard to survive defeats in Ashes series, especially successive Ashes series. May, Dexter, Denness, Gower, Gooch, Stewart and Atherton all finished their captaincy in close proximity to an Ashes defeat. It was and remains the ultimate accolade or disgrace for any England captain. Hussain failed to regain the Ashes in 2001 and 2002/3 and England once again had a poor World Cup in southern Africa. Hussain was now 35 and vulnerable.

Hussain had been England's one-day captain from the time he had been appointed Test captain. A veteran of 88 one-day internationals, his record was unexceptional: he had made a solitary century, averaged only 30, and his strike rate of 67 runs per 100 balls was relatively low even by the standards of the time. So Hussain's decision to quit the short form of the game was unsurprising. Stewart had stood in for Hussain as captain in one of the World Cup matches, but clearly was not a permanent successor. The choice rested between Marcus Trescothick and Michael Vaughan. Duncan Fletcher has written:

> 'Vaughan was always going to be the successor in my eyes because…I thought Marcus Trescothick a good deputy but not the main man. Vaughan had a bit of a mean streak in him

which I liked, and the ability to put players in their place if they stepped out of line – an essential quality for any leader'.

So Hussain led England to victory over Zimbabwe in the first two Tests of the summer, and Vaughan led England to victory in the final of the mini-tournament involving South Africa and Zimbabwe in the middle of the summer. Hussain found it difficult when he reappeared with the Test squad, many of whom had just played under Vaughan, for the first Test against South Africa at Edgbaston. 'I didn't know whether to stick or twist', Hussain wrote of that game.

'I didn't know whether to captain the side in my own way or in the way that Vaughan did it, the way I now perceived, rightly or wrongly, the boys wanted me to do it. I knew they had been shown a different way by Michael and they liked that way, and it became clear to me that I had taken the side as far as I could.'

Hussain was clearly suffering from a crisis of self-belief, perhaps exacerbated by the stress the controversy over whether England should play in Zimbabwe during the World Cup had generated just a few months before. By the end of the Edgbaston Test, he was ready to stand down. Fletcher has written 'so it came to the last day and again Hussain called me in for a meeting, with Graveney (chairman of selectors) there too. I looked into Hussain's eyes and knew it was over.' Vaughan took over as captain of the Test side as well as the one-day side.

This pattern of departing the scene as Test captain a relatively short time after relinquishing the captaincy of the limited-overs side was to become familiar over the next decade. Every new England Test captain since the inception of one-day internationals has, with the exception of Stewart for a very brief period, begun as captain of the side for both forms of the game, even when, as in the case of Atherton in 1993, or Andrew Strauss in 2009, he was not in the limited-overs team immediately prior to his appointment. All long-serving England captains over the last 20 years have, however, reached a stage when the increasing demands of the short form of the game have led them to stand down – or be stood down – from it. For Atherton, Hussain, Vaughan and Strauss, surrendering the leadership of the one-day side was the beginning of the end of their time as Test captain.

Vaughan enjoyed a golden couple of years of Test cricket at the start of his tenure as captain: in 2003, England drew the South Africa series 2-2; in the winter of 2003/4, they beat Bangladesh 2-0 and West Indies 3-0, though they lost 1-0 in Sri Lanka; in the summer of 2004, all seven Tests against New Zealand and the West Indies were won, and the following winter, England won 2-1 in South Africa. Then, following a 2-0 victory over Bangladesh at the start of the summer of 2005, came the famous 2-1 victory over Australia, and the regaining of the Ashes for the first time since 1989. Vaughan stood supreme as England captain.

For the next three years, the history of the England captaincy was dominated by Vaughan's fitness. His troublesome knee flared up during the tour to Pakistan at the end of 2005, causing him to miss the first Test (Trescothick stood in, as he had done once before in 2004) and play in some discomfort in the next two. He went to India with the touring party in early 2006, but it soon became clear that the operation which he had had in December had not solved the problem. With Trescothick also returning home before the series against India started, and Simon Jones having to return home injured too, in the week before the first Test England had lost three players and needed a new captain.

The Hero as Captain

There was little time for deliberation. In selecting Andrew Flintoff, Fletcher was choosing the greatest of the 2005 Ashes heroes, the people's favourite, the biggest personality in the side, and the man who wanted it most. The rationale was that for picking Botham in 1980 (an unhappy precedent) and to some extent Greig in 1975 (a happier one). In view of subsequent events, it is worth noting that Flintoff made a favourable first impression. *Wisden's* correspondent, Simon Wilde, wrote of the India tour in the 2007 edition:

> 'in the Ashes of 2005, he [Flintoff] already seemed the complete cricketer, but he now displayed the extra dimension: that of the caring considerate captain, tactically astute, at ease with responsibility, yet still fiercely passionate…Despite worries that he might be overworked, the captaincy enhanced rather than diminished his game.'

In the circumstances, a 1-1 outcome to the series, with England having the better of the Test which was drawn, was a good result.

In Vaughan's continuing absence, Flintoff captained England again during the first half of the summer of 2006 against Sri Lanka, but then he too succumbed to injury. With Trescothick still mentally fragile though back in the Test team, the next most senior player in the squad with serious Test captaincy qualities was Strauss. There was an issue as to whether Strauss should be appointed for the whole series against Pakistan for the rest of the summer (as he was) because Flintoff hoped to be fit again before the end of the series (he was not). And Flintoff wanted an assurance that he would be captain for the tour to Australia the following winter, while Strauss was unhappy about taking on the job if the assurance was given. On this, it appears things were left somewhat ambiguous.

With Vaughan still unfit for the winter of 2006/7, but Flintoff recovered, the selectors had to make a straight choice between Flintoff and Strauss. Miller favoured Strauss, Graveney was for Flintoff, and the deciding vote was Fletcher's, who plumped for Flintoff. There were positives in Flintoff's favour – his success in India the previous winter and his standing and presence in the team. But there was also apprehension about how Flintoff would react if he were not to be appointed. 'If Flintoff was not captain he would be a huge hindrance to the side' Fletcher has written. 'He would have teamed up with his mate Steve Harmison and they could have been difficult to manage, as the team management had discovered previously, and especially for someone like Strauss who would still have been learning the captaincy business on such a difficult tour.' This was a perfectly rational reason for preferring Flintoff to Strauss, but not an entirely comfortable one, carrying with it as it did an air of unspoken threat.

The tour to Australia, and the World Cup which followed, were famously disasters. England lost the Ashes in a 5-0 drubbing, and as usual failed to progress to the last four in the World Cup. Flintoff's leadership and off-field behaviour were heavily criticized, especially his drinking exploits culminating in the 'Fredalo' incident in the Caribbean during the World Cup, which led to him being fined and his credentials as an England captain shredded. Yet it could all have been different. Had Ashley Giles caught Ricky Ponting when he was on 35 on his way to 142 in the second Test, England might well have won and gone into the third

Test of an Ashes tour in Australia at 1-1 for the first time in 20 years. Who knows how they might then have performed, their morale intact rather than, as was the case, shattered through defeat? By such fine threads do reputations hang.

By the time of the World Cup, Vaughan was back as England captain after his long layoff. It might have been difficult for him to have resumed the reins had Flintoff led England to victory in Australia but as it was it was an easy decision provided he was genuinely fit. There was no question that he continued to be worth his place in the side, as he demonstrated in his comeback Test – the second against West Indies in 2007 when he scored a century. As chance would have it, he had been prevented from playing in the first Test due to a broken finger: with Flintoff now injured too, Strauss captained in Vaughan's absence. Vaughan captained England for the next 18 Tests.

By the winter tour of 2007/8 to New Zealand, Vaughan was beginning to experience the same doubts about continuing the captaincy as had Hussain nearly five years before. A big factor seems to have been his inability to establish the same sort of rapport with Peter Moores, who had taken over as England coach in 2007, as he had enjoyed with Duncan Fletcher. But perhaps the pressures on an England captain in the modern game are such that they can only be endured for a certain duration. Atherton resigned after 52 Tests and Hussain after 45. By the start of the 2008 season, Vaughan had captained in 45 too. Despite a series victory over New Zealand at the beginning of the summer, Vaughan gradually lost his lust for the captaincy, and he called it a day following defeat by South Africa in the penultimate match of the series, when England failed to prevent the visitors from chasing 280 in the fourth innings.

Vaughan did not want this to be the end of his Test career, and nor did his successor as captain. Hussain, Stewart, Atherton, Gooch, Gower, Gatting and Willis had all continued to play Test cricket for varying periods after they had relinquished the captaincy. Vaughan was only 33, he had scored three centuries in 18 Tests since he was restored to the captaincy and in this period averaged a respectable 36. No obvious candidate was being excluded from the side through his inclusion. He chose not to play in the last Test of the South Africa series, which was understandable, though electing not to tour India in the winter might have been a mistake: he had hoped to be selected in the party for the West Indies tour which followed later in the winter, but clearly that would have required dropping a batsman from among those who had gone to India, which would have been difficult. Effectively Vaughan's batting spot went to Owais Shah, and while he did nothing in the West Indies to cement an England place, in the fourth Test he was injured allowing Ravi Bopara to replace him and post a century. He would now be difficult to drop.

So the selectors demanded that Vaughan demonstrate his form in county cricket at the start of 2009, even though, unlike Bopara, he was centrally contracted. But Vaughan missed out when invited to play for MCC against Durham in April 2009, and was unable to produce the goods playing for Yorkshire either. It is difficult to avoid the impression that the selectors were unenthusiastic about recalling Vaughan; that they wanted to move on. Sensing this, Vaughan retired from first-class cricket in June 2009.

For the selectors, the timing of Vaughan's resignation as captain was inconsiderate. They had as little time to ponder about the next England captain as they had in India in 2006 when they appointed Flintoff: Vaughan had resigned on the Sunday, and the next Test would start on the Thursday. Potentially there were three candidates for the succession: Paul Collingwood, Strauss and Kevin Pietersen. Collingwood had been the one-day captain since the World Cup, but he resigned from that position at the same time as Vaughan – if not exactly in solidarity then for associated reasons.

Strauss had stood in for Vaughan when he was injured in the first Test of 2007 but while his place in the side was now secure, it had been less than a year since he had been omitted from the tour to Sri Lanka; and he was not in the one-day side. Pietersen was the stand-out batsman in the side, and his appointment offered the opportunity to revert to a situation in which there was a single captain for all England internationals. There was, however, no doubt that Pietersen was a volatile individual, and that he was less obviously a 'team man' than some of his predecessors. The word many commentators used to characterise his appointment was 'gamble'. It is interesting to speculate whether the selectors would have come to a different conclusion had they been under less time pressure. Their subsequent decision to jettison Pietersen certainly suggests second thoughts, and perhaps these second thoughts matured quickly.

Pietersen won his first Test as captain, against South Africa at the Oval, and England were victorious in the one-day series which followed. Pietersen was also praised for the way in which England responded to the terrorist attack on Mumbai during the series in India later in the year. While the team initially departed to the UK in the wake of the atrocity, Pietersen encouraged them to return to India after a short interruption. It was particularly appreciated by the Indian cricketing public. Both the Test and one-day series were, however, lost. Meanwhile, Pietersen's relations with Peter Moores were deteriorating, even more so than Vaughan's and Collingwood's had. Effectively, in a crisis which developed over and just after Christmas, he demanded Moores' resignation. Others have written about this in detail. Suffice to say here that, while the England and Wales Cricket Board accepted that they could not continue with Moores in view of the evidence of the lack of respect that he generated in a significant number of senior players, equally they felt that they could not tolerate a captain who sought to dictate terms to the Board. Had Pietersen not been on holiday in South Africa at the time, it might have been easier to reach an accommodation with him, though the evidence from the crisis the Board next faced with Pietersen, three-and-a-half years later, inspires little confidence that the availability of more time for negotiation would have made a settlement any easier. As it was, the rather bizarre outcome was that both Moores and Pietersen 'resigned'. This time there was only one candidate for the succession: Andrew Strauss.

Stablity Again

The success achieved by the England team under Strauss's leadership will be familiar to most readers: the Ashes victories of 2009 and 2010/1, the 4-0 defeat of India in 2011 resulting in England being acclaimed the top Test-playing nation. Strauss became the most respected England captain at least since Brearley, and he was regarded as having the job for the duration. For as long as England were winning, his own form was a secondary issue; and for as long as he was demonstrably worth his place as a batsman, he could survive a dip in the team's performances. The problem, in 2012, was that both were happening. England lost 3-0 to Pakistan in the United Arab Emirates, drew 1-1 with Sri Lanka away, beat the West Indies 2-0 at home, and lost 2-0 at home to South Africa, and with it their number-one status. In addition, Strauss's form as a batsman had unquestionably been on the decline since the start of 2011: in 19 Tests up until the end of the summer of 2012 he averaged a rather modest 32 – and that had been inflated by two centuries against an unexceptional West Indies attack. At the start of 2011, he had averaged 43. The decision he had to make was whether he was the man to lead England in the back-to-back Ashes series of 2013 and 2013/4, at the end of which he would be approaching 37. If not, he needed to make way for his successor during the winter of 2012/3. Against that background, and keen to avoid speculation about his future if things were not to go his way in the winter ahead, Strauss resigned at the end of the summer of 2012. No doubt coincidentally, he had the pleasing symmetry of having played 100 Tests and been captain for 50.

Alastair Cook had been Strauss's vice-captain since 2008/9, and had captained England in Bangladesh when Strauss was rested for that tour in 2009/10. He was also England's one-day international captain. Seldom in the history of England Test selection has an heir to the captaincy been so apparent, and his appointment as Strauss's successor was a formality.

At first, all went well for Cook. In the first Test following his appointment, against India at Ahmedabad, he made 176. It was in England's second innings in a match they lost, but his ability to master the Indian spinners was a fine example of leading from the front, and with two more centuries in the next two games, he was instrumental in reversing England's fortunes and securing a 2-1 series victory – the first for England in India since 1984/5. An inability to win in New Zealand in early 2013 was a minor setback, but wins in the home series of 2013, against New Zealand again and more importantly against Australia, suggested that the transition in the captaincy from Strauss was seamless.

It all went wrong, of course, with England's annihilation by Australia the next winter. Cook, who had made little impact with the bat in the home Ashes series, fared no better in the conditions in which he had been so dominant three years before. And as a captain, he provoked unfavourable comparisons with his opposite number, Michael Clarke, who seemed more innovative and less formulaic. Of course, it helped that Clarke had at his disposal an attack led by a rejuvenated Mitchell Johnson which proved more effective than England's. But four times in the series, England had Australia struggling in their first innings, only on each occasion to fail to drive home their advantage. There was speculation as to whether Cook could survive England's humiliation – though in the event Flower's resignation was deemed sufficient sacrifice.

This might have been expected to be England's nadir, but further nemesis awaited. After drawing with Sri Lanka at Lord's in a game they dominated, England were equally dominant in the second Test match when reducing their opponents to 277-7 in their second innings, a lead of just 169. There followed a partnership of 149 between Mathews and Herath, leaving England needing 350 to win. They lost by 100 runs and Cook was much criticised for his tactics. After a drawn first Test against India in the series that followed, England won the toss and fielded in the second Test in conditions clearly favourable to swing and seam bowling. But England's bowlers failed to exploit them and even while managing to reduce India to 145-7, were unable to prevent them reaching 295. India went on to win the match.

Cook's form had not returned. He had now gone 14 Test matches without a century, and England had gone 10 Tests without a victory. For the first time, certainly since Flintoff, a serious debate was under way in the media as to whether the England captain was up to the job. Many commentators called for Cook to go. Simon Barnes, in *The Times*, for example, wrote after the Lord's Test

> 'Cook's captaincy has been less than convincing. At the time when leadership has been most urgently required, he hasn't led. Players have consistently performed below their potential, his tactics have been iffy, and his entrenched belief that Asian cricketers can be subdued by the bouncer in any circumstances... has been shown to be utterly false. Not that he seems to have noticed, and his Plan A, B and C is to bowl James Anderson and Stuart Broad until they are incapable of standing.'

He was not alone. Brearley, for example, also believed that the time had come for Cook to go.

He might well have gone, had there been a plausible replacement. Matt Prior, the vice-captain in Australia, was now injured, Ian Bell, the vice-captain for the summer, was thought to be uninspiring and Joe Root too young. Broad had experience captaining England in T20 cricket and Anderson had once expressed aspirations to captain but neither was seriously considered with fast-bowling captains being such a rarity in international cricket. So Cook survived. In the next Test he was dropped on 15, went on to make 96, England won the match, and the next two which followed as India disintegrated like England had against Australia. Although Cook had, in April 2015, gone 17 Tests without a century, and victories under his captaincy have not entirely erased doubts about his tactical acumen, for the time being the post of England Test captain is not vacant. For Cook, the spotlight turned to his performances in one-day cricket. The selectors came late to the conclusion already reached by most England followers that neither as opening batsman nor as captain was he of the calibre of his international counterparts, and he was dropped only after the series in Sri Lanka a couple of months before the start of the World Cup. It remains to be seen whether he can defy the precedents of Atherton, Hussain, Vaughan and Strauss and continue for an extended period as Test captain while someone else skippers the 50-over side.

CHAPTER THREE

STRIKING A BALANCE

For the selectors of cricket teams, the choices are not just about the quality of the competing players; they are also about the mix of players in the side. The composition of the cricket team is guided by convention, but is not dictated by rules. There is always debate as to which combination of ingredients will generate the tastiest dish. A key to a successful recipe is to have bowlers who can bat, batsman who can bowl, and wicket-keepers who can bat. Such players may be regarded as all-rounders, though traditionally the term has been less frequently used in respect of wicket-keeper batsmen.

Generally, selectors will choose the best five batsmen and best four bowlers available. The area for debate in terms of striking a balance rests with the last two places – numbers six and seven in the batting order. Of course, where the same name appears among the five batsmen and four bowlers, the problem is much reduced. But even internationally over the last fifty years, that is extremely rare. Probably only Garry Sobers, Imran Khan and Jacques Kallis qualify over extended periods of their careers. England have had three great batting/bowling all-rounders in this timescale – Tony Greig, Ian Botham and Andrew Flintoff: while there were only moments when the second strings to their bows would have been sufficient in themselves to have included them in the Test side, their second discipline (bowling in the case of Greig, batting in the case of Botham and Flintoff) was strong enough to solve one of the selectors' problems. Greig was a very credible fifth bowler, while Botham and Flintoff were credible number-six batsmen.

For the best wicket-keeper also to be one of the best five or six batsmen is also relatively rare, though there are outstanding current examples in Kumar Sangakarra and A B de Villiers. Alec Stewart, whose place as a batsman in the England side was undoubtedly merited, arguably was also the best wicket-keeper in England in the second half of his Test career, and therefore could be regarded as the country's premier all-rounder of the last 50 years.

With Greig, Botham, Flintoff or Stewart in the side, the selectors' problem was much reduced – though not in this respect eliminated other than when, very briefly, the careers of two of them overlapped. In other circumstances, compromise had to be made – to play at six or seven a batsman and weaken the bowling, a bowler and weaken the batting, or a player whose second discipline, be it bowling or batting, was judged sufficient to offset the fact that he would not merit a place on the basis of his first discipline alone. This latter consideration applied equally to wicket-keepers.

Wicket-Keepers and All-Rounders

Some contemporary commentators have lamented a halcyon age when the choice of wicket-keeper was determined by glove skills alone, but if such an age ever existed, it was not in the last half century. Batting capability has always been an important consideration. England's wicket-keepers in the Antipodes in 1962/3 were John Murray and Alan ('A C') Smith. Murray went as first choice, but did not impress Ted Dexter, who wrote of him in his post-tour report 'not a class keeper standing up to the wicket. No doubt about his ability standing back. Batting, as usual, flattered to deceive.' He lost his place to Smith, of whom Dexter was more complimentary, while noting that he was 'not quite up to world-class standards.'

Nevertheless, it was Murray who was expected to be selected at the start of the 1963 season, and a major surprise when England instead recalled Keith Andrew, whose only other Test had been in 1954. It was a bold choice, for whatever Andrew's abilities behind the stumps, he was no sort of batsman, normally batting no higher than nine for his county. It is difficult not to regard this as other than a poorly thought-through decision, for he was dropped after just one game and a completely different strategy was adopted. This was to select a batsman who could keep wicket.

Jim Parks had come to keeping relatively late in his career, and he was no great stylist, but he played in 36 out of England's next 38 Tests, and did not let England down. In his report following the 1964/5 tour to South Africa, M J K Smith wrote of him 'I consider he is under-estimated as a keeper. Very safe catcher standing back and by no means below standard to the spinners.' His batting offered an important contribution to the balance of the England side in the mid-60s with an average of 32.

Unnatural Selection

He was a victim of the night of the long knives after the fourth Test in 1966, when he was succeeded by Murray. It was an extraordinary irony that Murray, who had been excluded from the England team by Parks's superior batting, should proceed at once to score a century, batting at number nine, which made a crucial contribution to England's victory in the Oval Test.

Murray, who was still only 31, might have been expected to have had an extended run. In the second Test of the 1967 series, he took six catches in an innings to equal the then word record. But he played only two further Tests. The selectors' eyes had been caught by Alan Knott, then just 21 but in his fourth season with Kent. His selection for the penultimate test of 1967 was more than just a hunch. He had received good reports from his tour of Pakistan with the MCC Under-25 team in 1966/7 *(Wisden's* correspondent Alex Bannister wrote in the 1968 edition 'his wicket-keeping could hardly be faulted' and that 'he batted with greater skill and resolution than many of the specialised batsmen'). He went to the West Indies in 1967/8 as reserve to the surprisingly recalled Parks. But Parks conceded 58 byes in the first three Tests of the series, including 33 in one innings, and scored just 48. Knott had his chance and took it, giving away just two byes in the last two Tests, and scoring two not-out fifties, the second of which enabled England to hold out for a draw with nine wickets down and thus win the rubber. He had demonstrated that he was just the man England were looking for and the job was his for a decade. He played in 87 out of 88 England Test matches from 1967 to 1977 in which time he averaged 34 with the bat and was generally considered the best wicket-keeper in the world.

But if England had finally found a decade of balance behind the stumps then the position of bowling all-rounder was considerably harder to fill in the years before Grieg. Probably the nearest England came to finding a classical Test-class all-rounder between 1962 and 1969 was Barry Knight, who performed the 'double' of 1000 runs and 100 wickets in the County Championship on four occasions. Principally a bowler he scored two Test centuries, although the second was immediately followed by being dropped (he shares this unfortunate distinction with Peter Parfitt, John Crawley and Ravi Bopara in the last 50 years). Dexter did not appear to be a fan of Knight. He wrote in his post-1962/3 tour report 'not too sure against fast bowling

– useful medium pace bowler and good in the field when giving his best. Bit of a playboy – he let these activities affect his performance on the field on a couple of occasions.' The tour manager, the Duke of Norfolk, was perhaps harsher on this latter point: 'as a tourist he complied with all orders and instructions but did not put first the necessity to keep fit to play cricket. It seemed that he was intent on sampling Australian hospitality to the full at the expense of the game.' When picking the team for the following winter's tour, the minutes of the MCC Selection sub-Committee record that 'it was agreed to recommend that in view of his adverse report on the recent Australian tour, B R Knight should be seen by the secretary of MCC before his departure to India.' This interview appears to have borne fruit, as the manager's report after the India tour said of him 'despite the fact that he did not like India, a fact that, in public, he concealed well, he was a great success on the tour both as a cricketer and a man. He tried very hard and I give him top marks.' Nevertheless, while he played in another 12 Tests for England, he never cemented his place.

At county level, both Fred Titmus and Ray Illingworth could be considered all-rounders. Each did the double on many occasions and Titmus scored useful runs in Test cricket, particularly on his three tours of Australia. But he never scored a Test hundred, and his career Test average of only 22 was that of a bowler who could bat. Illingworth was even less effective before he was appointed England captain: at the end of 1968, his Test average was just 16.

In the absence of an all-rounder other than Parks, England's default option in this period was to play only four front-line bowlers (that is to say, players who were expected to take a full share of the bowling load). Setting aside the India tour of 1963/4, when selection was dictated by the 11 men who happened to be fit, England played 60 Tests between the start of the 1962/3 tour and the end of the 1968/9 tour, and in only eight were five front-line bowlers picked. (Twice only three were selected.) Of the remaining 52, the attack comprised two quicker bowlers and two spinners on 30 occasions – a balance rarely repeated, and hardly at all outside Asia. Only in 18 of 205 Tests in the 70s and 80s did England play only two quicker bowlers, and only 13 times in 286 Tests since. Such a limited quick-bowling attack appears very foreign to students of the modern game, but it was not without its success. Of the seven Test victories in the period 1963-1968 against the three strongest

Unnatural Selection

Test-playing countries of the era – Australia, West Indies and South Africa – five were with attacks of only two front-line bowlers of medium pace or above.

One of the reasons why England managed with just four front-line bowlers was a willingness to use occasional bowlers. These ranged from the very occasional indeed, Ken Barrington with an average of five overs per Test and Brian Close with nine, through to the respectable first change bowlers, Dexter with 14 overs and Basil D'Oliveira with 22 overs. There was also the alternative spinning option of Bob Barber – average of 20 overs. The latter three were all at times regarded as genuine all-rounders, though their respective career Test bowling averages of 35, 40 and 43 indicate batsmen who could bowl a bit. Increasingly from the 1960s England captains have become more reluctant to use occasional bowlers, helped by reduced over rates. In the early 60s around 110 overs might be expected to be bowled in a day, making it much more difficult for a captain to manage exclusively with four bowlers than is now the case when 90 overs is effectively the maximum.

Basil D'Oliveira

The extent to which he was perceived as being an all-rounder was crucial in the events which led to the infamous 'D'Oliveira affair' in 1968. D'Oliveira was born and played his early cricket in apartheid South Africa, where, as a cricketer of mixed race, he was ineligible for selection for the Test side. Emigrating to England, he made his County Championship debut for Worcestershire in 1965 at the age of 33, and that season finished sixth in the national batting averages. He made his first Test appearance at Lord's in 1966, and scored three fifties in six innings against the West Indies that summer. His 88 was the highest score in England's dismal showing in the Headingley Test, and he survived the cull which followed it. He played in five of the six Tests in the summer of 1967, during which he scored his first Test century. He was to have less success in the ensuing tour to the West Indies, however: in five Tests he scored only one fifty and averaged just 22, while his enthusiasm for partying also gave rise to comment. There was a case, therefore, for not picking D'Oliveira at the start of the 1968 series against Australia. But he made the side for the first Test at Old Trafford, as one of seven specialist batsmen. Although a similarly balanced team had beaten West Indies at the Oval in 1966, the limitations of England's attack were exposed by the Australian batsmen, and England lost by 159 runs. England's top scorer in the match was D'Oliveira, who made 87 not out in England's second innings.

It was clear that England would play a fourth bowler in the second Test, and with Barrington expected to be back after injury, two of the batsmen who had played in the previous Test had to be omitted. Dennis Amiss and Barber were duly dropped but England also included Colin Milburn in the squad of 13 as cover for Barrington. When the final 11 was revealed on the morning of the match, however, both Barrington and Milburn were included, and D'Oliveira was left out. After his innings at Old Trafford, this was a harsh decision, and one apparently inconsistent with the rationale underlying the composition of the squad.

In his autobiography, Colin Cowdrey, England's captain, explains the omission of D'Oliveira thus:

> 'he was dropped from the side at Lord's, despite his excellent second innings batting at Manchester, because of his bowling. At Manchester I had used him as first change. He had bowled tidily, but without the thrust to keep the pressure on at that point in the game. At Lord's we wanted more of a seam bowler than a swing bowler to follow up the initial assault of Snow and Brown. We brought in Colin Milburn as a batsman and Barry Knight as a seam bowler. After talking the matter over on the eve of the game the selectors agreed that D'Oliveira was not a justifiable choice. Our thinking was right. Milburn scored 83 in England's only innings, and Knight took 3-16 in Australia's first innings of 78 all out.'

What is odd about Cowdrey's explanation is the implication that D'Oliveira and Knight were somehow alternatives: that D'Oliveira had been chosen for Old Trafford principally as a bowler. Of course, with only three front-line bowlers, D'Oliveira (and Barber) had to make a significant contribution to the attack. But he still bowled only 30 out of England's 218 overs – and not because he was hit out of the attack: he went for just 45 runs and took two wickets. Before that Test his best bowling figures in 14 Test matches were 2-38. In the West Indies he had taken 3-293 in five Tests. In first-class cricket in 1968 prior to the

Unnatural Selection

first Test he had bowled only 40 overs and taken only four wickets. The selectors could not possibly have regarded D'Oliveira as a front-line bowler when they picked him for the Manchester Test, and indeed his contribution as a bowler exceeded their legitimate expectations. His bowling was irrelevant to the decision to pick him for that match, or to drop him afterwards. The interesting question is not the selection of Knight, which requires no great explanation, but of Milburn ahead of D'Oliveira. Had England needed an opening batsman, the preference for Milburn would have been more understandable, but Milburn batted at three in a side with Cowdrey, Barrington and Tom Graveney – all of whom had occupied this position for England on many occasions. Somewhere in the selectors' minds the fact that D'Oliveira *could* bowl had hidden the fact that he was the most successful batsman.

    D'Oliveira's subsequent county form as a batsman was indifferent that summer. After Milburn's success at Lord's, and the return of Dexter for the fourth Test, there was no obvious opening, and when Cowdrey was injured England decided to blood the young Keith Fletcher rather than recall D'Oliveira – a decision undoubtedly merited on the basis of current form.

D'Oliveira's route back to the England side for the Oval was a circuitous one. The original squad chosen included five bowlers – John Snow, David Brown, Ken Higgs, Illingworth and Derek Underwood – but Cowdrey, who had played for Kent at the Oval the previous week, believed that the pitch might be more favourable to the medium pacer than the faster bowler. After the 12 was announced, he investigated the availability of first Tom Cartwright and then Knight as possible additions to the party, but neither was fully fit. He then approached D'Oliveira, whose inclusion was announced just as one of the opening batsmen in the squad, Roger Prideaux, fell ill. It appeared that D'Oliveira had come in as cover for Prideaux, but that was not the case. Although D'Oliveira's bowling had flourished to the tune of 55 first-class wickets at an average of 15, it remains curious that Cowdrey viewed him as an alternative to Cartwright and Knight. But the selectors sought no replacement for Prideaux. In the event, Higgs was omitted, Milburn moved up the order to open with John Edrich, and D'Oliveira made the final 11 alongside four specialist bowlers – 'mainly as a batsman though his bowling could be useful', as Cowdrey subsequently wrote. In the first innings, he scored

158, and took a vital wicket in Australia's second innings as England forced a famous victory.

The 16 players chosen after the Oval Test for the 1968/9 tour to South Africa were: Cowdrey, Graveney, Geoff Boycott, Edrich, Barrington, Fletcher, Prideaux, Knott, Murray, Brown, Snow, Bob Cottam, Cartwright, Underwood and Pat Pocock. One place was left open for another opening bowler depending on the progress of Jeff Jones's recovery from injury. Commenting on D'Oliveira's omission, the chairman of selectors, Doug Insole, said:

> 'the selection committee regarded D'Oliveira as a batsman from the point of view of an overseas tour rather than as an all-rounder as he is known here. He is put alongside seven other batsmen, including Milburn whom we left out. Fletcher is regarded as the most promising young middle-order batsman and we were worried about the age of the middle-order batting. He is also a fine utility fielder in spite of what happened at Leeds.' [the fourth Test, where Fletcher, included ahead of Phil Sharpe of Yorkshire, had dropped two or three slip catches which the Headingley crowd had made clear they would have expected Sharpe to pocket.]

With Boycott, Edrich, Cowdrey, Barrington and Graveney automatic selections, and a third opening batsman at least highly desirable to cover for injury, if D'Oliveira were to be included in the party it could only have been at the expense of Fletcher. And as Insole indicated, that would have made for a more mature batting line up than would have been ideal. But it is still very difficult to understand how this was sufficient to tip the balance in favour of a man whose scores in the recent series had been 0 and 23 not out, and against the man whose scores had been 9, 87 not out, 158 and 9. And in settling for D'Oliveira as effectively Prideaux's replacement for the crucial test at the Oval, they had indicated a preference for him over Fletcher which was now reversed. Nor is it easy to understand how D'Oliveira's bowling could be so easily discounted, especially in view of the rationale for his being called up for the Oval Test. It is one thing to challenge the notion that D'Oliveira could be regarded as a front-line bowler; quite another to reject the contribution he could make as a fifth bowler. Without D'Oliveira,

England would have been forced in South Africa to play five specialist bowlers, and carry a very long tail (none of the bowlers selected averaged above 17 in first-class cricket in 1968 or could be considered credible batting at seven), or rely on Barrington as a fifth bowler. In any case, if Cartwright's medium pace was going to be of value in South Africa, it is hard to understand why D'Oliveira's not dissimilar style of bowling would not have been of at least some utility: after all, he had been selected for the Oval Test precisely as a substitute for Cartwright.

Alongside the various omissions of David Gower more than 20 years later, and of Kevin Pietersen in 2014, the exclusion of D'Oliveira from the touring party to South Africa stands as the most controversial Test selection of the last fifty years. John Woodcock, in *The Times*, supported the decision:

> 'the fact is that D'Oliveira had a poor tour of the West Indies last winter, and although he got another 100 for Worcestershire yesterday, he has had only a moderate county season. As the selectors saw it, he does not rate as a Test match bowler overseas; he is an indifferent fielder, and beside the other batsmen he failed to make the grade. They have, I think, made the right decision, though there will be those, no doubt, who will accuse them of either prejudice or cowardice.'

But E W Swanton, in *The Daily Telegraph* wrote 'if justice has been done, it has scarcely been seen to be done. In the second place, has not cricket lost a golden chance to throw at least a temporary bridge between the divided sporting communities in South Africa?' And a *Telegraph* leader claimed that 'the MCC appear to have bowed to non-existent pressure'.

Looking back nearly 50 years, it is hard to say whether non-cricketing reasons had any part to play in the decision not to select D'Oliveira. Certainly all those involved deny such a suggestion. If the selectors had been minded to exclude him from the tour in order to avoid the risk of his inclusion causing its cancellation, they would hardly have chosen him for the Oval Test. Such an omission would have been quite uncontroversial, while if there was a predetermination not to pick him for South Africa, selecting him for the Oval was a very high-risk policy. They could also uncontentiously have omitted him from the side for the first Test of the 1968 series. If there was a conspiracy, it was a bungled one. It was also one to which the four Test selectors (Insole, Peter May, Alec Bedser and Don Kenyon) and captain during the summer of 1968 could not, judging by their decision making, have been a party. But the tour party was not picked by just these five. Also present at the meeting on the evening of the fifth day of the Oval Test were Arthur Gilligan, president of MCC, Gubby Allen, treasurer of the MCC, Les Ames, the tour manager, Billy Griffith and Donald Carr. According to Cowdrey, the meeting went on until two in the morning. It can only be speculation, but it seems likely that the position of D'Oliveira was the reason for this. Aside from the choice between Prideaux and Milburn, and possibly the inclusion of Bob Cottam, the rest of the party largely selected itself. It is at least plausible that, as had been the case 12 months earlier over the appointment of Close as captain for the West Indies, the majority of the selectors were outgunned by the additions to the committee. And their concerns would have focussed both on the implications for the tour going ahead with D'Oliveira in the party, and also, perhaps, on the scope for embarrassment in South Africa of D'Oliveira's evening lifestyle, as manifested in the West Indies.

Of course, this was not the end of the story. Shortly after the original party had been selected, Cartwright withdrew due to injury. D'Oliveira replaced him. This was consistent, up to a point, with the geography of D'Oliveira's route to the Oval Test. But it was hardly consistent with the explanation of the chairman of selectors for D'Oliveira's original exclusion from the tour party ('...regarded...as a batsman...rather than an all-rounder'). J A Bailey, assistant secretary of the MCC did his best:

> 'unfortunately the injury to Cartwright has not responded to treatment in the way that had been hoped. The selection committee therefore decided to replace him. They considered that there was no direct replacement for a bowler of Cartwright's specialist abilities and felt, therefore, that the balance of the touring party had inevitably to be altered. Basil D'Oliveira is being invited to join the touring party.'

It is difficult to understand the cricketing logic of deciding to replace a bowler with a batsman just because there was no like-for-like replacement bowler available. And it is in any case doubtful whether Cartwright was quite as unique as Bailey's statement implied. He had not played a Test match for three years, and on the 1964/5 tour to South Africa had taken 2-196 in his solitary Test appearance. It was easy therefore to see in D'Oliveira's late inclusion the influence of contrary non-cricketing pressures to those which had allegedly caused his original exclusion. Among those who took this view was the Government of South Africa, for whom it was now much easier to justify cancelling the tour on the grounds that the England selectors had responded to political pressure in picking D'Oliveira than it would have been had he been selected in the first place. Another 25 years would pass before the two countries met again.

Two Genuine All-Rounders

The struggle to find a balanced England team abated in the early 70s with Knott behind the stumps and Illingworth's batting transformed after assuming the captaincy. In only three of his 31 Tests as captain did he play just four bowlers, and in only two Tests was he the solitary spinner. He and Knott regularly filled the number six and seven batting positions and from 1972, the balance of the side was further enhanced with the arrival of Tony Greig.

It is perhaps easy to forget quite what an exceptional player Greig was, as his England career was a relatively short one. But he played in 58 successive Test matches, and was never dropped. During his time in the England team, he was the highest run scorer, with over 3500 runs, including eight centuries, at an average of 40. Though a less outstanding bowler, his career Test return of 141 wickets at 32 is comparable with those of, say Illingworth (122 at 31) or Phillip DeFreitas (140 at 33). While Illingworth was captain, Greig's place in the side offered the option either of playing an additional bowler, or extending the batting with Knott or Illingworth at eight. And on Illingworth's departure, Greig facilitated England's inclusion of five front-line bowlers in all but one of the Tests in which he played until he ended his career.

What changed in this period, however, was the assumption that a five-bowler attack necessarily implied two spinners. As we have seen, in the 60s, and under Illingworth's captaincy, two spinners were played frequently in four-man attacks and always where five operated. In all

Tests in the period 1963-73, England played two spinners in 77% of matches. Thereafter, the percentage has gradually declined: 54% from 1973/4 to 1980, 45% in the 80s, 14% in the 90s, and 16% since 2000. The 1973/4 series in the West Indies provided the first example of England playing four faster bowlers in a five-man attack, and the 1980 series against the West Indies the first example of playing no spinners in a four-man attack.

The change in balance was partly the consequence of the change in the regulations relating to the covering of pitches in the late 70s which eliminated the sort of wicket on which Underwood was so lethal in the fifth Test against Australia in 1968. Thereafter, pitches outside Asia were generally unsympathetic to conventional finger spin, although there have been periods in the last 30 years when the Oval and Old Trafford offered help to slow bowlers. Partly, it has been the consequence of the dearth of outstanding England spin bowlers between Underwood and Swann: at no time during this period have two spinners been among the best five bowlers in England. Increasingly, the role of the spinner has become exclusively defensive: to rest quicker bowlers, especially when one of a four-man attack, and to slow scoring rates when the quicker bowlers fail to break through.

The loss of Greig (never to return) and Knott to World Series Cricket at the end of 1977 meant that a new balance had to be struck. Serendipitously, the departure of Greig coincided with the arrival of Botham who had first drawn attention to himself in a match between Somerset and the West Indies in 1976. Botham found his way into the England one-day squad for the Prudential Trophy against the West Indies at the end of the season, playing in two matches, scoring 1 and 20, and taking 1-57 from six overs. He did not make the 1976/7 touring party, but made his Test debut for the third Test against Australia in 1977, at the age of 21. He was the youngest England cricketer to earn a Test cap since Knott in 1967. He bowled Greg Chappell to secure his first Test victim and took 5-74 in his first Test innings. From the first Test of the second England tour in the winter of 1977/8 he played in 65 consecutive Tests. Botham and Greig only twice played in the same side. Botham was not quite a like-for-like replacement for Greig: Greig was probably the superior batsman and Botham certainly the superior bowler. Within a year of his debut, however, Botham had scored his first three Test centuries, and had established himself in the number-six batting position vacated by Greig.

Problems Behind the Stumps

Alan Knott was to prove more difficult to replace. His longstanding understudy was Bob Taylor, who had been on three overseas tours with England. As a wicket-keeper, he was regarded as at least Knott's equal. He was also a useful batsman, and his 97 in the second innings of the Adelaide Test of 1978/9 turned the game and set up an England victory which clinched the series. But he was not a credible number seven batsman, as his Test average of 16 testifies, so the selectors faced three alternatives: play a second bowling all-rounder; find a wicket-keeper who could bat; or play only four bowlers. All three approaches were tried in the years ahead.

The first strategy was implemented through the selection of Geoff Miller. He was England's best off spinner in the late 1970s, and his career record of 60 wickets at an average of 31 makes him England's best off spinner between Illingworth and Graeme Swann (John Emburey took more than twice as many wickets, but at a significantly inferior average and strike rate). It was, however, his batting which made him attractive to the selectors following the departure of Greig and Knott. He batted in the top five for his county and so seemed capable of filling the number six or seven slot for England. Thus in the 26 Tests between the end of the 1977 season and the start of the 1980 season, Taylor kept wicket in 25, and Miller played in 21.

The second strategy was adopted in 1980, when Knott returned to the side following the end of his suspension for defecting to Packer. In fact, it was surprising that he was not recalled for the tour to Australia the previous winter, for which he was eligible. It seems that Mike Brearley favoured his inclusion, but was overruled by Bedser, as chairman of selectors, on the grounds that Taylor's loyalty and performance during Knott's absence should not be dismissed. At 34, five years younger than Taylor, he might have expected a further long run with the gloves, but after four Tests without reaching double figures, he was dropped. The selectors next looked to a new generation of 'keepers with batting potential, David Bairstow and Paul Downton each playing in three of the next six Tests. Neither, however, managed to score a fifty. England went into the 1981 season with no clear policy as to their wicket-keeper, and for the only time in the last 50 years, played three different glovemen in the series – Downton, Taylor and Knott. The recall of Knott was controversial. John Woodcock, writing in *The Times*, was unimpressed:

> 'There will be much resentment at Taylor's omission…Of Taylor's three matches this summer, at Lord's, Headingley and Edgbaston, England won two. He brought to the wicket-keeping job a standard not seen since he had last played for England. As an England slip fielder once put it 'Bob's timing is so good that you can't hear the ball hit his gloves…So why has he been dropped? The answer…[is] that England are planning to play two specialist spinners, Emburey and Underwood. If, to do that, they leave a batsman out, it is thought that Knott's batting will be more useful than Taylor's. If this view is based on Knott's much earlier record with the bat than his recent one…no one should decry it.'

In fact, England did not play two spinners in the game for which Knott was recalled, and indeed did so only once in the 13 Tests for which Taylor was not chosen in this period. Or rather, in 10 of these Tests, England relied on Peter Willey as their second spinner. He was a better batsman than Miller and a far inferior bowler (a Barrington rather than a D'Oliveira). But the selectors do seem to have regarded him as an alternative to Miller. Both made their debut in the 1976 series against the West Indies, but thereafter in their overlapping careers they played in the same side only twice.

Knott's batting in what proved to be his last two Test matches did match his earlier record. At Old Trafford, his 59 in England's second innings, following Botham's 118, helped set up England's victory. In the second innings of the final Test his 70 not out ensured that England secured a draw. He was unavailable for the 1981/2 tour to India, and subsequently signed up for the rebel tour to South Africa.

With the departure of Knott, the selectors reverted to Taylor, who played in the next 28 Tests. In all, he played 30 Tests at the age of 40 or over (a record for any England Test player in the past 50 years) and by the end of his career he was England's oldest wicket-keeper since Herbert Strudwick in the 1920s. But England struggled to achieve a balanced side. Miller played in seven of these 28 Tests, and Vic Marks, another off spinning all-rounder, in another six (but three times as part of a four-man attack); in the other 15, England had either to manage with just four bowlers or accept a tail beginning at number seven.

The problem of fielding a balanced side only grew as the 80s progressed. Taylor was dropped as England wicket-keeper at the start of the 1984 season, although many still regarded him as the best wicket-keeper, not only in England, but in the world. But the selectors were conscious that they would need every run they could find against the visiting West Indians, and Taylor's batting was certainly on the decline. His successor was Paul Downton, whose star had been on the wane since his selection three years previously. Jack Richards and Ian Gould were Taylor's understudies on the 1981/2 and 1982/3 tours respectively, while for the 1983/4 tour, the judgement was made (in the event correctly) that Taylor's fitness record was so good that no specialist reserve wicket-keeper need be included in the party. Downton was therefore perhaps fortunate to be selected: he was batting at eight for Middlesex, below Emburey and Edmonds, which hardly suggested that he was a significantly better batsman than Taylor. But he had a run of 23 Tests, all under Gower's captaincy, whose personal choice he seems to have been. As early as 1985, Downton's wicket-keeping was criticized for being below Test-match standard ('his performance with the gloves was uneven', wrote John Thicknesse in the 1987 *Wisden* of his performance in the West Indies in 1985/6). But crucially he did not deliver with the bat, failing to score a Test fifty and averaging only 10 against the West Indies in 1985/6. When Gower was relieved of the captaincy in 1986, Downton's fate was sealed.

For the next three years, the wicket-keeping gloves oscillated between Bruce French and Richards (though Downton was recalled for three Tests against the West Indies in 1988: it was his misfortune to play a disproportionate 16 of his 30 Tests against the strongest international team of the 1980s). French was Downton's heir apparent, having toured alongside him in the previous two winters. But he was no batsman. Richards, with an average of 40 and 1000 runs to his name in 1986 was chosen as the second wicket-keeper for the 1986/7 Ashes tour. In fact, his superior batting led to his supplanting French, and in his second Test he scored the first century by an England wicket-keeper since Knott in

1977. It is perhaps surprising that Richards did not cement his England place on the back of that achievement. But the consensus was that French was a sufficiently better 'keeper than Richards, especially to spin, to be preferred. French thus regained his place at the start of the 1987 season, and with a fifty and a 40 in his first two innings of the series, suggested that the margin of Richards' superiority as a batsman might be smaller than previously assumed. French was injured for most of the 1988 season during which first Downton and then Richards were recalled. But Richards fell out with Surrey during the course of the season, was released from his contract and disappeared from the county game.

But it was not just the absence of a wicket-keeper batsman that was creating problems for the selectors. There was also the availability, and later the form, of Botham. His run of successive Tests was broken when injury forced him home early from the 1983/4 tour to Pakistan; and he was then unavailable for both the 1984/5 tour to India and the 1987/8 winter tours. He was also suspended from all first-class cricket from 29 May to 31 July 1986 for bringing the game into disrepute by admitting in a newspaper article that he had used cannabis. He was injured for most of the 1988 season, but was recalled for the third Test against Australia in 1989 before succumbing to injury once more before the series was over.

The selectors faced a real challenge in deciding whether or not to pick Botham in his later years. He had been triumphant once more against Australia in 1985, but in his next 18 Tests over the period 1985-89 he took only 33 wickets at 48 each. He had scored a century at Brisbane in 1986/7, but thereafter had passed 50 only once. It was perhaps understandable that he was recalled in 1989: he was still only 33, his record against Australia was outstanding, and the selectorial cupboard was pretty bare. But it did not work, and the decision not to select him for the subsequent winter's tour to the West Indies was almost certainly the right one.

The desirability of finding bowlers who could bat in the absence of a wicket-keeper batsman, or of Botham (or of both), led the selectors down a number of blind alleys in the 80s and into the 90s. When Derek Pringle was first picked for England in 1982, while captain of Cambridge University, it was very much as an all-rounder. In *The Times*, John Woodcock described him as 'a fine prospect – a big strong all-rounder with the confidence of youth'. In his early Tests he batted at seven for

England, and when recalled in 1986 to fill the place made available by Botham's suspension, and in 1988 to fill the place made available by Botham's injury, it was at six. Pringle was less than three years younger than Botham, but played only 11 of his 31 Tests in the same side as him. But while there were times when his place was merited as a specialist bowler, he was not an all-rounder at Test level, as his batting average of 15 indicates.

Another attempt to find a substitute for Botham was the selection of Christopher Cowdrey for the tour of India in 1984/5. May, the chairman of selectors, described his choice as a 'hunch'. Certainly the empirical evidence to support it was limited – in first-class cricket in 1984, Cowdrey's batting and bowling averages were an unexceptional 31 and 30 respectively. While he played in all five Tests on the tour, where he batted at six and was used as an occasional bowler, he did nothing to justify the hunch. Later in the decade the selectors turned to David Capel. In 15 Tests (only one in the same side as Botham) he batted at six on 10 occasions, and seven on the other five. His career Test batting average of 16, and his bowling record of 21 wickets at an average of over 50, suggests a classic case of picking someone in the hope of providing balance. The reality was that neither Capel nor Cowdrey added much to the side in either discipline.

Throughout the 80s, England's preferred option was to play five specialist bowlers even when Botham was not in the team, even if it meant picking a bowler such as Pringle or Capel, who might not otherwise have made the side, to bat at six or seven. In nearly half their Tests, they played two (and once three) spinners. There was a distinct change of policy with Graham Gooch's appointment as captain at the end of 1989. During his era, until his resignation in 1993, England played just four specialist bowlers in 26 out of 37 Tests. Gooch took the view that in a day of no more than 90 overs, in which it was not unreasonable to expect any bowler to bowl 25 overs, four bowlers were sufficient. In terms of sheer stamina this was true, but it limited variety, and in general precluded the option of playing two spinners. Two spinners were picked only six times in this period, and only once (in India) as part of a four-bowler attack. Under Gooch, exclusively seam attacks became more common. It was unheard of in the 60s and 70s, and was rare in the 80s before Gooch became captain. Partly this reflected the available spin bowling options of the time, combined with a ruthless absence of sentimentality and recognition that England needed credible batting options at six and seven.

Jack Russell was first chosen as England's wicket-keeper at the end of the 1988 season.

> 'Quite why Russell has had to wait so long remains one of the year's bigger selection mysteries', wrote Alan Lee in *The Times*, 'as the opinion that he is the best wicket-keeper appears to be shared by every player and umpire on the circuit. Now that the woolly theory of picking an inferior wicket-keeper in the hope that he will make a few runs has been thoroughly exposed [he had replaced Jack Richards, who had failed to reach double figures in the two Tests he played in the series], the brilliant but undemonstrative Russell could have the job for years to come.'

Russell did indeed have the job for much of the next decade, playing in 54 Tests. But the 'woolly theory' continued to be debated. Lee's was the classic exposition of a case which overlooked the consequence for the balance of the rest of the side if a 'keeper was selected whose batting was limited. Russell's 94 on debut (as nightwatchman), albeit against a weak Sri Lanka, generated hopes that he might develop into a genuine wicket-keeper batsman, and he did indeed score two Test hundreds. But he was not the best wicket-keeper batsman of his day.

Alec Stewart – The Man for All Seasons

Alec Stewart first played for England in the West Indies in 1989/90 as a specialist batsman. An occasional wicket-keeper for Surrey, he was not even the reserve wicket-keeper on that tour. He was, however, selected in that capacity for the subsequent winter's tour to Australia, and replaced Russell for the fourth Test. The change was the consequence of the decision, for the first time in the Gooch era, to play five specialist bowlers as a consequence of doubts over the fitness of Angus Fraser. Stewart was retained for the fifth Test too, even though Fraser was not selected due to injury.

For the next seven years, the selectors oscillated between Russell (and a couple of his competitors) and Stewart. The issue was not just the traditional one of whether it was worth compromising on wicket-keeping standards in order to strengthen the batting, or allow an extra bowler to be played. While, in 1991, Russell was clearly the superior 'keeper, as Stewart's career progressed, the margin in Russell's favour reduced to the point where it probably ceased to exist. The issue was also whether by keeping wicket, Stewart's own contribution as a batsman might be diminished. The evidence was already there in that 1990/1 series: Stewart scored 195 runs in his first three Tests as a specialist batsman, but just 29 in his next two when keeping wicket. This disparity between Stewart's runs when keeping and runs when not was to endure. A further complication, especially when Gooch missed the 1993/4 tour to the West Indies, and then after his retirement a year later, was whether Stewart could reasonably be asked to keep wicket and open the batting. Stewart was at his best against fast bowling, and had particularly successful stints opening the batting in the West Indies in both 1993/4 and 1997/8. But in only seven of his 133 Tests for England did Stewart open the batting and keep wicket.

The selectors went some years without a clear strategy on these matters. Stewart was dropped altogether after the 1990/1 tour, but reclaimed his place for the fifth Test against West Indies in 1991 at the expense of Russell, who had had a particularly poor series with the bat. But Russell was back for the end of season Test against Sri Lanka, with Stewart playing as a specialist batsman. Russell retained his place for the next seven Tests, but was dropped for the fourth Test after another poor run of batting form, and Stewart took up the gloves. He had scored 348 runs in the first three Tests, but added just 49 in the last two.

Concerned that they needed a wicket-keeper batsman for balance, but worried about the effect of keeping on Stewart's form, the selectors next went left field in choosing the party to tour India in 1992/3 by omitting Russell altogether, and bringing in Richard Blakey, who had scored a lot of runs for Yorkshire in 1992. The decision was highly controversial. In *The Times* Alan Lee wrote that Russell had been '...yet again shamefully sacrificed for the shortcomings of others. [Keith] Fletcher [the England manager] confessed that the selectors felt it impossible to include a specialist wicket- keeper when nobody else was capable of doing the all-rounder's job. So Alec Stewart, greatly against his will, must keep wicket and drop down the batting order.' But this was far from fair. Russell's shortcomings were his own – no fifties in his last

21 Tests. Far from 'confessing' to making what was being implied to be some ethically dubious decision, Fletcher was exposing the difficulty he, his predecessors and his successors had or were to have in choosing a balanced side when there was no credible all-rounder. In the four winter Tests, Richard Blakey kept in two without replicating his county batting form, and Stewart the other two.

Stewart kept throughout the Ashes series of 1993, batting down the order (and with modest results), but Russell was recalled for the tour to the West Indies the following winter. The logic appeared to be that with Gooch unavailable, Stewart was needed to open (which he did with some success, scoring a century in each innings in Barbados) in which case he could not keep wicket. It was a formula which England were keen to continue going in to the summer of 1994, even though Gooch was back in the side. But now doubts were beginning to be raised about Russell. Alan Lee in *The Times* rightly predicted that 'Steven Rhodes seems sure to replace Russell and win his first Test cap… a better batsman than Russell, though not an immeasurably more effective one, his agile, enthusiastic wicket keeping has plainly been identified by the new regime after Russell's tour was blighted by missed stumpings'. The 'new regime' was that of Ray Illingworth as chairman of selectors, and there was more than a suspicion that Rhodes benefited from being a Yorkshireman (albeit one playing for Worcestershire).

Rhodes had a run of 11 Tests, in most of which Stewart continued to open the batting. He did not, however, demonstrate his superiority over Russell as either batsman or 'keeper, and was dropped after the 1994/5 tour to Australia. The gloves returned to Stewart, and when after three Tests he suffered an injury, Russell was recalled, holding on to his place after Stewart resumed his. But the pendulum swung back again for the final Test of the summer of 1996, when Russell was once again dropped. As Illingworth wrote subsequently 'when we met to pick the side for the final Test, knowing we had to win to save the series, we were back to the old problem – how to get five bowlers in without dropping Russell… We couldn't, so it was back to square one with Stewart keeping wicket on a one-off basis.'

In fact, Stewart was to have a run of 13 Tests as 'keeper, generally batting at three. Once again it was the desire to have Stewart open which led to the switch back to Russell on the 1997/8 tour to the West Indies, and it worked in the sense that Stewart had a successful tour as a batsman. But Russell's lack of runs was a problem, and his keeping in the first of the two Trinidad Tests was poor. He was not selected again after that series.

The situation became more complicated in 1998, with Stewart now England's captain. For familiar reasons, he resumed wicket-keeping duties notwithstanding his additional responsibilities, until the fourth Test of the 1998/9 Ashes tour, when the reserve wicket-keeper, Warren Hegg, took over. History repeated itself once again: Stewart, batting at four, had made just 112 runs in the first three Tests; opening in the last two, he scored 204, including a century.

This formula continued for the first three Tests of the 1999 summer, this time with Chris Read filling the specialist 'keeper role while Stewart opened. But Read, to a greater extent than even Russell or Rhodes before him, was unable to score the runs needed of a number seven, and it was back to Stewart for the fourth Test. And so, at last, it was to remain: Stewart kept wicket in the rest of his 44 Tests over the next four years, and never again opened for England.

Stewart's was a remarkable career for students of England selection policy. He played in a record-breaking 133 Tests for England, in 82 of which he kept wicket. But he kept wicket in eight different spells; only one of the interruptions was caused by injury. The selectors faced a real difficulty because of the disparity between Stewart's batting record when keeping and when playing as a specialist batsman. In Tests in which he did not keep wicket, he averaged 47, while in those in which he did, he averaged 35. Statistically, his batting when opening and keeping was marginally better than when batting lower in the order and keeping, which makes it perhaps surprising that the selectors' default position was that if Stewart were keeping, he would need to bat in the middle order. Notwithstanding the multiplicity of variables affecting these choices, it is remarkable that there was no consistent strategy for Stewart, not only between different selectorial regimes, but also within them. Only the Duncan Fletcher/Nasser Hussain regime adopted an unwavering policy.

Of the 152 Tests England played between Gooch's assumption of the captaincy in 1989/90 until Stewart's retirement in 2003, England played five bowlers on 79 occasions: 58 of these were when Stewart was keeping wicket. England played four bowlers in the other 73 Tests: 50 of these were when someone other than Stewart was keeping wicket. In the vast majority of cases, therefore, the choice as to whether Stewart played as a wicket-keeper was the choice as to whether to play four or five bowlers. As to the composition of the attack, other than in Asia, the default was to play one spinner and three or four seamers. On 30 occasions (out of 152) between 1989/90 and 2003, England played no spinner at all (four times when there were five bowlers in the attack).

There continued in the 90s to be a dearth of batsmen with second strings as bowlers (as there had been in the 60s) or of bowlers with a capability to bat at seven. Gooch and Graeme Hick were the nearest to occasional bowlers among the batsmen, but they were very occasional indeed. There was therefore a temptation for the selectors to pick as batsmen players who could bowl, but who were perhaps not worth their place in the side ahead of other batsmen. Dermot Reeve, Ronnie Irani and Adam Hollioake all failed in this category. Similarly, bowlers who could bat a bit but who would not have been picked for their bowling alone had brief runs in the side – Mark Ealham (eight Tests) and Ben Hollioake (two Tests – though he would almost certainly have played more, and perhaps developed into a genuine Test all-rounder, had he not been so tragically killed in a road accident). The two players who came nearest to fulfilling the role of a genuine all-rounder between Botham and Flintoff were Chris Lewis and Craig White.

Lewis's talent was one for which the adjective mercurial might have been invented. The gap between his natural abilities and his achievements presented the selectors with an enduring dilemma from the time he was first picked to replace the injured Ricardo Ellcock on the 1989/90 tour to the West Indies. At his best he looked an effective England bowler, and on three occasions he took five wickets in an innings. His century against India in 1992/3 – the only one by a bowler between Botham in 1986/7 and White in 2001/2 – suggested that he had the potential to be considered a genuine all-rounder. But his temperament and attitude were always suspect. In his early days he was vulnerable to a series of what appeared, at least in some cases, to be psychosomatic injuries and illnesses. His late appearance for the Sunday of the Oval Test in 1996 led to his dismissal from the squad for the impending one-day series, and to the end of his Test career.

That Oval Test, his 32nd, revealed Lewis at his worst. Illingworth assessed his performance:

Unnatural Selection

'It wasn't just that he had a poor game. It was how he played. He is a great striker of the ball, but he hardly raised his bat in anger in either innings. It wasn't exactly a crisis when he went in on the first day at 248-5, but he scored only 5 runs from 40 balls before he was bowled by Wasim. It was the same story in the second innings, when he scored four off 22 balls with a match situation in which runs were just as important as time. As for his bowling, he got the new ball, but still had five spells in his 23 overs for 112 runs because he was always too expensive.'

White was first picked in 1994 – another Yorkshireman (though Australian by birth) favoured by Illingworth as the new chairman of selectors. With Stewart having passed the gloves to Rhodes, England were desperate for an all-rounder to enable five bowlers to be selected. White played in four Tests with respectable but unspectacular results, before succumbing to injury. Thereafter he played only occasionally, until being called up unexpectedly for the 2000 series against the West Indies, at the age of 30, effectively as replacement for the injured Flintoff. It was an inspired selection, for he had done nothing in county cricket that season or indeed the previous one to suggest that he was Test quality. But, as the 2001 *Wisden* reported in its review of the series, 'White was a revelation, consistently generating more pace than anyone from a strong body action, and causing mayhem with his reverse swing'. He proved to be especially successful, particularly with the bat, in Asia on the winter tours to Pakistan and Sri Lanka in 2000/1 and India in 2001/2, but thereafter he found himself competing unsuccessfully with Flintoff and injury. Of the 22 Tests he played after his comeback, only five were alongside Flintoff, and once Flintoff was established, and fit, there was no space for him.

Balance Found

The selectors were quick to spot Flintoff's potential, and first picked him for England in 1998 at the age of 20. Unlike Botham two decades before, however, Flintoff did not immediately realise it. Injury restricted his early appearances in the Test side, as they were to later in his career. By the end of 2001, out of 37 Tests since his debut, Flintoff had played in only nine, and averaged just 17 with the bat and 55 with the ball. But the selectors did not lose faith, and thereafter Flintoff began to produce returns on the investment – first with the bat, with a spectacular 137 against New Zealand in 2001/2, and later, especially from 2003/4, with the ball. When fit he was England's best and fastest bowler over a period of five or six years.

He was omitted against his will for the fourth Test against Australia in 2009. Despite a chronic knee injury, he had bowled heroically in the second Test to make a major contribution to England's first victory in the Ashes at Lord's for 75 years, and scored 74 off 79 balls in the third Test. He was, however, judged not fit enough to play a full role as part of a five-man attack in the fourth Test. The insistence on five bowlers is, in retrospect, surprising in view of Andy Flower's and Andrew Strauss's four-bowler strategy since Flintoff's retirement, and some commentators judged that Flintoff's controversial absence had a psychological impact on the team which contributed to the defeat they suffered in this Test. Flintoff was recalled for the fifth Test, the knee having apparently eased with a short rest, but it was his last match for England.

With Flintoff in the side (as with Stewart keeping wicket – and for 19 Tests they played together), five bowlers was England's default balance. In 78 Tests for England, Flintoff was part of a four-man attack on only eight occasions. Mostly these were one-offs, driven by particular circumstances. For example, in the temporary absence of Stewart and White, England chose to opt for just four bowlers in New Zealand in 2001/2 to avoid having to bat rookie 'keeper James Foster higher than eight. Without Flintoff, and even with Stewart, the balance was more variable. Where two spinners were judged to be required, as in Pakistan and Sri Lanka in 2000/1, it was considered necessary to sacrifice a batsman rather than a third seam bowler – though White's presence as the third quicker bowler mitigated the extent to which the tail was thereby lengthened. For the other 24 Tests which Stewart played without Flintoff in 17 only four bowlers were picked.

Stewart and Flintoff at six and seven represented the best balanced England side since the 70s. But of course as Stewart approached 40, the issue of wicket-keeper emerged once again. He was not available for the tour of India in 2001/2 (a reaction to – albeit incredible – allegations that he had taken bribes from an Indian bookmaker during the 1992/3 tour to India). The England manager, Duncan Fletcher, took the view that Stewart could not pick and choose, and that he must therefore be considered unavailable for the subsequent tour to New Zealand. The selectors' choice of James Foster to replace him was a surprising one. Just 21, and having spent the first half of the 2001 season at Durham University, Foster's claims might have been thought to be considerably behind those of say Hegg (who averaged 48 in county cricket in 2001, and went on the tour as second 'keeper) and Read. Fletcher himself subsequently explained the decision thus 'yes he was raw and had some technical deficiencies in both his batting and his keeping, but I felt he was someone we could work with for the future. He really wanted to play for England, and his mental toughness was up with the best I had encountered.' Foster scored useful runs in both India and New Zealand but his keeping was below top class. Nevertheless, Fletcher claims that he would have been picked for the first home series of 2002, had he not broken his arm at the start of the season. As it was, Stewart returned to play another 18 Tests for England, retiring as England's most capped player at the end of 2003.

Following Stewart's retirement, England picked Read and Geraint Jones for the winter tour to the West Indies. Foster had not progressed as hoped while Jones, by contrast, had had an exceptional season for Kent in which he scored two first-class hundreds and averaged 45. Read had kept wicket in England's one-day internationals during 2003, a recognition that he was still regarded by many as the best 'keeper in England. But his batting had not improved, and while England won the first three Tests against the West Indies, Read's contribution was less than that required of a number seven. It seems that it was the match against a Carib Beer Xl before the third Test, in which both Read and Jones played, that persuaded Fletcher of the superior merits of the latter: while Read struggled against the spin of Dave Mohammed to score nine, Jones hit a breezy 66. Although Read survived for the third Test, Jones replaced him for the fourth.

    Jones embarked on an unbroken run of 31 Tests for England. A century in his third, against New Zealand, suggested that England might have found the wicket-keeper batsman they needed to succeed Stewart, but while Jones continued to pick up occasional fifties, his batting regressed rather than progressed. And there continued to be a powerful lobby for Read – not least Rod Marsh, the former Australian wicket-keeper and head of the National Academy. In 2006, Jones's runs virtually dried up, with a top score of 19 in five Tests. But did it make sense to return once again to Read, when the argument for replacing Jones was the need to strengthen the batting?

Fletcher apparently did not think so, and argued for Matt Prior, who had displaced Read as England's reserve wicket-keeper the previous winter, and had played in the one-day internationals. But he was overruled by the other selectors, and Read was restored to the side for the last two Tests against Pakistan. With scores of 38, 55 and 33, he seemed not to have diminished the batting, and indeed, as the 2007 *Wisden* put it, to have bloodied the noses of one or two critics. Unsurprisingly, he was picked for the winter tour of Australia, alongside Jones.

But it was Jones who was selected for the first Test of the winter. It was a deeply controversial decision, and one in which it seemed that Fletcher had used his personal authority as tour manager to overrule the collective will of the selectors. Fletcher did not believe that Read should have been on the tour at all – not just because of his limitations as a batsman, but also because of a technical flaw he had identified with his keeping. He claims that the new England captain, Flintoff, and other senior players, were of the same view. Not only was Jones back in the team, he was also appointed to the tour management committee.

It was, of course, a disastrous tour, and England lost the series after only three Tests. Jones was no more successful than the rest of the team. The pressure to recall Read became irresistible, and thus he came back for the final two Tests of the series for his fourth and final spell as England wicket-keeper. But he scored no more runs than had Jones.

Rebalancing

Although no longer England coach, Fletcher would no doubt have approved of the selection of Prior for the start of the 2007 season. It represented an unambiguous preference to have as England 'keeper the best batsman available in order to generate runs at number seven. It was the case for Parks 40 years on – though Prior proved to be both a better batsman and 'keeper than his fellow Sussex predecessor. Prior was the second-highest run scorer in first class cricket in 2006, with an average of 46, and his century against West Indies in 2007 was the highest-ever score by an England wicket-keeper on first appearance. Nobody suggested – at any rate in 2007 – that Prior was the best 'keeper in England, and a poor tour of Sri Lanka in 2007/8, in which he dropped three catches, and missed two stumpings, interrupted his career. Thereafter, Tim Ambrose replaced him for a sequence of 10 Tests, assisted by a century in his second, though – like Jones – he failed to sustain this momentum. Prior was England's first choice from the winter of 2008/9 for five years. During the period of England's supremacy in Test cricket which followed, his ability to score the runs expected of a front-line batsman, and quickly (a strike rate in the 60s), was a crucial factor. In May 2013, he was named England's cricketer of the year, averaging as he was, at the time, 44 – far better than any wicket-keeper of the last 50 years.

Alas, however, that proved to be his pinnacle. A combination of injuries and ruthless international bowling led to a dramatic fall from grace and he was dropped after the third Test match in Australia in 2013/4, to be replaced by Jonny Bairstow, who, while the reserve wicket-keeper for the tour, had previously played a number of Tests alongside Prior as a specialist batsman. In two Tests as wicket-keeper, Bairstow impressed with neither gloves nor bat, and England were keen for Prior to regain form in England colours in what was imagined to be the less demanding circumstances of home series against Sri Lanka and India. He was duly recalled for what turned out to be another four Tests, but it was not to be and he stepped down before being pushed in an attempt to sort out chronic injuries.

There were various candidates to replace Prior. Some commentators favoured the recall of Read or Foster, regarded as the best 'keepers in England though, at 35 and 34 respectively, only short-term solutions, and inferior to others as batsmen. Craig Kieswetter was mentioned earlier in the season as a potential candidate, but it would have been odd to choose him ahead of Jos Buttler, who had progressed from T20 to 50-over England 'keeper, and who had scored a brilliant century in a one-day international at Lord's earlier in the summer. In a previous era, such an innings might have catapulted Buttler into the Test side, but as it was, Alastair Cook, while praising the knock, expressed the view that Buttler was not yet ready. It was odd simply from a diplomatic perspective that Cook should have.

offered this opinion. That he held it at all seemed to reflect his intrinsic preference for the proven and conventional over potential and flair – a way of thinking reflected in his captaincy. In any case, the selectors did not share his view. Buttler was brought in as cover for Prior for the Lord's Test, and succeeded him thereafter. In three Tests he kept more than competently, and his batting on each occasion, albeit in reasonably benign circumstances, demonstrated how effective middle-order belligerence is in demoralising an opposition already under pressure. For the time being, at least, his place seems secure.

In the 42 Tests not played in Asia between Flintoff's and Swann's retirements, England adhered to a formula of three faster and one slow bowler in all but five – an unprecedented period of stability in the balance of the side. And yet in this period England arguably had more all-round strength than at any time since the 1970s. With Prior, Stuart Broad, Swann and often Tim Bresnan, England had rarely, if ever, possessed such a strong 'tail' and in that sense a greater opportunity to play five bowlers.

That England chose not to do so has been a deliberate and novel strategy of 'scoreboard pressure' – of believing that the weight of runs scored by the batsmen creates such pressure on the opposition that it is worth in itself the added value of a fifth bowler. The strategy was that of the great Australian sides in which Shane Warne played, and was enabled by the presence in the team of Swann – a spinner who could bowl long, uninterrupted spells on occasions when the energy of the three seamers needed to be preserved. For that period, the England selectors saw no need to play a fifth bowler, and so picking six specialist batsmen produced no opportunity cost. Just as Flintoff's presence in the side made it possible to pick only five specialist batsmen, so Swann's made it possible to play only four specialist bowlers.

There was, however, one exception to Swann's inclusion. When in the summer of 2012 Swann failed to match his previous standards (10 wickets in five Tests at an average of 59 compared with a previous average of 28) the selectors had pause for thought. Rather than play a fifth bowler, for the second Test against South Africa they dropped Swann and played four seamers (the first time England had played no spinner since 2003). England drew the match, but reverted to the previous strategy for the third Test. It was the only occasion on which

Walter Robins, chairman of selectors 1962-64 – 'a man of strange moods and unintelligible behaviour', according to Ted Dexter.

Doug Insole, chairman of selectors 1965-68. Did MCC overrule him over D'Oliveira's inclusion in the touring party of South Africa, 1968/9?

Insole and his selectors recommended Close as England captain in 1967, but MCC insisted on Colin Cowdrey (right).

Alec Bedser, chairman of selectors 1969-1981, and on the panel 1962-8, 1982-5. No man has more influenced England Test selection in the last 50 years.

Peter May, chairman of selectors 1982-8. The bouncers did not finish with May's retirement as a player, and he struggled with an increasingly intrusive and less deferential media.

Ted Dexter, chairman of selectors 1989-93. Led an unlikely triumvirate with Micky Stewart (then Keith Fletcher) and Graham Gooch, of whom he had earlier written 'has all the charisma of a wet fish'.

Geoff Boycott. Illingworth would have preferred him to Cowdrey as his vice-captain in Australia 1970/1.

Ray Illingworth, chairman of selectors 1994-6, with David Bairstow. Sought to exercise absolute power as both chairman and team manager, but the arrangement was short-lived.

David Graveney, chairman of selectors 1997-2007, at Nasser Hussain's resignation press conference in 2003. Hussain considered he was insufficiently assertive.

Selectors, captain and coach, 2003. Left to right: David Graveney, Rod Marsh, Michael Vaughan, Duncan Fletcher and Geoff Miller. Marsh and Fletcher frequently disagreed on selection matters.

The KP Fan Club: Alastair Cook, Graeme Swann and James Anderson.

Kevin Pietersen and Andy Flower in amicable discussion.

England's team for the First Test against Australia, 1968. Front row, l to r: Boycott, Graveney, Cowdrey, Edrich, D'Oliveira; back row: Knott, Barber, Pocock, Snow, Higgs, Amiss.

England winning the Fifth Test against Australia 1968. England Team l to r: Illingworth, Graveney, Edrich, Dexter, Cowdrey, Underwood, Knott, Snow, Brown, Milburn, D'Oliveira.

The unexpected selection, omission, and recall of D'Oliveira during the summer of 1968, and his omission and then inclusion for the winter tour to South Africa which followed, in part reflected the selectors' confusion over whether to regard him as a batsman or an all-rounder.

Brian Close (top) and John Snow (left). Both fell out with the MCC establishment, but were recalled when their Test careers seemed finished.

Tony Greig: never dropped by England in a career of 58 Tests.

Mike Brearley: a throwback to an earlier age, in that he played for England as a specialist captain.

David Steele (left) and Neil Mallender (below): county stalwarts who did a job for England.

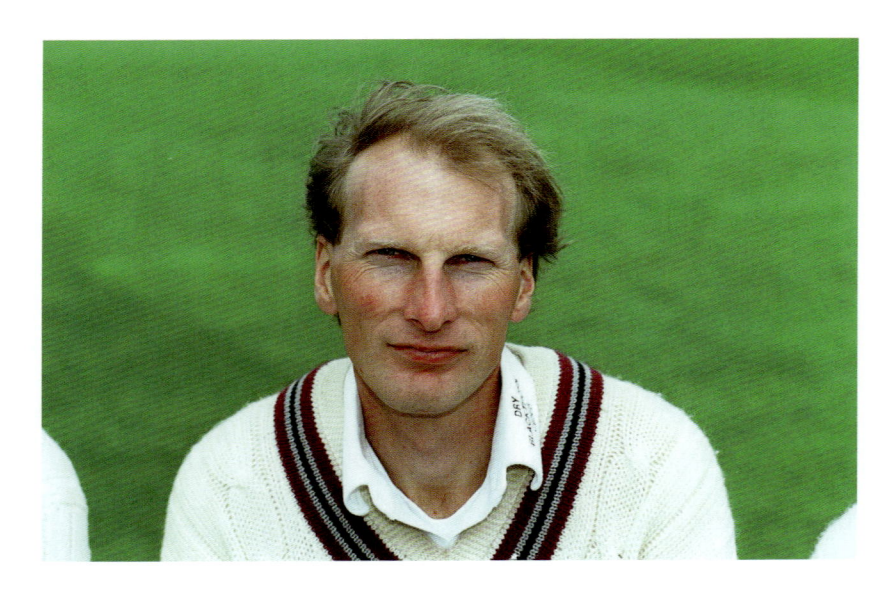

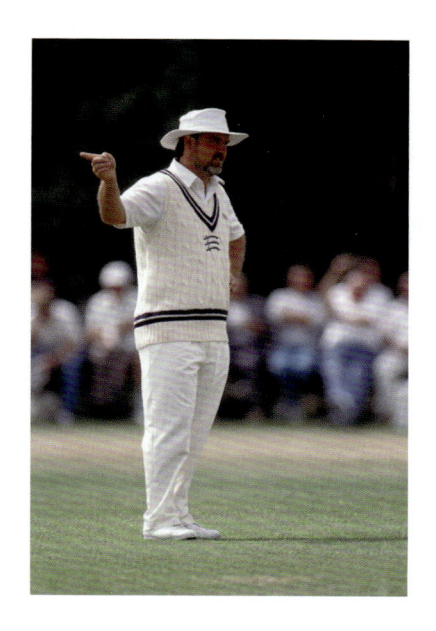

The four captains of 1988: Mike Gatting (top left); John Emburey (top right); Chris Cowdrey (bottom left); Graham Gooch (bottom right).

England's two best left-handed middle-order batsmen of the last half-century: David Gower (left) and Graeme Thorpe (right). Gower was dropped six times in his career, while the replacement of Thorpe by Pietersen in 2005 was one of the hardest decisions coach Duncan Fletcher had to make.

In the era of Shane Warne, England were desperate for a leg spinner of their own. But neither Ian Salisbury (left) nor Chris Schofield (bottom) was up to it.

In the absence of a traditional all-rounder, England were able to achieve balance in the side when they were able to play an outstanding wicket-keeper batsman (Alec Stewart, left) or an outstanding spinner (Graeme Swann, bottom).

Unnatural Selection

Swann was dropped after his initial selection.

The three quicker bowlers plus Swann strategy less obviously lent itself to Asian pitches, as exemplified by England's experiences in the UAE and Sri Lanka early in 2012. For the first Test against Pakistan, England played the same balance of four bowlers they had in England the previous summer – and lost. Persuaded that two spinners were necessary in the conditions, they played the next two Tests against Pakistan with two fast bowlers, with Monty Panesar joining Swann as a second spinner – and also lost. But the defeats in the second and third Tests were attributable to batting failures. Pakistan were dismissed successively for 257, 214, 99 and 365, with 24 of the 40 wickets falling to spin. Unsurprisingly, England retained the same balance of attack for the first Test against Sri Lanka which followed later in the winter – albeit with Samit Patel replacing the out of form Eoin Morgan. Patel was an all-rounder principally in the sense that he would not have been selected in the Test side as either a specialist batsman or specialist bowler. But with the reserve batsman, Bopara, injured, there was no alternative if Morgan was to be dropped. Patel batted at seven – below Prior – and was very much the fifth bowler. Again England lost.

For the next Test, England were keen to play Steven Finn to replace the injured Broad; but if no other change were made, this would mean a batting line up from seven down of Patel, Swann, James Anderson, Finn and Panesar. The selectors judged this too long a tail, and no doubt mindful too of two crucial catches Panesar had dropped in the previous Test, changed the balance of the attack by replacing Panesar with Bresnan. This was harsh on Panesar, who had taken 16 wickets in his previous three Tests that winter; and was a reversion to a formula adopted unsuccessfully for the first Test against Pakistan – albeit now with Patel in support as the second spinner. But in that England won, it was a balance that seemed to work. Arguably, however, the victory was achieved despite, rather than because of, the balance of the attack. Swann took 10 wickets in the match in 68 overs; Patel took one in 41 overs, and Bresnan 3 in 35. Had Panesar played instead of Bresnan, he might have been expected to have bowled most of the overs bowled by Bresnan and Patel, and to have secured more than the four wickets they managed given that the pitch was one on which Swann took 10. He might even have improved on the five runs Bresnan scored with the bat.

But when England returned to Asia in 2012/3, they picked up

where they had successfully left off the previous winter, playing three seamers, Swann and Patel in the first Test against India. But success did not repeat itself, and after defeat in Ahmedabad, Panesar was recalled to replace one of the quicker bowlers, and with instant success. In three further Tests, two of which England won, and the third of which was a draw, Panesar took 17 wickets. Patel became irrelevant as a bowler and the inevitable logic was to judge him purely as a specialist batsman. With a top score of 33 in five Tests, he was dropped and replaced by debutant Joe Root.

The nine Tests in Asia in 2012 presented a major challenge to the selectors in determining the balance of the attack. Fielding only two faster bowlers was counter cultural, and adopted with great reluctance. There was also reluctance to recognise the potential which bowling Swann and Panesar together in helpful conditions offered. It was a shock to discover, as the India series progressed, that these two were actually superior exponents of turning wickets than were the host team's spinners. Flower himself acknowledged that the omission of Panesar had been a mistake, and his inclusion thereafter had a major impact on the reversal of England's fortunes in that series.

The non-Asia strategy began to break down in the second half of 2013. For the final Test of the 2013 series, the selectors indulged in experimentation, which led to the introduction of Simon Kerrigan and Chris Woakes into a five-man attack. The Test after next was played in Adelaide, and the selectors concluded that the pitch was likely to spin, and that a second slow bowler was needed. Thus Panesar was selected alongside Swann (the first time England had picked two spinners in a Test in Australia for 22 years). As on previous occasions when a second spinner was chosen, the view was that three faster bowlers would still be required; but that as five bowlers would weaken the batting, some compromise would need to be made in the choice of the third seamer. Thus while Panesar replaced a specialist batsman, an all-rounder – Ben Stokes – was brought in to replace the man who for the previous Test had been regarded as the third best seamer in the touring party – Chris Tremlett. As it turned out, Stokes's bowling made more impact in the four Tests in which he was to play than did Tremlett's in the one he played, so in that sense nothing was lost. On the other hand, playing a second spinner was a mistake. The joint figures of Swann and Panesar in the match were 4-381, and of the 32 wickets to fall in the match, only 7 were taken by spinners.

For the third Test, England unsurprisingly reverted to one spinner, but more unconventionally played four seam bowlers – the first time that England had played four seamers and Swann since Flintoff. Thus Stokes was retained, despite an unexceptional debut at Adelaide. In that Perth Test, however, he did have an outstanding match, with a second innings century in a losing cause. This, combined with Swann's abrupt retirement after the third Test, pointed the selectors inevitably in the direction of playing five bowlers, with Stokes at six, which they continued for the rest of the series.

Come the start of the 2014 summer there was no spinner in England even close to offering the capability which Swann provided of bowling long uninterrupted spells from one end to enable three quicker bowlers to be rotated from the other once the shine had gone from the new ball. Panesar, who had bowled so effectively in India in 2012/3, had managed just eight wickets at 76 in his five Tests since. Two specialist spinners who were neither Swann nor Panesar – Kerrigan and Scott Borthwick – had each played one Test, but such was the lack of confidence of Cook in their ability that they bowled only 7% of the total overs. The selectors therefore reckoned that they must play at least four bowlers in whom Cook did have confidence – and if that meant they were seamers, so be it. The spin option would need to be provided by a batsman who was an occasional spinner. They might have reverted to Patel, who ticked the boxes but had performed with no great success in his previous Tests, and had had a disappointing season in county cricket in 2013. Instead, they turned to Moeen Ali. The season prior to his selection, he had finished eighth in the first-class batting averages, so he was a credible contender for a place as a batsman alone. His bowling was very much a second string, but the expectation was that he would be the filler in a five-man attack.

In the early Tests of 2014, this was how it turned out. A not out century in his second match, as England fought ultimately unsuccessfully to secure a draw against Sri Lanka, seemed to confirm his prowess as a batsman, though he was unable to make big scores in the series against India which followed. For his first four Tests, Cook used Ali very much as a part time bowler – a last resort. In these matches, he bowled just 15% of England's overs, despite England spending long periods in the field. In his fifth game, however, Ali seized his opportunity in the second innings when India were under intense scoreboard pressure to take 6-67, and establish himself as a very capable bowler at Test level.

Ali's development will be crucial to the future balance of the England team. If his batting delivers on the promise of his Headingley century, he could fill for England the all-rounder slot last filled by Flintoff, and enable England once again to play five front-line bowlers. If, on the other hand, his bowling delivers on the promise of his performance at Old Trafford, the selectors may feel confident of his playing the role vacated by Swann as part of a four-man bowling attack. It will be intriguing to discover how the balance will be struck if both options are available.

In striking a balance, selectors of different eras have faced radically different challenges. Those able to pick any two (or three) of Greig, Illingworth and Knott, or Stewart and Flintoff, or Prior and Swann, had an easy ride. And generally England sides were relatively successful in the times when those options were available. What is most interesting in retrospect is the variety of workarounds to which the selectors had to resort when they were not, and how short the shelf life was of any one of them. Thus, for example, only Taylor among wicket-keepers who were not all-rounders had a substantial unbroken run in the Test side – the limitations of his batting at least partially mitigated by the presence of Botham in the same side. And the periods outside those three set out above tended to be ones of considerable volatility as between including four or five front-line bowlers. The circle simply could not be squared: prior to Swann, an attack of four bowlers frequently proved inadequate, and so a change was made to five; but then the batting was exposed. Or players were picked in the hope that they would prove to be all-rounders at the Test level, only for their shortcomings in both disciplines to be exposed. This is not to criticize the selectors: denied all-rounders of the required quality, they had little option but to try different approaches in the search for one which worked. And this volatility was not confined to those years when Test selectors appeared to place less emphasis on stability anyway. Even recently, the evidence is that thinking can become muddled under stress. Thus, for example, the shock caused by the sudden departure of Swann was so disruptive that it led to the selection of a side for the fifth Test of 2013/4 which could offer the distinction of being the only one in the last 50 years in which two players (Boyd Rankin and Borthwick) played solitary Tests concurrently.

CHAPTER FOUR

SCORING THE RUNS: 1962-1995

A Decade of Stability

At the start of the 1963 season, England had available arguably a better quartet of middle-order batsmen than at any other time in the last half century. Ken Barrington, Ted Dexter, Tom Graveney and Colin Cowdrey rank respectively first, third, ninth and eleventh in the career Test averages of specialist middle-order batsmen who have played for England more than 10 times in the last 50 years. All four had toured Australia in 1962/3, but they were never again to play together in the same England side.

Someone with Barrington's outstanding record might have been expected to have been an automatic selection for England, and indeed he did appear in 45 of the 55 Tests England played between the start of the 1963 season and the end of the 1968. Injury and illness accounted for eight of the Tests he missed, but he was also dropped on two occasions. In 1965, after having scored 137 in seven and a quarter hours against New Zealand, he was left out for slow scoring, *pour encourager les autres*. The editor of the 1966 *Wisden* wrote that 'the selectors must be congratulated for, at last, taking drastic steps to cure cricket of the deadly disease of the defensive forward prod which has been a blight for too many years'. It is certainly true that Test scoring rates were slow in the 60s. England scored at an average of just 39 runs per 100 balls against Australia in 1964, compared with 63 per 100 balls against Australia in 2009. 'Positive cricket' was very much a mantra of the 60s, and it caused some to be dropped, and others to be chosen. After Barrington, later in 1965 Geoff Boycott was also dropped for scoring 16 in 140 minutes against South Africa, and again in 1967 after scoring 246 against India in nine and a half hours. Balls faced were not routinely recorded in those days, but it is estimated that Boycott faced 555 – a scoring rate of 44 per 100 balls which was certainly not excessively slow. But, as with New Zealand in 1965, England were up against weak bowling attacks that they might have been expected to dispatch more aggressively. Certainly, when Barrington scored 256 in over eleven hours against Australia in 1964, or 109 off 366 balls on a difficult wicket against Pakistan later in the summer of 1967, he was not penalised.

The other occasion on which Barrington was dropped was for the fifth Test of the 1968 series against Australia. It was a curious decision, for while his county performances in 1968 were uncharacteristically poor (his first-class average that season was only 24) he was still delivering the goods at international level. His scores in that series had been 75, 0, 49 and 46 not out. In fact, although selected for the winter tour of 1968/9, he was not to play Test cricket again, a heart attack in Australia later in the year ending his playing career prematurely.

There was never any thought of dropping Dexter. He was regarded as the new Denis Compton – a batsman with flair and aggression at a time when these qualities were perceived as being in decline. The problem the selectors faced here was in securing his availability. After he broke his leg in 1965, while still only 30, he effectively retired from county cricket. He made two brief attempts at a comeback. In 1966, he played two matches for Sussex in late May in a perhaps half-hearted attempt to win a place in the England team to play the West Indies. His scores were 2, 18, 0 and 63. The selectors unsurprisingly considered he needed rather more match practice than this to merit inclusion in the side, and he was passed over. He did not play first-class cricket again until July 1968, when he suddenly made himself available to play for Sussex against Kent. In a remarkable demonstration of his natural ability, he scored 203 the day before the England team was chosen for the fourth Test. This time the selectors concluded that they needed no further proof of his readiness to resume Test cricket, and he was immediately recalled. He did not embarrass himself, but neither did 97 runs in four innings represent a fairy-tale return. The final Test of the summer was his last.

Cowdrey did not have the ability to dominate an attack in the way of Dexter, nor could he accumulate runs with the same perseverance as Barrington. But he was a player of undoubted class, who always seemed to have time to play the fastest of bowlers. He had been a fixture in the England side for longer than either Barrington or Dexter, scoring a brilliant century in his third Test match at the age of 22 to play an important part in England's 3-1 victory over Australia in the 1954/5 tour.

Unnatural Selection

He was picked for the 1962/3 tour to Australia specifically as one of three opening batsmen – though in the event Geoff Pullar and David Sheppard opened in the first four Tests, and only the former's injury necessitated Cowdrey moving up the order to open in the fifth. Thereafter, his career was a series of peaks and troughs. He broke his arm in the second Test against the West Indies in 1963, joined the tour of India in 1963/4 late as a consequence, was briefly injured and then omitted when fit in 1964, before being recalled for the fifth Test.

He did not go to South Africa in 1964/5. The party for the tour was, rather oddly, chosen in two tranches. The selectors first met on 31 July, and selected 11 of the squad. At this point, Cowdrey had indicated that he would not be available to tour for family reasons. When they met again on 23 August to consider the remaining five members of the party, it was reported that Cowdrey might now be available after all. But the selectors were really after a third opening batsman. The minutes record that 'it was agreed that the remaining batting place be given to a recognised opening batsman, and for this reason it was decided that Cowdrey should not be considered for the place. After a full discussion, it was agreed that J M Brearley should be invited to join the tour.' It was a strange conclusion to reach only days after Cowdrey had scored 93 not out against Australia on his return to the England side. While it was the case that Cowdrey's own preference was to bat in the middle order, he had opened for England on a number of occasions, and his record as an opener was not inferior to that when he batted lower. In any case, the likelihood was that, as in 1962/3, he would be utilised in the middle order anyway unless one of the other two openers suffered injury. It is improbable that he would not have performed more successfully than the young Cambridge captain, who was not selected for the Tests and whose top score in the other first-class games was 68. M J K Smith wrote of Brearley in his post-tour report 'I do not think it is sufficiently appreciated how much the standard of University cricket is below [County] Championship' – which begs the question of why this appreciation was not recognised at the time the party was selected. Maybe the selectors were irritated by Cowdrey's vacillation over his availability.

But he bounced back in 1965, with three Test centuries in the next 12 months, before performing modestly against the West Indies in 1966 and being dropped when Brian Close took over as captain. It was the penultimate Test of the next summer before he found his way back into the England team, but his appointment as England captain for the West Indies tour of 1967/8 heralded a new purple patch, yielding four centuries in that series and the two which followed it. Injured in 1969, he returned to the England side for the Rest of the World series in 1970, and was selected for the Australasia tour which followed it. But he made just one fifty (against New Zealand) in four Tests. He played in the first Test of the following season, but was twice bowled by the in swing of Asif Masood in a way that suggested he was no longer the player of his heyday and was dropped. Soon after, he fell ill with pneumonia, and, at 38, his Test career appeared to be over.

Graveney returned from Australia in 1963 a veteran of 55 Tests in which he had scored over 3000 runs and averaged 42. In that career he had had some considerable triumphs – including, notably, an innings of 258 against the West Indies in 1957. But he had always been competing for a place in England's middle order against various combinations of Compton, May, Cowdrey, Barrington and Dexter. The 1962/3 tour, with May retired, might have seemed a last chance to establish himself. But in the three Tests he played in Australia he had failed to reach 50 and he was now 36. He continued to score heavily in county cricket, particularly in 1964 and 1965; and his claims on an England place were well represented in the press; *The Times* would have played Graveney in 1963 (ahead of Close) and in 1964 ('with due respect to Edrich and Parfitt, Graveney, as he is batting at present on all manner of wickets, is in a class above them both'); E W Swanton would have taken him to Australia in 1965/6.

Graveney's recall for the second Test in 1966 invites parallels with Cyril Washbrook's in 1956. Washbrook had been out of Test cricket for over five years, compared with Graveney's three, and Graveney was a mere youth at 39 compared with Washbrook's 41. Graveney, unlike Washbrook in 1956, was not himself a selector. But in both cases, the selection was a slightly desperate measure, prompted by an England defeat in the previous Test match in which the batting had been particularly disappointing. Both were to score 90s on their recall. For Washbrook, the recall was for just three matches. For Graveney, it was to be for an unbroken run of 24 over three years, during which he scored more runs than any other England batsman, including five centuries, and averaged nearly 50. Should the selectors be congratulated at the wisdom of their decision in 1966, or castigated for having failed to pick him earlier? It is difficult not to believe that Graveney would not have performed well had he been recalled sooner. His return, in 1966, was at the expense of M J K Smith, and Smith's inclusion was the major reason for Graveney's exclusion in the previous 20 Tests. The difference between their capabilities as batsmen was the price to be paid for picking a 'specialist' captain.

Graveney's Test career ended on a sad note. In 1969 he sought, and was refused, permission to play in a team he was raising to play against R B Simpson's Xl on the Sunday (ie rest day) of the first Test, for a bounty of £1000. He went ahead anyway. He was 'severely reprimanded' by the Disciplinary Committee of the Test and County Cricket Board, and suspended from Test cricket. He was not to play for England again.

Apart from Barrington, Dexter, Cowdrey, Graveney, Smith and, from 1966, Basil D'Oliveira, three other middle-order batsmen had interesting walk on parts in the years from 1963. For the first Test against the West Indies that year, the selectors turned to Close. The decision appears largely to have been based on early-season form. Dexter, it seems, was a particular fan of Close, and had argued for him to fill an opening-batsman's position. Close also offered an additional bowling option, though in the event it was seldom exercised. Close was to produce some legendary batting during that 1963 series, though ultimately his record of three fifties in five Tests was modest. He was not available for the 1963/4 tour to India, and was not again to be included in an England side until a new captain was required.

Another middle-order batting spot appeared in 1963 after Cowdrey broke his arm. The choice of Phil Sharpe as his replacement was a surprise. His unexceptional county form was not such as to demand inclusion ahead of, say, Graveney or Peter Parfitt. Nor was he regarded as an up-and-coming star (already a relatively mature 26, he had not previously played Test cricket). He was selected principally for his reputation as the best slip fielder in the country against the background of the gap which the absence of Cowdrey, himself a specialist slipper, created. Seldom since has fielding been such a major consideration in a Test selection decision. As it turned out, Sharpe was England's most successful batsman in the last three Tests of the series, but he continued to be regarded as primarily a Cowdrey substitute. Of the twelve Tests he played between 1963 and 1969 (plus one in the Rest of the World series in 1970), only twice was he in the same side as Cowdrey. This characterisation of Sharpe was to his disadvantage, for he enjoyed a Test batting average of 46, and might reasonably have been expected to have been chosen more often.

In contrast to the middle order, England began 1963 with two gaps in the opening positions. They had been filled the previous winter by David Sheppard and Geoff Pullar. But Sheppard had returned to the priesthood, and Pullar, who had not impressed Dexter in Australia ('he did not appear to be as enthusiastic as he should be') and had returned home early with knee problems, was injured. In fact, despite having been England's preferred opener since 1959, he was unable subsequently to recapture his form, and never played for England again, retiring from first-class cricket in 1968 at the age of 33. In the 15 Tests which followed the start of the 1963 season, 10 different openers were tried in an attempt to find an established pair.

The outstanding England openers from the mid-1960s were Geoff Boycott and John Edrich. Together they played in 185 Tests for England and scored over 13,000 runs. Their average opening partnership of 52 runs ranks third behind Graham Gooch and Mike Atherton and Marcus Trescothick and Michael Vaughan among England's principal opening pairings of the last 50 years. Between Boycott's first Test and Edrich's last, England played 114 Tests. But they opened together in only 21 of them.

The selectors seldom had any doubts over the quality of Boycott. He established himself as one of Yorkshire's opening batsmen only in 1963, but he did so to some effect, finishing second in the first-class averages that season. He was in the frame for the India tour of 1963/4, and selected to play for MCC against the Australians early in the following season. He made a favourable impression. Michael Melford, in *The Daily Telegraph,* commented that he 'successfully conveyed a look of class and an appetite for runs which could put him in time among the [Conrad] Huntes and [Bill] Lawrys'. His selection, at the age of 23, for the first Test against Australia, came as no surprise. From then until the first Test of the 1974 series, Boycott played in 63 out of England's 92 Tests, in which he opened the batting on all but one occasion. Of the 29 Tests he missed, 26 were due to unavailability – either injury or, in

1972/3, a refusal to tour India. Twice, as we have seen, he was dropped for slow scoring. The only other time he was dropped was for the first Test of the 1966 series against the West Indies, an interesting example of how sensitive the selectors of this era were to form in county cricket. Boycott started the season as an established England player with 20 Tests behind him, and an average of 39. He had had a successful tour of Australia the previous winter but he had an indifferent start to the 1966 season playing for Yorkshire, and was replaced by Eric Russell. Russell had also toured Australia, injuring himself in the first Test, and not regaining his place until the short tour of New Zealand which followed. He did nothing in New Zealand to suggest he was a superior player to Boycott, and for the second Test of 1966, Boycott replaced him. It was curious that Russell, older than Boycott and with much less Test experience, should have usurped him in the first place.

Boycott resumed his place in the England side after missing the winter tour of 1972/3, and retained it until 1974. In the first Test against India, he was twice dismissed cheaply, and was then omitted. It was probably more a case of Boycott being rested than dropped, and there was a degree of mutual agreement about the decision. Certainly Boycott had entered a period of disillusionment with England after Mike Denness had been preferred to him as England captain, and despite considerable success against the West Indies in 1973/4, according to John Woodcock in *The Times* 'he found it almost more than he could manage to enter into the spirit of the tour. On and off the field he was a figure apart.' He was picked for the 1974/5 tour to Australia, but subsequently withdrew. The chairman of selectors, Alec Bedser, said 'he asked to be released from the tour as he felt that he still needs more time away from international cricket. It is basically the same problem he had in June. He does not want to subject himself to the pressures of Test cricket yet.' He was not ready again until 1977.

The selectors were much more ambivalent about Edrich. A century against Australia at Lord's in 1964 in his sixth Test match might have been expected to secure him an extended run, but after two more matches he was dropped, and was not even chosen as one of the three openers for the 1964/5 tour of South Africa (like Cowdrey, being passed over in favour of Mike Brearley – 'bewildering inconsistency', according to Alex Bannister in *The Cricketer*). His style was less easy on the eye than some of his competitors, and this may have obscured the extent of his effectiveness. Recalled in 1965 when Boycott was injured, he scored 310 not out against New Zealand and followed it up with a successful tour of Australia in 1965/6 in which he scored two centuries. But he was passed over for the start of the 1966 series: apparently an unconvincing performance in the MCC v West Indians fixture at the start of the season was held against him. He was picked for only three Tests in that summer and the next. His selection for the Caribbean tour of 1967/8 was thus almost as surprising as his omission from that to South Africa three years previously, but he scored lots of runs in what proved to be an unbroken sequence of 38 Tests. He was unavailable to tour India in 1972/3, and as we shall see, this enabled Dennis Amiss to secure the opening position and exclude Edrich from it until Boycott withdrew his services. From 1974 until his final Test in 1976, Edrich played in 18 of England's 20 Tests, missing two due to injury.

Edrich's opening partnerships with Boycott were thus constrained by periods during which the selectors were unconvinced by Edrich, and by Boycott's absence from Test cricket in the mid-70s. They were also due to Edrich's success in filling the number three position for England: in 25 of his 77 Tests he batted there (and a further five at four). This in turn was due to strong competition for the opening position from two others in the 60s.

Bob Barber had not played Test cricket since 1961/2 in India and Pakistan, where he had not been regarded as a specialist opening batsman. But a century for Warwickshire against the Australians in August 1964 catapulted him into the England side for the final Test of the series. It was less the fact than the manner and timing of the innings which impressed the selectors. His century came before lunch on the opening day and altogether he scored 138, including twenty-two 4's, out of 209 in 135 minutes; and it happened days after the Old Trafford Test in which England had scored 611 in 293 overs. Barber's selection was unsupported by volume of runs in county cricket, but it was a recognition of the imperative for a more positive approach to batting. It was an inspired selection. Barber played in 16 of England's next 17 Tests, averaging just under 40, and playing one of the great England Test innings of the 60s – 185 off just 255 balls to set up a rare England victory over Australia at Sydney in 1965/6. By the standards of the day, it was a phenomenal scoring rate. Business commitments, however, limited Barber to only three more Test matches after the Australia tour. The selectors were desperate to have him in the side. They debated whether to pick him for the 1967/8 tour to the West Indies even though he would have to leave it early, before concluding that this was not sustainable, though they earmarked him as a reserve in the event that injuries occurred.

In Barber's absence in 1966, the selectors looked for another aggressive opening batsman, and immediately chose Colin Milburn. As *The Times*' cricket correspondent wrote commenting on the selectors' choice:

> 'Milburn fills the place that was Barber's in Australia, of a belligerent opening batsman who seeks the initiative from the time of taking his guard. His selection is a calculated risk, though it has been made that much easier by his splendid start to the season. He has made 700 runs at an average of over 60, and at his only meeting with Hall and Griffith, he hooked them off his eyebrows.'

He continued in this vein in his first two Tests, scoring 94 off 136 balls in the first and 126 not out off 170 balls in the second – again scoring rates unmatched by any other England batsman of the 60s apart from Barber. The downside to Milburn was his girth, which limited his utility in the field, and which was the key factor in his omission for the last Test of the 1966 series. The selectors varied their views about the weight to be placed on this dimension, and Milburn was picked erratically over the next three years, before an eye injury sustained in a car accident in 1969 brought his Test career to a premature end. There was to be no one else in the Barber/Milburn mould, someone who could consistently score at 60 runs per 100 balls in Test cricket, until Ian Botham.

Chopping, Changing and Waiting for Boycott

At the end of the 60s, England went from riches to rags in regards to middle-order batsmen. Within a year from July 1968 to June 1969, Barrington, Dexter and Graveney played their last Tests, while Cowdrey's injury and subsequent decline made him no longer an automatic choice.

Scoring the Runs: 1962-1995

D'Oliveira remained around until 1972, and Tony Greig came to fill the number six position very capably from 1972. But whereas England had five specialist middle order batsmen born between 1927 and 1935 who played 50 Tests or more (Graveney, May, Barrington, Cowdrey, Dexter), there was only one born between 1935 and 1951 who did so (Keith Fletcher) and only two others who played more than 20 (Denness and Graham Roope).

The potential of Fletcher was recognised early when he made his debut against Australia in 1968 at the age of 24, and was then selected, controversially, ahead of D'Oliveira, for the winter tour of 1968/9. But the selectors were impatient with his failure to deliver at Test level, and for some years he had no really extended run in the side – three Tests in 1969, six out of eight in the Antipodes in 1970/1, two in 1971, one in 1972. He was an enigma. Apart from 1969, he scored prolifically for Essex, but by the end of the 1972 season, and by now 28, he had played 15 Tests without scoring a hundred, and with an average of just 21. When selected for the winter tour to India and Pakistan, the selectors publicly declared (in a perhaps curious motivational tactic) that it was his last chance. But he took it. He played in 32 of England's next 33 Tests and scored seven centuries (including a double), while averaging 57. It was a transformation.

Fletcher's purple patch was brought to a halt by the Australian bowling attack of Lillee and Thomson in 1974/5. Fletcher was one of several England batsmen to offer little resistance to the fearsome pair, and while he scored a century in the sixth Test, this was when Thomson was absent and Lillee was injured after six overs. Fletcher was retained for the first Test against Australia in England the following summer, but another failure led to his being dropped. What was now surprising was that the selectors, having made the strategic judgement that Fletcher, for all his successes prior to the winter, was not up to at any rate the task of dealing with that Australian attack, should recall him after just one more Test. It was a consequence of a decision to dispense with Amiss, another who had failed to handle Thomson and Lillee in Australia and England, and Graham Gooch, who had made his debut in the first Test of the series. In a later era, one might have expected, in these circumstances, Gooch to have been given a third try rather than reverse the decision to drop a senior batsman. Certainly it was not a successful move and Fletcher was immediately dropped again.

Unnatural Selection

His subsequent recall for the 1976/7 tour to India was not unreasonably based on his success in the sub-continent four years previously. Fletcher was still only 32, and might have been expected to prosper in an environment where extreme pace would be absent. But he did not, and also failed once again in the Centenary Test against Australia at the end of the winter. His Test career seemed over.

Denness's career has been considered elsewhere, in the context of his captaincy. Roope was first selected for the England tour to India and Pakistan of 1972/3. At the age of 26, he was the nearest thing to a young debutant batsman since Fletcher in 1968 – a reflection, as we shall see, of the preference of Illingworth for seasoned pros. He was not a success. According to John Woodcock in *The Times* 'to watch him play the Indian spinners...was not a recommended way of relaxing'. It might not have helped that he played his first two Tests as an opening batsman after Amiss and Barry Wood, who had failed to score a fifty between them in the first three Tests, were dropped. But Roope did no better. That he played as many as 21 Tests in the 70s without scoring a hundred is a reflection in part of the difficulty England had in finding a stable middle order, and in part on the importance the selectors attached to his outstanding slip fielding. Roope's catches/matches ratio is unmatched by any other England fielder in the last half century.

It is paradoxical that four of the new middle order batsmen who England tried from 1969 to 1975 were instant – or near instant – successes, but in no case was the consequence a long Test career. In 1969 John Hampshire of Yorkshire was preferred to Fletcher. This was itself a controversial decision: Fletcher had performed reasonably well in Pakistan the previous winter, and at that point was the up and coming man. In the 1970 *Wisden's* report of the tour, E M Wellings wrote 'Fletcher...did splendidly, batting consistently and raising fielding standards considerably'. Hampshire, by contrast, was 28, had a solid but unspectacular record for Yorkshire, and his county form at the start of the 1969 season was underwhelming. Yet it was an inspired selection. He came into the side for the second Test and scored 107 against the West Indies. Three low scores followed, and he was dropped for the first Test against New Zealand in the second half of the summer for Fletcher. It is difficult to understand why the selectors undertook this *volte face*: the evidence for the contentious preference for Hampshire over

Fletcher had surely been enhanced, rather than diminished, by events. Hampshire himself was modestly unsurprised by the decision (for which he received no explanation from his captain or the selectors): he did not regard his century as an especially convincing one, and he continued to struggle in county cricket, though that had not prevented his original selection. Hampshire had a run of four Tests against Australia and New Zealand in 1970/1 – Ray Illingworth, it seems, would have preferred him to Cowdrey from the start of the tour, but was overruled; and was recalled for singleton Tests in 1972 and 1975 – in all cases despite, rather than because, of his county form. It was as if the selectors did not really know what to make of him.

Frank Hayes also made a century on debut against West Indies, at the age of 26, in 1973. He was rewarded with a prolonged run in the side, playing in six of England's next seven Tests (all against the West Indies). But his century proved not to be portentous. He scored just 97 more runs, and he was no more successful when recalled for two Tests (also against West Indies) in 1976.

David Steele was 33 when he made his debut in the second Test against Australia in 1975. He had been a solid county batsman for many years, but had never been seriously canvassed as a Test player. True, he found an unusually rich vein of county form in 1975, but his elevation to Test status was a major surprise. In *The Times*, John Woodcock wrote of him 'he is prematurely grey, but resolutely dogged. It was this doggedness which earned him a place, a feature which has been conspicuous by its absence in one or two recent performances'. 'Positive cricket' was now history, and nobody complained about Steele scoring at less than 40 runs per 100 balls as he accumulated 365 runs in three Tests against Australia that summer. After England's batsmen had disintegrated in the face of Australia's fast bowlers the previous winter, Steele went a long way towards restoring some pride in English cricket, while his unpretentious appearance and approach appealed to the wider sporting public. As winner of the BBC Sports Personality of the Year in 1975, he is an unlikely member of a select quartet of England cricketers similarly honoured, Jim Laker, Botham and Andrew Flintoff being the others. He played another five Tests against the West Indies in 1976. Taking his eight Tests as a whole, he was England's highest run scorer, with a century and five fifties, and overall only Edrich had a higher average.

Unnatural Selection

Yet Steele was never again picked for England. His omission from the party to tour India in 1976/7 was as unexpected as his original inclusion against Australia. Instead the specialist batting places went to Amiss, Brearley, Bob Woolmer, Derek Randall, Graham Barlow and Fletcher. Of these, only Amiss, who had been recalled for the last Test against the West Indies and scored 203, was an automatic choice. Brearley and Woolmer got in ahead of Steele, as they were openers and three were required. Randall (25) and Barlow (26) had not played for England before and were regarded as being the most promising of the younger generation. For both, the route to tour selection had been via inclusion in the England sides during the one-day internationals at the end of 1976, in which each had scored an 80. Fletcher returned on the basis of his reputation, gained on the 1972/3 tour of India, of being a good player of slow bowling. It was, effectively, Fletcher who was preferred to Steele. It was said that Steele did not play spin bowling well, though as his Test career had required him to face almost exclusively fast bowling (in 16 Test innings he had not once been dismissed by a slow bowler), it is difficult to know on what evidence this conclusion was reached.

Of the six specialist batsmen who went to India, only Amiss averaged over 30 in the Tests. In addition Randall, who had a dismal tour, came back with his reputation enhanced after his brilliant innings of 174 in the Centenary Test in Melbourne which followed it. Fletcher averaged just 16 in Tests that winter. So Steele would not have had to perform very well to have justified being selected ahead of him. On the other hand, Steele in 1975/6 was essentially a good county batsman enjoying a purple patch. He never again reproduced his county form of 1975, and even in Tests his performances generally declined during the 1976 series after he had scored a century in the opening match. Perhaps the selectors were ahead of the game in recognising that purple patch coming to an end.

Bob Woolmer had caught the selectors' eye as early as 1972, when he was first picked for England in the series of one-day internationals against Australia. Regarded then as a bowling all-rounder, he was arguably the prototype of the specialist one-day utility player which was to become particularly fashionable in the 90s. When finally he was picked for the Test side against Australia in 1975, he was 27, and batted at eight. In his second Test he was up the order to five, in which position he scored his maiden Test hundred. In 1976, having begun to open the batting for Kent following an injury to Brian Luckhurst, he was opening for England. After a poor tour of India the following winter, he seemed to have cemented for himself the number three position in a highly successful series against Australia in 1977 in which he score two hundreds and averaged 56. The time which he appeared to have to play the ball provoked comparisons with Cowdrey, but he had signed for Packer, and was ineligible to play for England during his prime years. Subsequently he was selected for two Tests in each of the 1980 and 1981 seasons, but was unable to repeat his achievements of 1977, and by then there was a new generation of England middle-order batsmen competing for places.

With nobody besides, for a period, Fletcher (and for a shorter period Denness), establishing themselves in England's middle order between 1969 and 1976, the selectors were forced to consider some more unorthodox approaches. One was to play three opening batsmen. Edrich not infrequently batted at three, and he was to do so again in the first five Tests of England's Ashes winning series against Australia in 1970/1, and for most of the Tests against India and Pakistan the following summer. He also batted down the order in Australasia in 1974/5. On the first of these tours, Boycott's opening partner was Luckhurst. He first played for England against the Rest of the World in 1970, at the age of 31, and, on the back of his performances there, was selected for Australia where he proved to be an outstanding success. He followed this up with another excellent season in 1971, such that after his first 13 Tests he had scored over 1000 runs at an average of 48. In 1972, his form deserted him and he was dropped for the final Test. Thereafter he had two recalls, one in 1973, and one to the 1974/5 touring party to Australia, but neither was happy. He was a classic – but still relatively unusual – example of a batsman making a successful entry into Test cricket at a mature age while in peak form. Steele, of course was another, and Clive Radley (picked at the age of 33), who had eight marvellous Test matches in 1977/8 and 1978 before losing form in Australia in 1978/9, was a third. None of these late developers was able to sustain his early success.

The other opener who emerged to allow Edrich to bat lower was Dennis Amiss. His potential was identified when he was chosen for the final Test of the 1966 series against the West Indies. At this time he was a middle-order batsman, and for the next couple of seasons struggled to find a place in the Test side when competition was so hot. Only in 1971

Unnatural Selection

did he enjoy an extended run of four Tests, but he managed just one fifty and was dropped. By then he had played nine Tests at an average of 19, was 28, and might have imagined his time had passed. In 1972, he transformed himself into an opening batsman, and with neither Boycott nor Edrich available for the 1972/3 tour, he forced his way back into the side. He did nothing on the India leg of the tour, when he was dropped, to justify his selection. But a maiden century in the first Test against Pakistan transformed his fortunes. In the remaining 38 Tests of his career he scored 3264 runs at an average of 55. In his *annus mirabilis*, 1974, he scored 1369 runs. Unusually, he reserved his best performances for the West Indies, against whom he scored two double-centuries and averaged 70. By contrast, he always struggled against Australia, against whom he averaged just 15. Like Denness, Fletcher, Luckhurst, and David Lloyd, he had no answer to Lillee and Thomson in 1974/5, and was dropped after two more failures against Australia in 1975. He returned triumphantly for the final Test against the all-powerful West Indies in 1976, where he scored 203 as Michael Holding took 8-92. He was successful in India in the winter of 1976/7, but once again struggled against Australia in 1977, and was dropped after two Tests to accommodate the returning Boycott. Thereafter he joined Packer. He continued to score prolifically in county cricket during 1978 and 1979, and although when eligible to be selected for England again he was 37, it is perhaps surprising that he was not given an opportunity. But by then the opening positions were firmly occupied by Boycott and Gooch, although in view of his record against the West Indies, he might have had more success in 1980 and 1980/1 than say Wayne Larkins, Brian Rose or Bill Athey, who were chosen ahead of him. Fletcher sought to have Amiss in his party for the 1981/2 tour to India, but was overruled: Boycott was by then 41 and Fletcher was 37; a third player of that vintage was regarded as pushing it.

Nevertheless, on three occasions, the selectors did turn to middle-order batsmen from a previous era. In 1972, M J K Smith was recalled. Aged 39, he had last played for England in 1966, and indeed had retired from county cricket at the end of the summer of 1967 before returning in 1970. Even in his prime Smith was unable to translate his success in county cricket into performances at the Test level. Perhaps the selectors were inspired by the consequences of their decision to recall Graveney in 1966, but Graveney had always been a better player. Smith played three

Tests and scored 140 runs before being dropped.

In the first Test of the 1974/5 series in Australia, both Edrich and Amiss suffered broken bones at the hands of Australia's pace attack as England plunged to a heavy defeat. A replacement batsman was required, and Cowdrey was summoned. It was a move which smacks either of excessive sentimentality, or desperation. Cowdrey was to celebrate his 42nd birthday in Australia. He had not played a Test match since 1971, and had not scored a Test hundred since February 1969. His last tour of Australia, in 1970/1, had been disappointing. He had had a reasonable county season in 1974 but in averaging less than 40, it was his least successful for many years. Someone like John Jameson, who had an outstanding summer, who was 33, and who had played four Tests over the previous three years, would have been a more conventional choice. Barry Wood of Lancashire and Mike Harris of Nottinghamshire were also considered. But, Denness has written, 'right from the start the player I had in mind was Colin Cowdrey. We were looking for someone who was a good player of quick bowling, who could open if necessary, who had Test-match experience, and who was willing and keen enough to come out and work hard for us.' As it was Cowdrey played five Tests without scoring a fifty.

The selection of another veteran, Brian Close, at the age of 45, for the first Test against the West Indies in 1976 – his first since 1967 – was one of the most controversial of the last 50 years. The background was the match between MCC and the tourists a week and a half before. MCC had fielded six batsmen in contention for Test places – Amiss, Brearley, Alan Butcher of Surrey, Roope, Randall and Richard Gilliat of Hampshire. They were bowled out for 197 and 83 by Andy Roberts, Michael Holding and Vanburn Holder. Gilliat alone passed 50. West Indies then moved on to Somerset, whom they also beat easily. But Close scored 88 and 40 (and the young Ian Botham 56). The selectors appeared to conclude that the younger generation were not up to the challenge that the West Indies bowlers posed, and Greig pressed successfully for Close to be recalled to the Test team.

It is hard not to conclude that Close was chosen for what he represented as much as for what he was likely to achieve. Even in his prime, he had had only two full series in the England side and he had never scored a Test hundred. The recent experience of Cowdrey in

Unnatural Selection

Australia was hardly a happy precedent for the recall of heroes of the past. Nevertheless, Close did as well as anyone in the second Test, with scores of 60 and 46, and found himself asked to open in the third. His partner was Edrich, and their combined age was 84! The pitch for that Old Trafford Test turned out to be one favourable to the West Indies fast bowlers. England were dismissed for 71 in the first innings. Edrich and Close were required to open the second on the Saturday evening. The 1977 *Wisden* reported the session thus:

> 'the period before the close on the third day brought disquieting cricket as Edrich and Close grimly defended their wickets and themselves against fast bowling, which was frequently too wild and too hostile to be acceptable. Holding was finally warned for intimidation by umpire Alley after an excess of bouncers. Lloyd admitted after the match "our fellows got carried away. They knew they had only 80 minutes that night to make an impression and they went flat out, sacrificing accuracy for speed"'.

Although Edrich and Close survived the session (and with 24 and 20 respectively were England's highest scorers as they were dismissed for 126 to lose by the awesome margin of 425 runs) it was judged that, in those pre-helmet days, two such mature batsmen could not reasonably be subjected to such an attack again. Thus it was, for both of them, their last Test.

In 1977, Boycott returned to the England fold. It is not clear precisely when he indicated to the selectors that he was available once more. It was certainly before the second Test, for which he was not selected. The selectors might have been inclined to make Boycott wait even longer, in view of his failure to make himself available for England for three years for what seemed selfish, or at any rate self-indulgent, reasons, were it not for the presence in the side of four, soon to be five, players whose moral position seemed no more worthy. Boycott had, at least, rejected Packer's overtures. As it was, he was recalled for the Trent Bridge Test at the expense of Amiss. He ran out Randall in front of Randall's home crowd, but went on to score 107. He followed this up with 191 in the next Test at Headingley, in the process scoring his 100th century in front of

Scoring the Runs: 1962-1995

his home crowd. Thus he re-established himself as England's premier batsman. From the time of his recall, Boycott played in 45 of England's next 49 Tests, missing just four due to injury.

The drought in the production of England middle order batsmen ended in 1951 with the birth of Derek Randall – the first of five players born between then and 1957 who dominated England's batting line up from the late 70s to the early 90s. As we have seen, Randall ended a modest winter tour of 1976/7 with his century against Australia in the Centenary Test. Big hundreds were Randall's speciality, but he could go through long lean spells between them. Thus he was dropped in 1978 following a disastrous winter tour, but toured Australia in 1978/9. Coming in at 0-1 in the second innings of the Sydney Test, with England having conceded a first-innings deficit of 142, his 150 swung the match, which England went on to win by 93 runs. But he scored just 135 runs in his next seven Tests, and with competition for middle-order places now much stronger than in the early 70s, he was dropped again after the second Test of the 1979/80 series.

The Age of the Three Gs

Graham Gooch was selected for the first Test against Australia in 1975 at the age of 21, after only 30 first-class games. He was the youngest batsman to be picked for England since Cowdrey in 1954/5. He owed his place to an innings of 75 for MCC against the Australians earlier in the season, but he was to have less success in the two Tests he played, famously starting with a pair at Edgbaston, and doing only slightly better at Lord's. His case illustrates the difficulty selectors have with promising players who do not immediately make an impression. Were they premature in picking Gooch at such an early stage in his career or were they wrong not to persevere with him despite his early setbacks? When Gooch returned to the England side in 1978 it followed his transformation into an opening batsman. After scoring just 837 first-class runs at an average of 27 in 1977 as a middle-order batsman, as an opener in 1978 he scored 1254 at an average of 42. Even so, he only found his way back into the England side thanks to an injury to Boycott. When Boycott recovered, Gooch retained his place, Brearley moved down the order, and Boycott and Gooch opened together in 24 Tests.

Mike Gatting was even younger than Gooch when selected for

Unnatural Selection

the winter tour of 1977/8, and made his debut in the third Test against Pakistan at the age of 20. He was picked on potential (his county season in 1977 had been unspectacular, and he had yet to score a first-class hundred), and as a result of his good fortune in playing for the England captain's county, Middlesex. As we shall see, different selectors over the years had a faith in Gatting which was only occasionally repaid. By the end of the 1984 season, he had been in and out of the England side, but had appeared in 30 Tests without having scored a hundred and averaging just 23. No other England batsman of the last 50 years enjoyed selection beyond 30 Tests with a record of this modesty unless he was the captain.

David Gower, by contrast, made an immediate impact following his debut in 1978 at the age of 21. With the insouciance for which he was to become renowned, he struck his first ball in Test cricket for four. In his fourth Test he scored his first century and it seemed unquestionable that England had found the successor of at least one of Dexter, Barrington, Cowdrey or Graveney.

The debut of South African born Allan Lamb was delayed until 1982, when he was 27, as he completed his naturalisation as an England player. He was awaited with the same expectation as was Graeme Hick nine years later. In each of 1979, 1980 and 1981 Lamb had scored more than 1700 runs for Northamptonshire at an average of over 60, finishing third, first and third respectively in the first-class averages. He was selected immediately on qualifying to play for England, and began an unbroken run of 45 Tests. He established a reputation for being a fine player of fast bowling, and his greatest moments for England were against the West Indies, against whom he scored six of his 14 Test centuries and against whom he scored more runs than against any other opponent. Only Gooch scored more runs for England against the West Indies in the 1980s.

From 1978 to 1981/2, Boycott, Gooch and Gower formed the kernel of England's batting, with Brearley when he was captain, and usually one of Randall or Gatting (rarely did they play in the same side). From 1982, the default middle order was Gower, Lamb and either Randall or Gatting. There was, in fact, no particular reason why Randall could have expected a resumption of his Test career at the start of the 1982 season. He had played the last of his 27 games for England on the 1979/80 tour of Australia. His Test average was a modest 27. He was now 31. His selection for the series against India, ahead of Gatting (who had toured India the previous winter) was thus unexpected, and unpredicted. *The Times'* cricket correspondent wrote 'there seems to me no future in giving him priority over Gatting who is six years younger and in prime form'. But this was one the selectors got right. Randall played in 20 out of the next 22 Tests. During this period he averaged over 40 and only Gower and Botham scored more runs for England. He had a particularly good tour of Australia in 1982/3, when he topped the Test averages. Against this background he was unfortunate, following a good tour to New Zealand and Pakistan in 1983/4, to be dropped after only one Test against the West Indies in 1984, in which he made 0 and 1. He was replaced in that series successively by Gatting, Paul Terry and Chris Tavare, whose scores were 1, 29, 8, 1, 7, 16 and 49. Randall would not have had to have played very well to have improved on that. As it was, his Test career was over.

    He was passed over for the 1984/5 tour to India on the grounds of his lack of success there in 1976/7 – though similar considerations were not applied to the case of Gatting, who was selected despite averaging only 13 in India in 1981/2. But Gatting's triumph over Randall was now complete. He embarked upon a run of Test form in which he scored 2419 runs at an average of 62 over the next 28 Tests in which he played. The selectors' uncharacteristic perseverance with him had finally been justified.

The rebel tour to South Africa following the 1981/2 tour to India left a gaping hole in England's opening batting positions, with Boycott, Gooch and Amiss all banned. Not since the first Test in 1978/9 had neither Gooch nor Boycott opened for England, and they had opened together in 20 of the previous 23 Tests. Boycott had missed the last two Tests in India and the one in Sri Lanka which followed, on the grounds of 'physical and mental tiredness' – a condition from which he had sufficiently recovered a month later to depart for South Africa.

    These bans offered opportunities to a number of largely untested players. Geoff Cook had opened with Gooch in the Test in Sri Lanka. The captain of Northamptonshire, Cook was already 30 when chosen for his first overseas tour, and although he had had a good season in 1981, it was not significantly superior to that of a younger generation of openers – Wilf Slack (26), Alan Butcher (26) and Graeme Fowler (24) – who might have been thought better long-term prospects. There was some speculation that Cook's century in the 1981 domestic one-day final at Lord's might have weighed unduly with the selectors. Others saw in his selection the creation of another option for a future England captain. Cook played a total of seven Test matches, before the selectors concluded that he was not good enough.

The other spot went to a man whom the selectors probably regarded as being as close to a like-for-like replacement for Boycott as was available. Chris Tavare had made his England debut in 1980. Following a recall for the fifth Test in 1981, in which he made 69 and 78, he established himself in the number three position, where he batted for Kent, though he opened with Gooch in the last two Tests in India after Boycott's departure. A dour batsman, Tavare was to record some remarkable slow-scoring statistics in a Test career in which his average strike rate was just 30 runs per 100 balls: 35 in 240 balls in the Madras Test of 1981/2, 14 off 95 balls at Lord's against Sri Lanka in 1984, and 63 minutes to get off the mark against Australia in Perth in 1982/3. From the fifth Test against Australia in 1981 to the second against New Zealand in 1983/4, Tavare had an unbroken run of 26 Test appearances, 18 of them opening. He filled a gap when England were shorter of opening batsmen than at any time since 1963, but his career average of 32 was, ultimately, inadequate. When dropped in 1983/4 he was only 29, but he was to play just three more Tests for England.

Tavare had three other opening partners in addition to Gooch and Cook during his 18 Tests in this position. Randall was called on to open on a couple of occasions and, while this was not his normal position, he did score a century against Pakistan. Graeme Fowler was picked for the last Test of the 1982 series, and played in 21 of the next 27. He has the curious distinction of being dropped just one Test after scoring a double-century. He made 201 in the Madras Test of 1984/5, but poor form at the start of the 1985 season, combined with the return of Gooch after the South Africa ban, conspired to lose him his Test place. Injured in the middle of the season, his form was so bad by the end of it that he could not make the Lancashire side. He did not play Test cricket again. Chris Smith, who was born in South Africa, made his England debut in 1983, the first season in which he was qualified to play for England, and his first full season in Hampshire's first team. He forced his way into the England team through the weight of runs he scored in the County Championship early in the season, and played in six out of the next seven Tests, and a couple more a little later. But he did not make the same impact as other Southern African émigrés in the 80s and beyond.

Aside from Gooch, who returned to the England team after completing his suspension in 1985, England's most successful openers in the 1980s were the Nottinghamshire pair of Chris Broad and Tim Robinson (though they only opened together on three occasions). Broad had the misfortune of making his debut against the powerful West Indies attack of 1984. In four Tests he performed better than some, less well than others, but finished the international season with 86 against Sri Lanka. He might have expected to have been selected for the winter tour to India. Instead, Robinson was preferred. The chairman of selectors, Peter May, said 'Broad is unlucky, if not very unlucky'. He paid tribute to Broad's 'bravery' against the West Indian fast bowlers, but expressed doubts about his ability to play spin. Steele might have sympathised with him. However, Robinson did prove to be an inspired choice. In 11 Test matches in 1984/5 against India, and in 1985 against Australia, Robinson scored 934 runs at an average of 62. Both series were run feasts for England, which came to an abrupt end in the Caribbean the following winter. He was found out by the West Indies' fast bowlers, and scored just 72 runs in four Tests. He played a further 14 times for England over the next four summers, but failed fully to re-establish himself.

Robinson's demise reopened the door for Broad, who was brought back for the 1986/7 tour to Australia in a move no less surprising than the preference of Robinson to Broad two years earlier. Robinson had scored heavily against Australia in 1985, and had a superior county season to Broad in 1986. But again the selectors made the right decision, for Broad was even more successful in Australia than Robinson had been in India. He played in another 13 Tests, with reasonable success, before being dropped after a single bad performance against the West Indies in the second Test in 1988. It came on the back of a winter in which he had scored three Test centuries, but also one in which he had shown ostentatious dissent to umpiring decisions (see Chapter Two). The 1989 Wisden reported that when Broad was given out lbw he left looking 'unhappy' with 'his expression of disappointment caught by the television cameras'. For some commentators, this was the last straw, and there appears to have been disagreement among the selectors as to whether to retain him. As it was, he was given a 'final warning' about his 'unacceptable shows of disappointment', but retained in the squad of 13 for the third Test. If this was a defeat for the disciplinarians on the selection committee, they secured their victory a few days later when it came to whittling the 13 down to 11, and Broad was omitted to accommodate the returning Gatting, with Martyn Moxon moving up to open. It is difficult to imagine that Moxon would have been preferred to Broad but for the incident in the previous Test, so effectively the selectors had, on reflection, surreptitiously substituted a ban for their final warning.

If finding an opening partner for Gooch (and two openers when Gooch was unavailable) proved troublesome for England, it might have been expected that Gooch himself, Lamb, Gatting once he had cemented his place and Gower would be automatic choices for England in the 1980s and beyond. Between them, in total, they played 393 Test matches for England. It did not, however, work out quite so simply.

Gooch played every Test for England from 1985 to 1986, but declared himself unavailable for the 1986/7 tour to Australia. That probably counted against him when in 1987 the selectors were considering an opening partner for Broad, who had distinguished himself in Australia. As it happened, Gooch endured a poor run of form in county cricket that season – itself coinciding with his brief spell as captain of Essex. And the recalled Robinson seized his opportunity by scoring 166 against Pakistan in the first Test. But when Robinson moved down to three in the final Test, it was not to accommodate Gooch but Moxon. Moxon was by then 27, probably a little old still to be regarded as promising, and had played two Tests in 1986 without convincing the selectors to pick him ahead of Bill Athey as Broad's opening partner the previous winter. It needed Gooch to score a century in the MCC v Rest of the World bicentenary match at Lord's at the end of 1987 for the selectors to recall him to England colours.

Gooch was never again dropped by England although he chose not to tour New Zealand in 1987/8, and West Indies in 1993/4. He also asked to stand down from the fifth Test against Australia in 1989 after a poor series in which he was repeatedly out lbw, in particular to Terry Alderman. But he was back for the sixth Test, and became England captain after it. In 34 Tests at the helm, he averaged 59, compared with 36 in the 84 in which he was not. The selection issue for Gooch which next arose was how long he should continue to play for England after relinquishing the captaincy in 1993. He was by now 40. Recalled at once after missing the 1993/4 tour to the West Indies, a double-hundred against New Zealand in the first Test appeared to confirm that his powers were undiminished. Despite modest performances in the other five Tests, he continued to score heavily in county cricket. His selection for the 1994/5 tour to Australia was, therefore, understandable. But it proved a tour too far. Gooch managed only a solitary fifty in the series, and announced his retirement from Test cricket towards the end of the tour.

Lamb, as we have seen, had an unbroken run of 45 matches for England, starting with his debut. But after a wonderful 1984 season, in which he scored four Test centuries, his form gradually declined, the centuries dried up, and he was dropped for the first time in 1986. Selected ahead of him was Bill Athey, who had first been chosen as a 22-year-old back in 1980, though he never fulfilled the early promise which had prompted that selection despite a reasonable run of Tests in the mid-1980s. Lamb was in and out of the England side for the next couple of years, but re-established himself as one of only two batsmen (the other was Gooch) to deal competently with the West Indies attack of 1988. Thereafter he was a regular in the England side when fit. A couple of poor Tests against Pakistan, and advancing years (he was by then nearly 38) brought his Test career to an end in 1992.

  Despite being England's premier batsman of the 1980s, and ranking alongside Gooch as the outstanding batsman of his generation, Gower was dropped six times during his England career. The greatest of batsmen have had vicissitudes in their early career – though Gower had an unbroken opening run of 21 Tests in which he averaged 44 – and the greatest of batsmen face a waning of their powers at the end of their career – but Gower was dropped for the last time at the age of just 35.

  He was first omitted in 1980 after the first Test against the West Indies, in which he had scored 20 and 1. He had, it was true, had a disappointing, though hardly disastrous, tour of Australia the previous winter; and he had a modest season in county cricket in 1980. But even at this early stage in Gower's career, county form was no guide to Test performance. His average for Leicestershire in 1978 was 25, and for England 55; in 1979, the comparable figures were 34 and 72 respectively. Gatting who, not for the last time, replaced Gower, had a first-class average at the time of his selection of nearly 80. But in four

Unnatural Selection

Tests against West Indies, he scored only 172 runs at an average of 25. The probability must be that Gower would have done better: on the tour to the West Indies which followed, he averaged 54.

Gower was next dropped for the final Test against Australia in 1981 – though in this case it was more a case of resting him with the series won. The third occasion was for the fifth Test against the West Indies in 1988. He had had a fairly average series, with just 211 runs – though only Gooch and Lamb had performed better. He was replaced by debutant Mathew Maynard, who made 3 and 10, and was then himself dropped. Blooding a new player against the dominant West Indies side of 1988 when there was a much less demanding end-of-season Test against Sri Lanka to come was harsh on Maynard and that easier opportunity was gratefully taken by Kim Barnett.

Gower was back as England captain in 1989, but as we have seen, was replaced by Gooch at the end of the series. Gower was not selected for the 1989/90 tour to the West Indies. The chairman of selectors, Ted Dexter, explained the decision in these terms: 'although David did contribute more than some during the series with Australia the remainder of his form was extremely sketchy. I am sure his shoulder has been troubling him and it was felt that a winter off would be the best thing.' Gower was not, it is true, the batsman he had been in 1985, when he had scored 732 runs in a series against Australia. Although he had scored a hundred against Australia in the 1989 Ashes, he had not averaged over 40 in a Test series since 1986/7. His shoulder injury, on which he was indeed due to have an operation in the autumn of 1989, was undoubtedly a limitation, not only on his fielding, but also on his ability to follow through when driving. But it was far from clear that the operation on his shoulder would prevent him embarking on a tour which did not get under way until the following February. And it was certainly open to the selectors to have selected Gower, had they wished, on the stipulation that he would need to prove his fitness following the operation.

Another reason for excluding Gower might have been his modest record against the West Indies. But, by and large, everyone struggled against the West Indies in the 80s. It was a lot to ask of the three young middle-order batsmen chosen ahead of Gower (Rob Bailey, Alec Stewart and Nasser Hussain) to make a significant impact, and indeed they did not: none scored a fifty in the 10 Tests they played between them. The likelihood, again, must have been that a man with 106 Tests behind him and an average of 43, and still only 32, would have improved on this.

There were undoubtedly other factors which influenced the decision to drop Gower. One was the sense of creating a clean break with the disastrous series of 1988 and 1989 in which England had lost seven, won one (against Sri Lanka) and drawn four Tests. In this sense, Gower's omission has something of the rationale underlying Cowdrey's when he was dropped from the side as well as the captaincy in 1966. Another was the desire to break up the Gower/Botham/Lamb circle in the England party, which some regarded as exclusivist and subject to different rules from the rest (Botham too was omitted – though the cricketing reasons in his case were clearer cut). And then there was the personal antipathy which had developed between Micky Stewart, the England coach, and Gower. It seems as if the initiative to exclude Gower came from Stewart. In his autobiography, Gower wrote that when Gooch 'talked me through the decision as best he could [he implied] my omission had been more or less presented to him' by Dexter and Stewart. Gooch's autobiography is rather delphic on the point: 'I attempted to explain the reasons to him [Gower] and that, having been given the job after just a bit of experience of it before, I was now determined on a fresh, dynamic attitude, or England would go on failing' Whatever Gooch's precise position, it appears that he at any rate did not, or could not, dissent from Dexter's and Stewart's decision.

Gower was recalled for the one-day internationals against New Zealand at the start of 1990, but was not picked for the Test team until India arrived for the second half of the summer. Some commentators were critical of his treatment by the selectors. In *The Times*, Alan Lee wrote:

> 'Gower did, of course, fail twice in the one-dayers, but in the very recent past this has been ruled inadmissible evidence. Alec Stewart made two noughts in three balls in successive one-day internationals in the Caribbean, whereupon his father, Micky, likened his misfortune to bagging a pair in a Test match and said: 'we are not in the business of dropping batsmen for that'. If Gower had been an experimental choice in the Texaco series, or even a limited-overs specialist, his transitory appearance could be justified. But he is one of the most distinguished England cricketers in two decades, and the flippant way in which he has been treated insults his dignity.'

Unnatural Selection   147

Gower was included in the squad for the tour to Australia in 1990/1. After the third Test in Sydney, few people's place in the side looked more secure than Gower's. His last seven innings, starting from the second innings against India at the Oval the previous summer, had been 157 not out, 61, 27, 100, 0, 123 and 36. But after two more Tests, he was dropped again. Two incidents were primarily responsible.

During the match against Queensland soon after the third Test match, Gower and John Morris, both of whom had already batted in England's innings, absented themselves from the ground, without the permission of the captain. Their purpose was to visit a nearby airport, from where they boarded two 1938 Tiger Moths, and in the course of their flights, persuaded the pilots to 'buzz' the cricket ground. Later, both posed for pictures by the aircraft which subsequently appeared in the press. Gooch was not impressed. He wrote in his autobiography:

> 'The unwritten rule in cricket is that if you are playing you ask the captain (or manager) if you can leave the ground. I assumed that as David hadn't asked, he expected me to say 'no', and I would have. The press took the manager Peter Lush by surprise when they asked him about the prank soon afterwards, and when Peter came back to the pavilion to see David about it, we discovered that he and Morris had actually returned to the airport to pose for press photos in the cockpit, dressed in 'Biggles' outfits...That let us down badly, I thought. What if the rest of the team, especially the younger ones, thought that sort of behaviour was par for the course?'

Gower and Morris were both fined £1000. Rob Steen, in his biography of Gower, claims that Lush, Stewart and Gooch were all for sending Gower straight home, and that only Lamb, as vice-captain a member of the Disciplinary Committee, persuaded them to settle for a fine. Gower considered the fine to be exorbitant. Certainly it was in stark contrast to the decision not to fine Broad for his ostentatious dissent in Pakistan three years before, which arguably was much more damaging to the reputation of the England team. The 1992 *Wisden's* correspondent, John Thicknesse, commented:

> 'for all their dereliction of duty in leaving without permission

a game in which they were playing, it was a harsh penalty for an essentially light-hearted prank, reflecting all too accurately the joyless nature of the tour. Impressive though Gooch's captaincy was, a hair shirt was usually to be found hanging in the wardrobe.'

The second incident was the manner of Gower's dismissal in the first innings of the fourth Test. Replying to Australia's 386, England were 160-3 with one ball to go before lunch, when Gower chipped McDermott to Hughes who had been specifically positioned at backward square-leg for the shot. The loss of Gower precipitated a collapse and England were all out for 229 – though they did go on to draw the match. However ill-conceived the shot, it surely did not merit the reaction of Gooch. In Gower's words:

'when the slating arrived, it was worse than I had expected. It was a rare bad day for me in the series, and yet I was made to feel that I had not scored a run for years...at the Perth press conference [after the fifth Test, Gooch] talked about players' careers being on the line, people having to look at themselves honestly and decide whether they had given of their best, weeding people out the following summer, and, once again, I had the feeling that somewhere in that little lot, there was a reference to me.'

Effectively, Gower was dropped after the 1990/1 series because, whatever his actual achievements in Test matches (he averaged 45 on that tour) his attitude and the lackadaisical appearance of his batting were at odds with the ethos of the England captain and team manager. Gower was advised by Gooch to demonstrate his commitment by scoring runs in county cricket. But Gower failed this test. He did not score a century for his new county Hampshire between May 1990 and June 1992. Supported by this form, the selectors resisted calls for his return. Graeme Hick had now qualified as an England player, and much was expected of him, and the young Mark Ramprakash had also emerged. With this promise the selectors thought they could manage without Gower.

Gower did, however, score runs in county cricket in the first half of the 1992 season. By the end of June he was averaging 65, and after

Unnatural Selection

Pakistan had beaten England in the Lord's Test in a match in which England's batsmen had performed pretty moderately, he was recalled. His scores in the three Tests that followed were 73, 18 not out, 31 not out, 27 and 1. These were not, however, sufficient for Gower to win a place in the touring party for India and Sri Lanka the following winter.

The seven batsmen chosen ahead of Gower were Gooch, Stewart, Atherton, Robin Smith, Hick, Neil Fairbrother and Gatting. The first four were automatic choices. But Gower's claims were surely stronger than each of the last three. Hick turned out to be a successful selection, but at the time he was picked he had played in 11 Tests and averaged just 22. The case for Fairbrother was argued by Gooch in his autobiography thus:

> 'in the three Texaco one-dayers at the end of the Pakistan series we had included, instead of David, the left-handed Neil Fairbrother, who scored 62, 33 and 15 and it goes without saying, fielded like a quicksilver demon. David had admitted his throwing arm in the field was now a liability in the one-day game, and on the upcoming tour of India and Sri Lanka there were to be four Tests and all of eight one-day internationals.'

Nonetheless, in Fairbrother's seven Tests prior to the tour, he averaged just eight. He was to make his only Test fifty against India that winter, and scored one half-century in the eight one-day internationals: this was not a performance to justify his selection.

There was no question that Gower was a better Test batsman than both Hick and Fairbrother. The case against him in comparison with these two was his age (35), when taken alongside Gooch (39) and Gatting (35). England's new team manager, Keith Fletcher, explained 'the thing which concerned me about David was that it would have given us three batsmen in their late 30s. I would not want England to lose three established players at the same time.' It was a similar argument to that which had been used to justify Fletcher's inclusion in England's 1968/9 touring party to South Africa ahead of D'Oliveira, and was equally suspect. If age were so important, why was the 40-year-old John Emburey in the party?

But even if it was considered essential to include no more than two batsmen in their late thirties, the case for Gatting ahead of Gower was thin. Gatting had played his last Test in 1989, before departing on the rebel tour to South Africa. The five-year ban on him, and the other rebels, had been cut short following South Africa's readmission to Test cricket, and expired in October 1992, making him once again eligible for selection. The argument for his inclusion was his outstanding county season in 1992 (2000 runs at an average of 67) and his successful tour to India in 1984/5. But not only had Gatting not played Test cricket for more than three years: his record in those Tests he had played immediately prior to his suspension had been less than electric. Since the summer of 1987, he had played in ten Tests and averaged 20; in the same period, Gower had played in 21 Tests and averaged 42. Gower also had the advantage of being left handed, which might have been expected to be useful against India's leg spinners and slow left-armers, who were to prove England's undoing.

The issue was the more emotive because many felt that notwithstanding the lifting of the ban on the South African rebels, Gatting's decision to lead the tour in 1989/90 was self-serving and morally wrong and that he deserved no favours. A motion of no confidence in the England selectors tabled by dissident members of the MCC was only relatively narrowly defeated (by 6135 to 4600). The editor of *Wisden*, Matthew Engel, writing in the 1993 edition, was sympathetic to the dissidents and his comments encapsulate many of the issues of the period:

> 'There was no sustainable cricketing case for the omission of Gower from a Test series against India. No one seriously made one. Selectors have always had their own secret agenda: prejudices against certain players considered to be unsuitable tourists. In the old days men were sometimes omitted because they did not buy their round at the bar; these days they are more likely to be left out because they do.
>
> 'There are many criticisms which can legitimately be made of Gower as a cricketer and, above all, as a captain; Graham Gooch's period of captaincy since 1989 has been marked by a dedication and determination that has often been quite magnificent. But the English cricket public...have remained loyal to their Test team in a manner unmatched elsewhere

in the world. The modern player who has most reciprocated that loyalty has been Gower. Between 1978/9 and 1986/7 he went on nine successive winter tours. The following year, understandably, he asked for a break. Since then he has been willing to play for England any time anywhere...He did not go on any rebel tour nor is there any evidence (as there is for some who subsequently trumpeted their loyalty) that he seriously contemplated it. The contrast with Gooch – his decision to go to South Africa in 1981/2, his refusal, for understandable family reasons, to tour Australia in 1986/7, his need to have Donald Carr fly out to Antigua in 1986 to persuade him to stay because some politician had criticised him, the fact that he planned to skip the (abandoned) India tour of 1988/9 until he was offered the captaincy, even his insistence on not going to Sri Lanka this year – is very stark.

'This party for India was chosen last September at a moment when reconciliation was being offered all round, to John Emburey for instance. Now Emburey is a fine cricketer and a nice man. But he is the only person in the whole shabby history of these enterprises who actually signed up for rebel tours of South Africa on two occasions. Short of standing on the square at Lord's and giving a V-sign to the Long Room, it is hard to see how anyone can have shown greater unconcern about whether he plays for England or not. For him, forgiveness was instant. For Gower there was none. The whole business reflects badly on English cricket; the dissidents were right to make themselves heard.'

Why did the selectors take a decision which they must have realized would provoke a public outcry? There is no evidence to suggest that it was long premeditated. Had they determined on not taking Gower to India early in the summer, it would have been easy enough not to have recalled him against Pakistan. True, the availability of Gatting for India had only been made possible by the meeting of the International Cricket Conference (ICC), which lifted the ban on the 1989 rebels, a few days after the third Test match of 1992 – that is after the decision to recall Gower. But if the selectors only saw a future for Gower in the continued absence of Gatting, they could have saved themselves a lot of trouble by postponing a decision to recall Gower by one Test and awaiting the outcome of the ICC meeting. That they did not suggests that there was no conspiracy. Rather, it seems that the selectors entered the meeting to select the party for India in a mind-set in which Gatting's place in the side was a fixed presumption which was not debated. The dynamics of the meeting may then have been such that the case for Hick and Fairbrother were made, and suddenly there was no room for Gower. Nobody stopped to think how running the logic from a different starting point – the fact that Gower had had a successful recall to the England side that summer in which in the three Tests he had played he had scored more runs than anyone bar Gooch and Smith, and should therefore be inked in the list from the start – could lead to a different outcome. And so, Gower was dropped by England for the sixth and final time.

As for Gatting, he played in England's next six Tests, scoring three fifties and averaging 31 and succumbing, in the first Test against Australia in 1993, to Shane Warne's famous first ball in an Ashes series. With other England batsmen struggling, it was a respectable performance – but no more. His recall at the age of 37, for the winter tour to Australia of 1994/5 was therefore all the more extraordinary. In his book, Illingworth, by then chairman of selectors, describes the rationale for the decision as follows:

> '...he had had a good season [in county cricket] – only Gooch scored more runs – and I had not forgotten that he was unlucky to be dropped after his last innings for England of 59 at Lord's when he got the wrong end of a marginal lbw decision against Shane Warne. We knew Warne would be a problem, and as Gatting has always played slow bowling well, none of us had any reservations about picking him. Obviously at that stage we could not second-guess what the side would be for the first Test in Brisbane, but with fielding so important on the Australian big grounds, I could not see a situation, other than injury, where Gooch and Gatting would play in the same side. The captain [Atherton] was perfectly happy to have both in their party for their ability as well as their experience.'

This last point is disputed. In his book, Atherton recalls 'in my diary,

Unnatural Selection

against Gatting's name, I had this entry: 'too old, liability in the field, recent Test record not good, another left hander needed to counter Warne'. In the event, Gooch and Gatting both played in all the Tests. For the first and second, they were preferred to John Crawley, even though Crawley had performed better than Gatting in the warm-up games. Thereafter, injuries to Stewart, Craig White and later Hick offered no choice. Although Gatting made a century in Adelaide, his 182 runs overall at an average of 20 did not justify his selection. Like Gooch, he announced his retirement from Test cricket before the end of the tour.

CHAPTER FIVE

SCORING THE RUNS: 1989-2014

Bringing in the New

For the 1989/90 tour to the West Indies, England's batting needed substantial rebuilding. Among the batsmen who had represented England in 1989, Mike Gatting, Chris Broad, Tim Robinson and Kim Barnett had been banned for signing up to the South Africa tour, and David Gower was out of favour. This left only three shoe-ins for the Caribbean: Graham Gooch, the new captain, Allan Lamb, and Robin Smith. Smith, the younger brother of Chris, became an England-qualified player in 1985, and made his debut in 1988 at the age of 24. He made a fifty in his second Test, and two centuries against Australia in 1989, thus becoming one of very few positives England could take from that nightmare Ashes defeat. His early Test form was stunning: by the end of 1989 his average was 50, and it was to remain just below or just above that figure for the next three years.

The South African rebels aside, five other batsmen had played for England in 1989: Chris Tavare, Martyn Moxon, Tim Curtis, John Stephenson and Mike Atherton. None had scored a half-century, and none was picked for the West Indies. In the case of Tavare, Moxon and, to a lesser degree, Curtis it might reasonably have been concluded that they had had their chances, and their time had passed. If Stephenson had been a little lucky to have been picked for the first time to open in the final Test of the 1989 series, he was unlucky to be so quickly discarded and never recalled: if he was the next opener in line in August 1989, what had happened for him to have been overtaken by the time the winter squad was announced in September? Mike Atherton had been selected for the last two Tests of the series at the age of 21 after spending the first half of the season captaining Cambridge University. Clearly, he was a name for the future, but like Stephenson, had to be content with a tour to Zimbabwe with England 'A'.

In an apparently conscious effort to select batsmen not tainted by the disasters of 1989, the selectors recalled one old pro, and tried three relative youngsters. Wayne Larkins had played six Tests between 1979 and 1981 without scoring a fifty, before signing up for the 1982 rebel tour to South Africa. He was recalled to the England side in 1986. In *The Times*, John Woodcock wrote:

> 'I can think of no more unexpected choice since the Second War than that of Larkins. What makes it so surprising is that owing to a football injury to his ankle, which kept him idle until the end of May, he has played only six first-class innings this season...his scores have been 8, 10, 12, 0, 11, 2 and 9 not out.'

In the event, injury prevented him from playing in that 1986 Test, and he was not a serious contender for a Test position for the next three years. His county form in 1989 was rather better than it had been in 1986 – he scored 1787 runs at an average of 42. But Larkins was now 35; and other, younger, openers had comparable or better records during that season – Mark Benson, Neil Taylor, and Stephenson. Larkins seems to have been very much Gooch's choice – indeed Ted Dexter, chairman of selectors, remarked that 'Graham said that he would feel more comfortable going in to bat with Larkins than anyone else'. Gooch wanted a partner who could carry the attack to the West Indies bowlers, and Larkins was judged to be more capable of doing so than his competitors.

Larkins made an important fifty in the low-scoring Trinidad Test that winter, but his series average of 25 was hardly such as to justify his selection. It is therefore even more surprising that he should have been chosen to tour Australia the following winter. By then, England had an established and successful opening partner to Gooch in Atherton, and it is hard to understand why as the reserve opener the selectors should turn to a 36-year-old with no history of achievement in Test matches, and a poor county season behind him. Perhaps his 207 for Northamptonshire against Gooch's Essex, days before the party was chosen, clinched it for him. Hugh Morris of Glamorgan, who was 27 and had had an outstanding summer, was a much more obvious candidate. As it was, Larkins played in three Tests in Australia, averaging just 23, before his Test career came to a close.

The other three batsmen for the West Indies were Rob Bailey, Alec Stewart and Nasser Hussain, aged 26, 26 and 21 respectively. Bailey had played one Test in 1988, had been selected for the abortive tour to India the previous winter, but failed to make it ahead of the other 13 specialist batsmen England picked in 1989. He did not shine in the West Indies, and was not called upon again. For Stewart and Hussain, it was the start of long and distinguished Test careers – though in both cases this was despite, rather than because of, their performances on their first tour. Both had had a strong 1989 season, and were unsurprising selections. An exact contemporary of Atherton, Hussain might have been chosen ahead of him in the Ashes series (he was in the squad for the Oval Test, but omitted). But having plumped for Atherton ahead of Hussain in August, it was certainly odd to reverse the preference in September. Probably, it was down to the change in captain: that Hussain played for Gooch's Essex no doubt worked to his advantage (though it did not to Stephenson's). Atherton, however, had the better deal: with centuries against Zimbabwe in each of the unofficial Tests on the 'A' tour, he was back in the England side at the start of the 1990 season in the role of opening partner to Gooch. Hussain was not selected again until 1993.

Hick and Ramprakash

The England batting line up of the early 90s revolved around Gooch, Atherton, Smith, Stewart and Lamb, with occasional appearances from Gower; and, from 1991, Graeme Hick and Mark Ramprakash, who both made their debut in the first Test against the West Indies of that summer. Both players were to prove a major headache to the selectors.

Hick was born and brought up in Zimbabwe, but began playing for Worcestershire in 1985 at the age of 19. His first six seasons for his county were awesome. He averaged over 50 in each of them, and between 1986 and 1990 scored over 10,000 runs, each season finishing in the top seven in the national averages. In 1988 he scored 2713 runs, including 405 not out against Somerset. He became qualified to play for England in 1991, and unsurprisingly he was selected at the first opportunity under a wave of public and media scrutiny and rampant optimism.

Things did not, however, go according to plan. Although he made 86 in an early Texaco Trophy match, he made next to no runs in the Test series which followed, and was dropped after four matches. He had no more success in New Zealand in 1991/2, nor against Pakistan in 1992. After 11 Test matches, Hick had scored just one fifty, and averaged 18. But the selectors remained convinced of his ability, evidenced not least by his success in one-day internationals, where at this stage of his career he averaged nearly 40. They kept faith in him, and he was included in the party for the 1992/3 tour to India and Sri Lanka. In the third Test, Hick's 14th, he rewarded the selectors' commitment to him with an innings of 178. It seemed that, at last, Hick had broken the mental barrier of scoring runs at the highest level for his adopted country. Indeed, including that series, Hick's next 31 Tests produced for him 2322 runs at an average of 51. By now, however, the selectors were becoming more fickle. In 1993, he was omitted after only two Tests in which he had scored a respectable 140 runs in four innings. It was one of those moments when the selectors seemed to feel compelled to make changes to counter charges of complacency in the face of successive defeats. Hick was dropped along with Gatting, Chris Lewis, Neil Foster and Phil Tufnell. Two of the new batsmen brought in, Graham Thorpe and Hussain, were notable successes, the other, Mark Lathwell, wasn't, so perhaps on balance the selectors got it right. But Hick was back for the final Test where his 80 and 36 were important contributions to England's only win in that series.

Hick's omission in 1995 was interesting because it was largely determined by a logic which related to the batting order. Hick had batted at three in the first three Tests, ahead of Thorpe at four and (in the second and third Tests) Smith at five. Hick had been out for three in both innings of the third Test when, on a poorly-prepared pitch at Edgbaston, England had lost in three days. The selectors decided that a change needed to be made specifically in the number three position, but were reluctant to move up either Thorpe or Smith. So they brought in Crawley, and with only five specialist batsmen required, and Thorpe and Smith retained, there was no room for Hick. Had Thorpe or Smith been considered suitable to bat at first drop, no doubt Hick would have been retained. As events turned out, Smith was injured during the fourth Test, and Hick (who had complained publicly about being dropped) replaced him for the fifth, batting at five – where he scored a century.

But Hick's Test form was to desert him totally in 1996, when he scored only 43 runs in four Tests. After the second against India, England's team manager, David Lloyd, asked Worcestershire to rest Hick before the next Test on the grounds that he was tired, but it had no positive effect. He was dropped after the first Test against Pakistan in the second half of the season, and omitted from England's touring party the following winter

Unnatural Selection

for the first time since he became an England qualified player. It was a harsh call. Hick was still only 30, and his career Test average was a respectable 36. He had done well in South Africa the previous winter but was seemingly still suffering from over-inflated expectations. But by now Hussain and Thorpe were established at three and four, while Crawley and Knight, with whom he was competing for the last batting place(s), had both scored centuries in the last two Tests of the 1996 series.

The selectors seemed to have lost confidence in him. Despite his excellent one-day record, he was omitted from the one-day internationals at the start of the 1997 season, and not chosen again for Tests until the end of the 1998 summer. A century against Sri Lanka secured him a place in the party to Australia the following winter, but he was not a success in the Tests although he again scored heavily in the one-day internationals. After that tour he played another 12 Tests over the next two years, but no longer was he an automatic selection, and he scored just one century (against Zimbabwe) and one fifty.

The Hick enigma was assessed by Ray Illingworth in his book on his period as chairman of selectors:

> '...Test cricket is the hardest form of the game, and temperament does play a big part. [Hick] could remain the mystery of the modern game. He has so much destructive talent, but is so easily subdued when he should be the one imposing himself on the opposition. I don't know what the answer is. In fact, there is no answer other than in his head. The problem for the next chairman is that Hick is bound to score masses of runs for Worcestershire, but the only thing that that reveals is that he is in form. So often he has been in great county form only to be rolled over in Test matches.'

He might have added that a critical part of the mystery was why Hick at all stages of his career scored heavily in the one-day game even when he went through periods at the start and end of his career when he was unable to put together a decent run of scores in Tests. But it is interesting to speculate whether, had the selectors been more tolerant of his blip in 1996 and more mindful of the runs he had scored for England over the previous three years, he would have regained his confidence and form.

Scoring the Runs: 1989-2014

Ramprakash was 22 when he made his debut in 1991, and had forced his way into the side on the back of a successful 'A' tour to Sri Lanka in 1990/1 (he scored 158 in the first unofficial Test) and consistent runs in the County Championship since his debut four years before. He enjoyed a run of six Tests with a top score of 29 before being dropped, though he was in the party which toured New Zealand in 1991/2, and later joined the 'A' team tour to the West Indies. The selectors were convinced of his class and potential and, especially from 1994, by his heavy scoring for Middlesex. But how long could they keep selecting him in Tests while he failed to deliver? From 1991 to 2001, he was selected for at least one Test in nine out of 11 home seasons, and between 1993/4 and 1997/8, for four out of five winter tours. His first fifty was not scored until his 10th Test, and when he was selected ahead of Hick for the West Indies tour of 1997/8, he was averaging only 17 after 20 Tests. No previous England batsman – not even Gatting – had delivered so little after this number of opportunities. But Hick had broken through after a difficult start: maybe all Ramprakash needed was a first century to set him on his way.

That elusive hundred came in the fifth game of the series, and on the back of it, Ramprakash enjoyed an unbroken run of 18 Tests, with reasonable success – 1116 runs at an average of 41. But there were no more centuries, and after a very moderate series against New Zealand in 1999, he was dropped for the winter tour to South Africa. Rather as Gooch a decade earlier, the new Duncan Fletcher/Nasser Hussain regime was looking for a break with the past after England's humiliating defeat by New Zealand in 1999, and Ramprakash (along with Hick) took a hit. It was not the end for him: he played another 14 Tests for England, and scored a hundred against Australia in 2001. But the consistency wasn't there, and there were others to offer competition. His last Test was in the winter of 2001/2. In his book, Fletcher wrote 'on that trip I saw it in his eyes that he was mentally shot at this level. I realized that we were wasting our time investing in him at international level.' He continued to score heavily in county cricket, but the selectors resisted media pressure to recall him at the age of 40 in the wake of England's defeat by Australia at Headingley in 2009.

The dream for selectors is when a debutant makes an immediate impact, although there have been cases where that has not guaranteed the individual an extended run in the side. More difficult for the selectors is to decide how long to persevere with someone who appears to have Test potential. Is it wise to back him with an extended run, or to withdraw him from the front and reintroduce him at a later date? And does exposure to Test cricket at a young age help to develop a cricketer, or does it retard development? Among the selectorial dilemmas in this context, and among batsmen, in addition to Ramprakash and Hick, were the cases of Dennis Amiss, Keith Fletcher, Gooch, and Gatting. All played more than 50 Tests for England, all were picked at young ages, all had shaky starts to their Test careers, but for all there came a period when they blossomed. Amiss, Fletcher and Gatting were dropped after their first Tests, Gooch after his first two, Hick after four and Ramprakash after six. Only Hick had an extended run again in less than three years after his debut. For all these batsmen, their best days for England came at the age of 27 or over. Would they have had more successful careers had their debuts been deferred until then (on the Strauss/Trott model)? Or were their early traumas in the Test arena a necessary learning experience? And did, ultimately, the selectors get an adequate return on their investment?

It may well have been that in these cases, selection at an early age did more harm than good. But it is difficult to criticize the selectors. Some players – Alan Knott, David Gower, Ian Botham, Alastair Cook – demonstrated that they were ready for Test cricket at the age of 21, or very soon afterwards. In prospect, there was no reason to regard Amiss, Fletcher, Gooch, Gatting, Hick and Ramprakash as less ready when they were first selected. When they did not immediately score runs, returning them to county cricket and trying again in two or three years' time made sense. Where the selectors might be criticized in the cases of Amiss, Fletcher and Gatting was in failing to offer them a reasonably prolonged spell in the Test team at early stage in their career. For Amiss it was five years after his debut before he played four Tests in succession for England; for Fletcher it was over four years, and Gatting two-and-a-half.

Perseverance was self-evidently justified in the case of Gooch, Amiss and, to a slightly lesser extent, Fletcher, who ended up with highly successful Test careers. It probably was in the case of Gatting and Hick too, in that they both reached Test averages of around 40 at the ages of 29 to 30, only to decline thereafter when most batsmen might have been expected to sustain or improve their returns. Ramprakash, however, has ultimately to be judged a poor return on a considerable investment. No other specialist England batsman who has played in 50 Tests has scored fewer centuries, nor had a career average as low as 27. In retrospect, the selectors would probably have been better showing more confidence in Hussain, a year older than Ramprakash, who made his debut just over a year earlier. After three Tests at the age of 21 in the West Indies, Hussain had only four more opportunities before establishing himself in the England side at the age of 28 in 1996. By then, Ramprakash had had 19 opportunities. The choice between Ramprakash and Hussain manifested itself most starkly in the 1993/4 tour to the West Indies. Both were selected, having both played in the final Test against Australia in 1993. At that stage Ramprakash averaged 20 from 10 Tests, Hussain 26 from seven. It was hardly a decisive advantage for Hussain, but Ramprakash was preferred then and subsequently, with continuing lack of success, until 1996. Probably, then, Hussain should have been picked earlier, and Ramprakash less. But it is more than possible that Hussain's subsequent success was enhanced by being spared regular exposure to Test cricket before he had fully matured as a batsman. Ramprakash's frequent exposure in his early 20s to the powerful West Indies attack of the 1990s served only to increase the brittleness of a delicate temperament, making it harder for him to score the runs expected of him when he reached his late 20s.

The Atherton Years

By 1995, Lamb, Gower, Gatting and Gooch had all moved on and England's batting now focussed on Atherton, Stewart, Smith, Thorpe, Hick and Ramprakash. Thorpe had been on each of the first four 'A' tours, on three of which he had had outstanding results, topping the batting averages on two. *Wisden's* correspondent, Richard Streeton, wrote in the 1991 edition of his 1989/90 tour '...Thorpe, a virtually unknown left-handed batsman before the start, did more than hint at an emerging talent of the highest quality. His mental flexibility to adjust his strokeplay to the needs of the moment was remarkable in one so young.' A few weeks older than Ramprakash, it was only when the selectors' patience with the Middlesex player began to strain that Thorpe got his opportunity – and he took it in some style with a century on debut against the 1993 Australians. After a disappointing tour of the West Indies the following winter, the return of Gooch and the new chairman of selectors' preference for a five-bowler attack squeezed him out of the side for the first four Tests of 1994. When England decided to revert to six specialist batsmen for the second Test against South Africa that summer, Thorpe returned, scoring three successive seventies and securing himself a place, when available, for a decade.

The problem for the selectors with Smith was the opposite of that for Hick. While Hick had taken a dozen matches to find his feet in Test cricket before he began to perform consistently, Smith started like a train and then slowed down. Always a fine player of fast bowling, he was unable to master the Indian spin attack on the 1992/3 tour (though he made a century in Sri Lanka) and fell victim to spin on seven occasions in the first five Tests against Australia in 1993. At this point he was dropped for the first time in his career, despite a career Test average of 46. It was, however, the right decision. Hick replaced him, and his first innings 80 was a significant contribution to England's solitary victory in the last Test.

It was assumed that Smith would have a good tour of the West Indies in 1993/4, where slow bowlers were unlikely to feature prominently in the opposition's armoury. But it was not to be. In the 1995 *Wisden*, Alan Lee, reported thus:

> 'The greatest single failure among the party was probably Robin Smith, though this judgement must be influenced by the fact that he began the tour burdened by so many hopes and expectations. He was, unarguably, the most accomplished player of fast bowling in the side and his role as the foundation of the batting was taken as read. He was a banker, but like so many odds-on favourites, he failed to deliver. His technique developed an alarming blip, his bat coming down crookedly from the direction of second slip, and his confidence nose-dived. He was confessing that his tour had been a 'disaster' even after making 175 in the last Test in Antigua and, when Fletcher [then England coach] publicly warned that Smith was being distracted by his commercial activities, he was voicing a common concern.'

The Antigua century ensured Smith held his place for the first series of 1994 against New Zealand, but his scores were modest against a modest attack, and Atherton was keen to get Crawley into the team. Atherton discerned, too, a surprisingly fragile confidence for one with Smith's record. But he was still only 30. With West Indies touring in 1995, Smith's special talents were once again in demand, and he played reasonably well, making crucial contributions of 61 and 90 to help England secure victory at Lord's, before suffering a fractured cheekbone from a ball from Ian Bishop in the fourth Test. His last Test for England was in Cape Town in 1995/6, where his 66 was England's top score. But that was that. He was perhaps unlucky not to be considered in 1996; and better county form in 1997 might have put him in the frame for a third West Indies tour. No other England batsman in the last 50 years with Smith's sort of record played his last Test at such a young age.

It was a curious end as Atherton reflected:

> 'It could be argued that a man with such a fine Test record should have played more than he did, but difficult decisions have to be made and they are made in good faith and for the right reasons. In 1996 Smith was thirty-two years old and his average had dropped from the low 50s to the low 40s and we decided to move on. Who can say if it was the right thing to do? But I was keen to follow the example of other test playing countries that seemed to realise, before it was too late, when a player was past his best. In England we rarely did.'

Perhaps Smith suffered from the lesson learnt from Gatting's recall.

John Crawley drew himself to the selectors' attention with an outstanding 'A' tour to South Africa in 1993/4, in which he scored 779 runs at an average of 65, including 286 against Eastern Province. He followed this up in May 1994 with 281 for Lancashire against Somerset in a match in which the England captain played. It seems that it was Atherton who pressed for Crawley's inclusion in the side for the first Test against South Africa at the expense of Robin Smith and ahead of Graham Thorpe. The Selection Committee split 2-2 on the issue, though Illingworth chose not to press his own preference for Thorpe. 'At the end of the day' said Illingworth 'we went along with the captain'. On this occasion, the captain did not get it right, as Thorpe was to prove a much superior player, and although Thorpe was in for the next Test, it was

Unnatural Selection

after England had lost in a game in which Crawley scored 9 and 7. Over the next three years, Crawley regularly did enough to suggest that he was potentially a batsman of the highest calibre without quite producing the performances to make him an automatic selection. His centuries in successive Tests against Pakistan and Zimbabwe in 1996 indicated that he had established himself at Test level, but a disappointing series against the West Indies in 1997/8 saw him being dropped for Ramprakash, whose big hundred in Barbados marked the start of a period in which he commanded a regular Test spot. Crawley was back at the end of the 1998 season, alongside Ramprakash, when Hussain was injured, and scored 156 not out against Sri Lanka. He had the misfortune to be omitted for the next Test after Hussain returned from injury for the first Test against Australia in 1998/9. An injury to Thorpe enabled Crawley to be recalled for the second Test, but a poor series saw him dropped again at the end.

Crawley was competing with Thorpe, Hick, Ramprakash, Smith (until 1996) and, from 1996, Hussain for a place in England's middle order. Hussain was identified as an England batsman as early as 1989 but after that early tour to the West Indies, he was not called upon again until 1993. Following England's defeat in the first two Tests – which actually made it seven in a row – he was brought in, along with Thorpe, to replace Gatting and Hick. 'Talented beyond question, Hussain can be bracketed with one of his rivals for the place, Mark Ramprakash, as a flawed temperament', wrote Alan Lee in *The Times*. 'He has made four centuries this summer, and is a brilliant all-round fielder, but must have been a borderline selection'. Lee would have preferred Gower or Mathew Maynard. Hussain toured the West Indies the following winter, but the recalled Hick, Ramprakash and Maynard were variously picked ahead of him in the Test team. It was not until 1996 that Hussain got another chance, effectively returning in place of Smith, and ahead of Crawley and Ramprakash. A century against India in the first Test, and consistent runs thereafter, secured Hussain the number-three spot for the next three years, and with his appointment as captain following in 1999, he enjoyed eight years as an automatic England selection when fit. With the benefit of hindsight, he should probably have played for England more in the early 90s, instead of Crawley or Ramprakash. But that was not a view shared by contemporary commentators.

Atherton played his first two Tests for England batting at three, but when picked at the start of the summer of 1990, it was to open in place of Larkins. He began with 151 against New Zealand – England's youngest centurion since Gower in 1978 – and commenced a fruitful opening partnership with Gooch which was to endure, with occasional interruptions until the end of 1994/5. In terms of average (57) it was England's most successful opening pairing since Len Hutton and Cyril Washbrook. The preferred alternative to Gooch was Stewart and, towards the end of Gooch's career, he often moved down the order to accommodate Stewart at the top. But there was unease about asking Stewart to open when also keeping wicket, and from 1995, after Gooch's retirement, other options had to be explored. It led to some bewildering juggling of both sides and batting orders over the following two years until the emergence of Mark Butcher restored a degree of stability.

Ramprakash had been earmarked as the reserve opener to Atherton and Stewart in the West Indies in 1993/4, but did not seem to relish the role. Smith opened in the first Test in 1995, a position in which he had scored a century against Sri Lanka in 1992/3. His preference for fast bowling created some logic for this, but inviting someone who batted in the middle order for his county to open in Test matches has seldom worked satisfactorily, and the experiment was abandoned after one match. Stewart moved up to open, but when he was injured in the third Test, it was decided to replace him with a specialist opener.

The selectors went for Nick Knight, who had been one of the openers on the 1994/5 'A' tour to India and Bangladesh. The more successful opener on that tour had been Jason Gallian, who had made his senior debut in the third Test of 1995 batting at six. But he too was injured, and Knight had his chance. It was then Knight who was injured in the fifth Test, allowing Gallian to return for the sixth. For the following winter's tour to South Africa, the selectors chose whom they regarded to be the best seven batsmen, and took no reserve opener: Stewart partnered Atherton in the Tests with Russell keeping wicket and Crawley and Smith deputised where necessary in the provincial games.

The absence of a clear strategy for establishing an opening pair – so intimately linked to the decision on the wicket-keeper – was exemplified in the pattern of selection in the summer of 1996. It was agreed to retain Jack Russell as wicket-keeper, which cleared the way for Stewart to open in the first Test against India. Instead, he was dropped for the first time since 1991. It is true that in the last three Test series he had averaged a disappointing 26; but he was a veteran of 52 Tests, with a career average of 38. To replace him, the selectors chose Knight who scored 27 and 14, and was then injured for the second Test. Stewart was recalled and with 20, 66 and 50 he did enough to retain his place when Knight was fit again for the first Test against Pakistan in the second half of the season. But curiously, Knight was picked to open, and Stewart moved down to three in the order. Hussain was injured, so nobody was dropped. But why move Stewart from the opening position when he was not keeping wicket? And why choose Knight ahead of Crawley (who in fact returned for the second Test at the expense of a bowler) or Smith – both of whom had been thought to be among the best seven batsmen in England when the squad to South Africa had been chosen the previous winter, and both of whom were scoring plenty of runs for their counties? Crawley could have slotted straight in to Hussain's position at three where he batted for Lancashire; or, if Smith had been chosen, Hick could have moved back from five to three.

An alternative to Knight does not seem seriously to have been considered – though why he should have been regarded as an automatic selection is something of a mystery; while according to Illingworth, the decision to open with him ahead of Stewart appears to have been determined by the desire for a right- left-hand combination. But it was an arrangement which survived only one Test. When Hussain came back from injury for the second, it was decided that he should reoccupy the number three position in which he had scored two centuries earlier in the summer. According to Illingworth, this

> 'meant that Stewart either had to open or bat at five or six, so we put him up with Mike [Atherton] and Knight dropped to six. Although we knew we would lose the left-right opening combination, we thought we'd get more from Stewart at the top rather than in the middle. Also, with Knight and Russell coming in at six and seven, the two left handers would be useful if we were in trouble.'

The logic is less than compelling: if the left-right combination was sufficiently important to deny Stewart the position in which he batted best, was moving him from three to five (to keep Thorpe at four) really such an issue? And why was having two left-handers specifically going to be helpful 'if we were in trouble'? That is not to say that this decision was the wrong one: Knight scored his maiden century batting at six in that Test; rather that the decision to move Stewart from opener to three to accommodate Knight in the first place was dubious.

    The saga was not quite over, because for the third and final Test, it was decided to improve the balance of the side by asking Stewart, once more, to take over as 'keeper. This might have been the time to open with Knight, and move Stewart down the order. Instead, Stewart opened. Knight retained his place on the winter tour, but now he opened once more while Stewart kept wicket and batted at three, Hussain moving to four. After playing in the Texaco Trophy at the start of 1997, Knight was considered to have displayed a technical weakness around off stump, especially to the in-swinging delivery. He went on to be one of England's most successful ever one-day internationals, but he played only six more Tests, and with no success.

Atherton's new partner was the success story from the 1996/7 'A' tour, Mark Butcher. He became Atherton's default opening partner for the next three years when Stewart was keeping wicket, generally slipping down to three, where he was more successful, when Stewart was not keeping and thus available to open. He also opened with Stewart when Atherton was injured.

Duncan Fletcher's Men

Michael Vaughan was first selected for the new-look England touring party to South Africa in 1989/90. Originally chosen as the 'reserve' batsman, he leapfrogged Darren Maddy to play in the first Test of the series. Seldom can a debut innings of 33 be regarded as so portentous, but coming in at 2-2 and soon finding England at 2-4 with Donald and Pollock bowling in conditions which were much to their advantage, Vaughan made a very favourable first impression. He later scored a critical 69 in England's victory in the controversial final Test of that series. Mainly because of injury, it took him a couple of years to cement his place in the team, which really happened in the winter of 2001/2. His *annus mirabilis* was 2002, with 1481 runs at an average of 62, and a year later, he was England captain.

    Marcus Trescothick came to Duncan Fletcher's attention when

he scored a century for Somerset against Glamorgan (where Fletcher was then coach) in the summer of 1999. Fletcher was sufficiently impressed to press for Trescothick to be included in the 'A' team tour to Bangladesh and New Zealand the following winter. Trescothick did not star, the big success being Vikram Solanki. According to the 2001 *Wisden's* correspondent, Ralph Dellor

> 'in both countries [Solanki] stood out as the batsman who appeared ready to step up. Not only did he score 597 first-class runs – no one else reached 400 – at an average of 59.70, but there was an unmistakable touch of class about the way he made them.'

When, however, injuries to Hussain and Knight necessitated additions to England's one-day squad in 2000, it was Trescothick, not Solanki, who was asked to step up. As it turned out, Solanki was never to be given an opportunity at Test level, though he played 51 times for England in one-day internationals (the highest number by any England player who has not played in Test matches).

Strong performances in the limited-overs competition between England, Zimbabwe and West Indies led to Trescothick being selected for the third Test against West Indies which followed. With Stewart keeping wicket and Butcher for the moment out of favour following a disappointing tour of South Africa, England needed a new opening partner for Atherton. Ramprakash had been invited to fill the role, but once again had not taken to it. With 66 on debut and 78 at the Oval, Trescothick embarked on a career of 76 Tests during which he was never dropped. His well-documented battles with depression caused him to pull out of the series against India at the start of 2006, and then to return early from Australia towards the end of the year. With that his Test career was over.

Atherton, increasingly debilitated by his back condition, retired at the end of the 2001 Ashes series at the young age of 33. But by now, England had a potentially strong and settled batting line up of Trescothick, Vaughan (promoted to open after Atherton's retirement), Butcher (his career revived after a match-winning 173 not out in England's solitary victory over Australia in 2001), Hussain, Thorpe and Stewart. But it was only in the three Tests against Sri Lanka at the start of 2002 that this sextet played together. Trescothick was injured for the first three Tests against India in the second half of the season, while Thorpe temporarily dropped out of Test cricket because marital problems were distracting him. Stewart retired at the end of 2003.

So there continued to be opportunities for others. Crawley was recalled in 2002 after nearly four years, on the back of a strong showing in county cricket that season and Hussain's general preference for experience ahead of potential. He played in eight out of 15 Tests over the summer and following winter, scoring a century against India. Robert Key was picked as the most promising of the next generation of batsmen. He played 15 Tests over the course of the period 2002 to 2004/5 – in all cases as substitute for Thorpe or Butcher when they were either unavailable or injured.

The year 2004 saw the debuts of two batsmen who were to be of enormous significance to England in the years to come. But their routes to the Test team were very different.

Andrew Strauss was unusual in making his first Test appearance at the age of 27. Since 1990, the majority of England batsmen had made their debut at 25 or younger. Those who have been older than Strauss were generally not conspicuous successes: the oldest – Alan Wells, 33 in 1995, was an eccentric selection which endured for a single Test. Others first selected when older than Strauss – Chris Adams, Hugh Morris, Aftab Habib and Anthony McGrath – played a grand total of 14 Tests between them. The exceptions were Paul Collingwood – though here the circumstances were slightly different, as he had 42 one-day international games behind him – and Jonathan Trott. Strauss was, then, a late developer. He had attended the ECB National Academy in Australia in 2001/2, but did not especially star. He had not previously been selected for 'A' team tours. A strong showing in county cricket in 2003, however, pushed him into the one-day squads for the winter tours to Bangladesh, Sri Lanka and the West Indies. When Vaughan was injured for the first Test against New Zealand in 2004, Strauss was called up. His 112 and 83 in that match not only secured him his place for years to come, but also pulled down the curtain on the 36-year-old Hussain's career. Conscious of Vaughan's returning for the second Test, and mindful of the dilemma the selectors would face in accommodating him, Hussain, who had himself scored a century (in the process running out Strauss) as England successfully chased down 282, decided to quit while he was ahead.

Ian Bell came into the side at the end of the summer of 2004 to replace the injured Thorpe, and immediately made an impression with a score of 70. Only 22, he had played Under-19 internationals for England, made his England 'A' debut at the age of 18, and excelled with the ECB National Academy in Australia in 2001/2 and in Australia and Sri Lanka in 2002/3. Unlike Strauss, therefore, his potential was apparent from an early age. He caught the attention of both Fletcher and Vaughan while practising with the England squad in New Zealand in 2001/2. For South Africa in 2004/5, Butcher and Thorpe were fit again, and the selectors decided to retain Key, who had made a double-century against West Indies earlier in the summer. And at Fletcher's insistence, Collingwood was chosen ahead of Bell for the final 'batting' space because his bowling offered a degree of cover for the injury-prone Flintoff. But Butcher once again suffered injury in South Africa, while Key failed to distinguish himself. For both, their Test careers were over.

Someone, however, who did distinguish himself, in the one-day games at the end of the tour, was Kevin Pietersen. Newly qualified for England, his three centuries in seven internationals marked him out as a player of unusual quality. So, at the start of 2005, the selectors were faced with an embarrassment of riches not seen for over 40 years. Strauss, Trescothick, Vaughan and Thorpe were the four established batsmen, who had all had strong winters; alongside them, the explosive Pietersen and the promising Bell. With Flintoff at six, there was room for only five against Australia in the Ashes series to come.

In reality, the choice was two out of Thorpe, Pietersen and Bell. In his account of the decision, Fletcher suggests that Bell was a given, and that it boiled down to Thorpe or Pietersen. Certainly, after Bell had been picked with Thorpe, and ahead of Pietersen, for the two Tests against Bangladesh which preceded Australia, and he had scored 65 not out and 162 not out, it would have been difficult to drop him. But Pietersen could have been picked ahead of him for the Bangladesh series. Fletcher says that Pietersen's poor early-season form with his new county, Hampshire, counted against him. There was also, it seems, concern about Pietersen or Thorpe batting at four – Pietersen because he was batting five for his county and Thorpe because five had been his England spot since the winter of 2003/4 – although he had batted successfully enough at four earlier in his career. Bell batted three for Warwickshire, and so was a plausible at four for England with Vaughan at three. As between Thorpe and Pietersen for Bangladesh, Fletcher and Vaughan were mindful of Thorpe being on 98 England caps. Thorpe it was who played, scoring 42 not out and 66 not out.

But Vaughan was determined to have Pietersen for the Ashes, while Fletcher described the choice between Pietersen and Thorpe as one of the hardest he had to make. A number of factors now conspired to swing the selection Pietersen's way. Thorpe had his 100 Test caps, he was 35 and was suffering from a recurring back problem, which limited his appearances for Surrey following the Bangladesh series. He had also told the selectors that he would be taking up a coaching position with New South Wales at the end of the season, thus effectively ending his international career. Finally – and perhaps surprisingly – Fletcher thought a right hander would be better at five because of the problems caused by Shane Warne when bowling into the rough.

Pietersen was, of course, one of the great successes of the England Ashes-winning team of 2005. His selection ahead of Thorpe was unquestionably the right one. But Bell's contribution was limited. As it turned out, Thorpe lost motivation and hence form with Surrey that season, but it might have been different had he still been in the England side, and he might have offered more than did Bell at that stage in his career.

The Super Six

The 2005 batting line up did not survive long. By the second tour of the winter of 2005/6, England had lost Vaughan to his recurring knee injury, and Trescothick to depression. In Alastair Cook, England quickly found a more than adequate replacement for Trescothick. Like Bell, he had been an Under-19 international, had toured Sri Lanka with the 'A' side in 2003/4, and was with the 'A' team in the West Indies when called up to join the England squad in India at the beginning of 2006. He had already scored a double-hundred against Australia for Essex in 2005. He made his England debut at the age of 21, scoring 104 not out in England's second innings (the youngest England Test centurion since before the War). Despite dips in form in 2010 and 2013/14 he has never been dropped since. When Trescothick returned for the summer of

Unnatural Selection

2006 he moved down to three, but since 2006/7 he has been England's opening batsman for an astonishing unbroken run of 100 Test matches.

The replacement for Vaughan was only marginally more difficult. Collingwood started his England career as a one-day specialist. He had toured Sri Lanka and Bangladesh as a reserve batsman in 2003/4, and played a couple of Tests when Hussain was injured, and again when it was decided to play a sixth specialist batsman. But Key was preferred to him as the reserve batsman in the winter of 2004/5. When, for the Oval Test of 2005, Simon Jones was injured, England decided again to play a sixth batsman, and Collingwood was called up. Perceived mental toughness, and relative success in the one-day series against Australia earlier in the summer, seem to have been the main reasons for the choice. While he only scored 7 and 10, the 72-minute duration of his second innings in a partnership of 60 with Pietersen was critical to England's Ashes-winning draw. In the third Test against Pakistan in the first part of the winter of 2005/6, in for Strauss (given leave to depart to attend the birth of his child), Collingwood scored 96 and 80, and made his maiden Test hundred against India in the next Test after that when he was in for the injured Vaughan. He was now a fixture in the side, and when Vaughan returned in 2007, it coincided with injury to Flintoff, and Collingwood retained his place as England reverted to playing six specialist batsmen.

Andrew Strauss was dropped for the Sri Lanka tour of 2007/8. It was an interesting decision by the selectors as he was by now extremely well established as an England player, with 43 Tests and an average over 40. There was no other opener challenging to replace him but he had averaged only 27 in the 12 Tests since he last scored a century. It was not a disastrous run, and considerably better than the form his replacement, Ravi Bopara, was to show – 42 runs in three Tests; and England were to miss Strauss's slip fielding in a series characterised by dropped catches. In this context, the decision to drop him must be counted a mistake. On the other hand, Vaughan has argued that Strauss's omission enabled him to return to the England side for the second half of the winter of 2007/8 refreshed, and certainly his form for the next two years was stronger than it had been in the run up to his being dropped. But was this a case of *post hoc ergo propter hoc*?

Collingwood was omitted for the second Test against South Africa in 2008. He had played in the previous 33 Tests for England, 37 overall, and averaged over 40. His summer had been unproductive, but it had only been six Tests since his last century. Flintoff, however, was fit again for the first time since 2006/7, and it was decided to include him at the expense of a specialist middle-order batsman. Vaughan was captain, and Pietersen and Bell had both made big hundreds in the first Test so Collingwood had to go. For the third Test, England reverted to six specialist batsmen, with Flintoff at seven. The Edgbaston pitch was expected to turn, allowing Monty Panesar to bowl a lot of overs, and three seamers were deemed to be sufficient. Collingwood returned, and scored a second-innings century. While an additional bowler was brought back for the final Test of the series, by then Vaughan had relinquished the captaincy and with it his place in the side, and Collingwood was retained – for the rest of his Test career.

Bell was dropped in the wake of England's dismissal for 51 in the first Test against the West Indies in 2008/9. He had 46 Tests behind him, and a career average of over 40, though in his previous six Tests, since his 199 against South Africa, he had scored a modest 214 runs. There was a perception that he lacked mental toughness, especially for the number three position which he had filled since Vaughan's departure, and exemplified by the fact that all his six Test centuries had been scored in matches in which other England payers had also scored hundreds – in other words, when there was less pressure on him personally. But undoubtedly his omission was also driven by a view that England's humiliation could not be without consequence for the composition of the team. He was replaced by Owais Shah for the next four Tests, but Shah failed to take his opportunity in benign batting conditions, and also fielded poorly. Bell would surely have done better. As in the case of Strauss, it can only be conjecture as to whether Bell's successes since his return for the third Ashes Test of 2009 were in any way consequential on having to force his way back into the side. Many commentators believe so. On the other hand, there were no better conditions for batting than the pitches on which England played and the bowling attack they were up against during the rest of that West Indies tour, and there must be a strong likelihood that Bell would have returned to form and confidence had he been retained.

Along with Shah, the other batsmen brought into the England side in 2009 to fill vacancies in the middle order in 2009 were Ravi Bopara and Jonathan Trott. Bopara's progression to the England

Unnatural Selection

team was typical of the 21st century Test player. Picked, at the age of 21, as a replacement on the England 'A' tour to the West Indies in early 2006, with bowling a useful second arrow in his quiver, he quickly progressed to the limited-overs team, playing in the 2007 World Cup. This kept him in the selectors' eye, and after an outstanding county season in 2008, the decision to drop Strauss for the Sri Lanka tour at the end of that year gave him his first opportunity at Test level. Alas, three ducks in five innings was an inauspicious start. Strauss was soon back in the side, and Bopara fell behind Shah as the next cab in the rank. The dropping of Bell against the West Indies the following winter gave Shah his chance, and then an injury to Flintoff opened the door to Bopara for the fourth Test. He seized it with a hundred, but when England chose to alter the balance of their side for the fifth Test, playing five bowlers in Flintoff's absence, Bopara was omitted. Despite just 99 runs in four Test innings on the tour, Shah continued to be preferred to the centurion – an arguably commendable commitment to giving new players a fair run in the team. But when Shah failed in the final Test of the winter, he was replaced by Bopara, who responded with successive centuries in the two Tests against the West Indies in England at the start of the summer of 2009. He seemed to have cemented the number three position, ahead of Bell, and indeed Vaughan.

But Australia proved a sterner test than West Indies, and in four Tests, Bopara failed to reach fifty. There was a feeling that he lacked the necessary chutzpah for the pressure of the occasion. A change was inevitable for the deciding final Test following England's disastrous batting in the fourth, and unsurprisingly, Bopara was dropped. Bell, by now, had already been recalled – replacing the injured Pietersen. There were calls in the media for the return of Ramprakash (who was having an Indian summer in county cricket, but was now aged 40) and even for Trescothick (also scoring heavily in county cricket). The choice of Trott was far from obvious. At 28, he was England's oldest debutant Test batsman since Adams, and before him Wells – hardly happy precedents. Born in South Africa, he had been playing county cricket for Warwickshire since 2003, qualifying for England in 2006. He scored consistently, aside from a disastrous season in 2007, which was when he was first seen in England colours – paradoxically, in view of his subsequent reputation, in the T20 side. Two undistinguished matches indicated no special talent, but he toured with the England Lions in 2007/8 and 2008/9. His was not a case of catching the selectors' eye through a high-profile innings: he had scored 0 for England Lions against the touring West Indians early in 2009, and 19 and 14 not out in England's Ashes warm-up game against Warwickshire. Rather, it was through the sheer volume of runs he was accumulating in county cricket.

Trott's instant success, with a century in the final Ashes Test of 2009, cemented his place in the England team, and instigated a period of unparalleled consistency in the selection of England batsmen. For 15 successive Tests, England's preferred batting line up was Strauss, Cook, Trott, Pietersen, Bell and Collingwood, all of whom averaged over 40. For two Tests against Bangladesh in 2010, Collingwood was rested, and for the four against Pakistan which followed, Bell was injured, but otherwise the preferred line up was the actual line up. For a period of 18 months, the selectors had no decisions to make on the composition of England's top six. Indeed, with Prior, Swann, Anderson and Broad also automatic selections when fit, the only issue in this period was the identity of England's third seamer.

Starting Again

In the two years following the Ashes tour of 2010/1, England lost four of this distinguished sextet. Collingwood announced his retirement during the final Test of the series. He seemed to have a replacement in waiting in Eoin Morgan, who was the reserve batsman on the tour. Morgan had made his one-day international debut for Ireland at the age of 19 in 2006, and England lost no time in picking him for its own one-day side as soon as he became England qualified in 2009. For the next five years, the combination of runs scored and strike rate arguably made him, along with Pietersen, England's most effective ever limited-overs batsman. Unlike Pietersen, however, he had nothing like as comparable a record in first-class cricket. The question for the selectors was whether Morgan's undoubted talents could be transferred from the one-day to the Test arena, or whether his modest results in county cricket were evidence of technical weakness which would manifest itself in the longer international game.

The first opportunity for Morgan came in 2010, when England decided to rest Collingwood for the two Tests against Bangladesh, following which Bell was injured for the series against Pakistan.

Unnatural Selection

Preferred to Bopara, he had an unspectacular summer – one hundred, but no fifties. It was not enough to keep out Bell when he was fit again for the 2010/1 Ashes series, but alongside Bopara and other Test hopefuls, he played for England Lions against Sri Lanka at the start of the summer of 2011. While Bopara scored 17 and 29, Morgan scored 193. It was another example of performance in an early-season match against the tourists swaying the balance. But despite a second Test century in the summer of 2011, his batting average drifted south rather than north, culminating in a disastrous three Tests against Pakistan in 2011/2 in which he scored just 82 runs in six innings. Flaws had entered into his game, notably an extraordinarily low crouch in his stance. For the time being, at least, his career was stalled.

Then at the end of the summer of 2012, Strauss retired and for other reasons Pietersen was also, for the time being, ruled out for selection. The selectors were thus confronted with a much cleaner sheet of paper when they came to select the batsmen for the 2012/3 tour of India than they had for several years. For the seven spaces available, only Cook, Trott and Bell from the super six of previous years could be inked in. During the previous summer, England had picked Jonny Bairstow, Bopara, and James Taylor in a search for a sixth batsman to fill the slot previously filled by Collingwood and then Morgan, and then, for the final Test, the place previously held by Pietersen.

Bopara would have been the selectors' preference at the start of 2012, just as he might have been in 2011 but for that Lions game. But he was injured; and while he returned to play in the first Test against South Africa, he then ceased to be available for personal reasons. The precedent of 2011 might have led the selectors to choose Taylor, who had scored a century for the Lions against the West Indies. Instead, they went for Bairstow, a graduate of England Lions tours, who had caught the eye on his one-day international debut in 2011 with a match winning 41 not out off 21 balls. A good start to the County Championship, along with a fifty in the match in which Taylor scored a hundred, clinched his place. But a highest score of 18 in three Tests against the West Indies, and an apparent weakness against the short ball, led to his replacement by Bopara when the latter recovered from injury. And then, when Bopara became unavailable, Taylor was called up for his debut. One Test later, however, and Pietersen was also unavailable. The selectors recalled

Bairstow, and he repaid their faith with innings of 95 and 54 against one of the strongest bowling attacks in the world.

So one can imagine that Bairstow's was the fourth name to be inked in for India. But who to fill the other three, bearing in mind that at least one needed to be an opening batsman? Morgan and Bopara offered Test experience, though neither had established themselves at that level; Taylor and Joe Root, at 22 and 21 respectively, represented the next generation; Michael Carberry, 32, and Nick Compton, 29, were the pick of the county circuit. Consciously, or more probably not, the selectors went for one from each pairing – effectively placing weight on three quite different selection criteria, albeit ones that had always been in play over the last 50 years. Morgan, it was hoped, had overcome the technical weaknesses which had constrained him earlier in the year, and his continuing success in one-day internationals demonstrated his mental resilience at the highest level, while there continued to be residual doubts about Bopara in this respect. Root, like Taylor, had scored a century for the Lions against the West Indies earlier in the season. While Taylor was the man in possession, his two Tests against South Africa had not offered conclusive evidence of Test potential. Crucially, however, Root was an opening batsman, and thus a credible long-term successor to Strauss. With Strauss's retirement at the end of the summer of 2012 – the second of the sextet of 2010/1 batting stars to quit – Carberry, along with Trott, was the only player who had experience of opening the batting for England (each had done it once). But his county form in 2012 was very moderate – an average of just 30: there was little sense in picking a player of his maturity unless he was in outstanding form. Compton, by contrast, was – 1494 runs at an average of 94.6. Thus the selectors went for international experience in Morgan, youth and potential in Root, and current form in Compton.

When it came to the Test series in India, however, Pietersen was back in the fold, and with the initial decision to play Samit Patel as a batting all-rounder there was space for only one out of Compton, Root, Bairstow and Morgan. One option would have been to retain Bairstow, and open the batting with Trott, with Bell at three. The indifferent record of makeshift openers, however, pointed to utilising a specialist for the role and, one suspects by a narrow margin, the selectors preferred current form to future prospects in choosing Compton ahead of Root. When, however, after the decision was made to play two specialist spinners, and Patel failed to justify his position as a specialist batsman, it was Root, not Bairstow, who replaced him at number six. The choice seems largely to have been made on the basis of Root's 166 for the Performance Programme side to which he was seconded for a game prior to the fourth Test, and perhaps of Bairstow's failure to make an impact when he replaced Bell, who temporarily returned home for paternity leave, in the second Test.

Compton was only moderately successful in India, with one fifty and no hundreds. Root, however, scored 73 and 20 not out on his debut, thus raising the issue as to whether he, rather than Compton, would be a better bet as Strauss's replacement. For the time being, however, the selectors stuck with Compton, with Root retained in the number six position, for the five Tests in the back-to-back series with New Zealand that preceded the 2013 Ashes series. With centuries in each of the first two of these, Compton appeared to have justified his selection, but his form deserted him for the two Tests back in England. Managing to score just seven off 45 balls in the second innings of the second of these Tests, when England were pushing for quick runs, served to emphasise his loss of touch in a way that a first ball duck might have avoided. In addition, with his maiden century earlier in the match, Root appeared to confirm that he was the Test batsman of quality which he had long promised to be. The selectors decided to elevate him to the opening position, where he batted for Yorkshire, at Compton's expense.

In scoring 180 in his second Test in this position, Root looked to have secured the opening spot for a generation. And while his returns in the rest of the series were less impressive, he went to Australia for the 2013/4 Ashes series inked in as Cook's partner. The reserve opener was Carberry, recalled at the age of 33 after a strong 2013 season in county cricket. He had played a solitary Test in Bangladesh four years before, but had not toured with England – nor even England Lions – since. The expectation was that Root would open with Cook, and that Gary Ballance would bat six. But while Ballance made nought and four in the first two warm-up matches, Carberry made 78 and 153. The selectors now decided to capitalise on Carberry's form by selecting him to open, with Root reverting back to six. On a famously horrendous tour for England batting, Carberry did slightly better than some of his team mates, though a solitary fifty hardly counted as success. With time against him, it is not surprising that the selectors looked elsewhere at the start of the summer of 2014.

This time, the selectors reverted to taking the top product from the England Lions. Sam Robson, Australian by birth, had nailed his colours to England's mast in 2013, and subsequently toured with the Lions to Sri Lanka in 2013/4, where he scored five centuries. Early runs in county cricket in 2014 helped his cause too. With a century in his second Test match, against Sri Lanka, Robson appeared to have secured the vacancy left by Strauss. But after this Robson regressed. An indifferent series against India followed, in which deficiencies in his technique were exposed, and concerns raised about how he would fare against a more challenging attack than the 2014 tourists offered. Dropped for the tour of West Indies in early 2015, he has, at least for the moment, drifted towards the end of the queue for England places.

An injury to Pietersen sustained during England's series in New Zealand in early 2013, followed by Root's elevation to the opening position on his return to fitness, once more opened up a vacancy at six. The selectors were consistent in returning to Bairstow to fill it on the back of the promise he had shown against South Africa in the final Test of 2012. He had a run of seven Tests in this position, but in this period averaged only 29, with just two fifties. While he was selected for the winter to Australia in 2013/4, it was as reserve wicket-keeper, and although he played in two Tests in that role, further batting failures confirmed that he had fallen behind the competition.

Consistency with decision making in 2012 might have suggested the selection of Taylor as Bairstow's successor. Overlooked for the India and New Zealand tours of 2012/3, he captained the Lions on their tour that winter with some batting success. But while he had a decent season in domestic cricket in 2013 he was leapfrogged by Ballance when it came to selecting the party for Australia the following winter. The Zimbabwean born Ballance had toured with the Lions in 2012/3, and followed it up with an outstanding season for Yorkshire in 2013. There was some speculation that his selection ahead of Taylor was because he was left handed, and that left handers were less vulnerable to the left-arm bowling of Australia's Mitchell Johnson, who had emerged as a potent threat in the one-day internationals at the end of the summer. Taylor had once more to be content with a Lions tour: his 242 not out in the second unofficial Test against Sri Lanka ensured that he remained on the selectors' radar.

Trott, like Tony Greig and (so far) Cook was never dropped by England in Test matches. He quickly secured the number-three position after his century on debut, and has batted there more often than any other England batsman. Never in the past 50 years have the selectors needed to trouble less about filling a historically difficult role, with Trott consistently averaging around 47. During the tour to Australia in 2013/4 he succumbed to a stress-related illness and went home after the first Test. Out of international cricket for 18 months, he resumed his Test career in April 2015 against West Indies as an opening batsman.

In the short term, he was not replaced as a batsman, as England chose to include an extra bowler for the next four Tests in Australia. But there was still the question of who should bat at three. For three Tests, the position was filled by Root, but failures in the last two of these led to his being dropped, and Bell moving up the order. Many commentators felt that as England's best and most experienced batsman, Bell was Trott's most obvious successor. But he failed in his one match in the position, and subsequently announced in public (surely the sign of a player confident of his position) that his own preference was to bat at four.

With Pietersen's Test career apparently coming to an end after the Ashes winter of 2013/4, and Trott unavailable, the selectors faced a real problem with England's middle order at the start of 2014. Only Bell was a certainty. Root was recalled, and Ballance, who had replaced Root to make his debut in the final Ashes Test (without distinction), retained. Neither Bell nor Root was asked to return to number three. Instead, the job of filling this pivotal position fell to the least experienced of the trio, whose normal batting position for his county was at five or six: Ballance.

The decision was unexpected, but it brought immediate success. Ballance took to the position with the same alacrity as had Trott, and had an outstanding summer in 2014, with over 700 runs, including three centuries, at an average of 70. Root, too, excelled on his recall at five, with even more runs than Ballance and at an average of 97. Ballance, Bell and Root now look as established a middle order as did Trott, Pietersen and Bell only a year before, though it will be tested by Australia in 2015 in a way it was not by Sri Lanka and India in 2014.

CHAPTER SIX

TAKING THE WICKETS – THE QUICKS

Trueman and Statham

BEFORE the start of the 1963 season, Fred Trueman and Brian Statham had opened England's bowling together on 34 occasions, and since 1959 they had been England's openers in 22 out of 30 Tests excluding those Tests on tours when one or both were rested. But Trueman was now 32, Statham nearly 33. The question confronting the selectors was how much longer they could continue to be a potent combination. The issue seemed less imminent in Trueman's case. He had taken 34 wickets in eight Tests in Australia and New Zealand the previous winter, topping the Test averages. Indeed, Trueman's finest series still lay ahead of him, for in 1963 he was to take 34 wickets at an average of 17 against a West Indian line up including Conrad Hunte, Rohan Kanhai, Basil Butcher and Garry Sobers. No England bowler since has taken so many wickets in a five-match series. Trueman was consciously rested from the 1963/4 tour to India in order to conserve his energies for the Ashes the following summer. He was successful enough in the rain-affected first two Tests, in which he took 9-185, including a five-wicket haul at Lord's. He was, however, punished savagely by Peter Burge in the third Test, in which Australia recovered from early setbacks to win. John Arlott wrote that when Trueman took the second new ball there 'came this incredible series of medium paced long hops which rose in a simple arc and, in what must have seemed like a bowler's nightmare, Burge…hooked him with murderous ease.'

It was perhaps unsurprising that the selectors should have dropped Trueman's new ball partner after that Test, Jack Flavell, who had also been complicit in the failure of the second new ball to bring the Australian first innings to a swift conclusion. But Trueman's case was quite different. He was a veteran of 64 Tests, had had an outstanding series the summer before and had taken 297 Test wickets. No fast bowler in county cricket was obviously superior: Fred Rumsey, who replaced him, offered little beyond the variety of being a left-armer, and he played a total of just five Tests for England. Although Trueman had been dropped before (controversially, again, during the 1961 Ashes series), his omission after one poor Test seems impulsive. Contemporary commentators thought otherwise. *The Times'* correspondent wrote 'had he [Trueman] been chosen, it could only have been on past performance – and because of alarming shortage of possible successors. Except on isolated occasions, Trueman this season has been neither especially fast nor instinctively accurate.' His omission, however, may have worked to his advantage. On a feather-bed pitch at Old Trafford for the fourth Test, Australia scored 656-8 and England replied with 611. It was not an occasion to be a fast bowler. Trueman was recalled for the fifth Test, where famously he became the first player to take 300 wickets in Test matches. He was still probably the best fast bowler in England, but if the selectors had judged Rumsey to be superior for the fourth Test, it is difficult to understand why they should have reversed that judgement on the basis of a solitary Test match in which the conditions were so unfavourable to bowlers.

Trueman's performance at the Oval was insufficient to secure him a place on the winter tour to South Africa in 1964/5. Perhaps the selectors were concerned about whether the new captain, M J K Smith, would be able to handle him. In his report of the 1962/3 tour to Australia, the tour manager, the Duke of Norfolk, had written of Trueman

> 'a fine bowler when it suited him. The least easy person in the team to control. Slack in his ways and not prepared to willingly lend any help in off the field duties. His general manner off the field, although improved from earlier days, still left a good deal to be desired.'

Alternatively, the selectors might have concluded that 300 Test wickets was a summit and there was nothing to be gained from continuing the climb – though Trueman himself wanted to go to South Africa. But the selectors, having, rightly or wrongly, apparently decided to move on from Trueman, puzzlingly recalled him, for his final two Tests, against New Zealand at the start of the following summer. The priority was surely to have used that series to establish the pair of opening bowlers they wished to lead the attack in Australia in 1965/6 – a tour for which

Unnatural Selection

they could hardly have expected Trueman to be a candidate if he was not in the squad for South Africa the previous winter. It is curious – at least to 21st century eyes – how the selectors did not take a more strategic approach to managing the exit from international cricket of the then most successful bowler in Test history.

Statham had done less well in Australia in 1962/3, taking just 13 wickets at an average of 45. He was picked to partner Trueman for the first Test of 1963, but his return of 0-121 seemed to provide further evidence that his best days were over. His zip, it was said, had gone. He was to be recalled to the colours on two further occasions. In the final Test of 1963 he was only slightly more successful than he had been in the first. But two years later, at the Oval, and at the age of 35, he produced the best figures (5-40 off 24 overs) in South Africa's first innings, of any England opening bowler since Trueman in the Edgbaston Test of 1963. There was some speculation about whether he might be included in the touring party to Australia the following winter. The selectors, no doubt wisely, and having noted Statham's reduced effectiveness in the second innings of that Oval Test, decided to put their faith in a new generation.

Paradoxically, however, in their search for a successor to Statham, the selectors had initially turned to older men. Statham's replacement for the second Test in 1963 was Derek Shackleton, who was six years his senior, and whose three previous Test matches had been played in 1951. Just as some batsmen were pigeon holed as being strong against spin or pace but not both, so opening bowlers were frequently selected on the basis of a hypothesis about their special suitability for specific pitch conditions. Shackleton was regarded as a horse for a course. The Times' correspondent described him as an 'automaton' who 'for more than a decade...has been known as a Lord's specialist'. In those days, the Lord's pitch was thought to favour the medium pacer rather than the fast bowler as such (though in fact the key bowlers in 1963 turned out to be Trueman, Wes Hall and Charlie Griffith). The selectors probably did not intend when they chose him to give him more than one Test, but Shackleton bowled his medium pacers sufficiently well (7-165 from 84 overs!) to keep his place for the rest of the series. He went for just 2.1 runs per over during his four Tests, though the theory that restricting the West Indies stroke-makers was the way to overcome them failed to prevent England losing the series.

A similar rationale underpinned the view the selectors took in 1964 in picking the side to tour the following winter. It was considered that pitches in South Africa would be green and sympathetic to those who moved the ball off the pitch rather than those who relied on pace. Thus they picked only two fast, or fastish, bowlers – John Price and David Brown. The other two seam bowlers who went – Tom Cartwright and Ian Thomson – were both rated by the *Playfair* annual of the time as 'RM' – right arm medium. Thomson, who replaced the originally selected Tony Nicholson of Yorkshire, who was injured, made his Test debut at the age of 35. He and Cartwright were undoubtedly highly effective bowlers in English conditions, but they had no success in South Africa, and it is difficult not to believe that a more conventional opening bowler would have offered more than one of them. But the theory that South African pitches were sympathetic to medium pace prevailed, leading to Cartwright's selection for the 1968/9 tour, alongside Bob Cottam – a medium pacer who normally bowled first change for his county, Hampshire.

The Next Generation

In the 28 Tests between the start of the 1963 series, and the second Test of the 1965/6 Ashes tour, 15 different players opened the bowling for England, as the selectors sought to find successors to Trueman and Statham. The pair that seemed briefly to fit the bill was Brown and Jeff Jones. In his book of the 1965/6 tour, John Clarke wrote:

> 'for the future of England the most exciting by-product of the tour was the emergence of Brown and Jones as partners with the new ball. These two, magnificently keen, of excellent temperament, and the one complementary to the other in the goods they purveyed – right arm [Brown] and left-arm [Jones] – learnt much as they went along, I fancy, and learning raised hopes that what looked like being for a long time a vacuum in England cricket might be so no longer'.

Alas, it was to be a false dawn. Plagued by injury, as his son was to be a generation later, Jones was to play only seven more Tests after the 1965/6 tour, and made little impression in them. Brown played in another 18 over the next three years with rather more success, his last when still only 27 and arguably at his peak. An unconvincing couple of 'Tests' against the Rest of the World in 1970 resulted in his omission from the 1970/1 tour to Australia – though the bowler chosen ahead of him, Ken Shuttleworth, had failed to take a wicket in the one match he played in that series.

The England bowler with the best career Test-bowling average in the last 50 years (among those bowling more than 100 overs) is Ken Higgs. Making his debut at the relatively mature age of 28 in the last Test against South Africa in 1965, he had an outstanding record over the course of the next two home series, though he was not an automatic selection. Partly because he was not as fast as Brown, Jones or Snow, he was regarded, rightly or wrongly, as a specialist for English conditions, and while he went on two winter tours, he played only one Test match outside New Zealand, where pitches were similar to English ones. Dropped after one indifferent game against Australia in 1968, he was in the squad for the final Test, and had he been available, would probably have been picked for the 1968/9 tour to South Africa. Thereafter, age was increasingly a disadvantage for him in relation to his competitors, and he was not called on again.

One experiment in the fast bowling laboratory of the mid-1960s did, however, offer a sustainable product – John Snow. He made his debut in 1965 at the age of 23, but was not selected for the 1965/6 tour to Australia. Almost a victim of the night of the long knives after the Headingley Test of 1966, he made a useful contribution with both bat and ball to England's subsequent victory at the Oval and was England's first-choice opening bowler for the 1967 Tests. But it was not until the 1967/8 tour of the West Indies that the selectors were to discover that in Snow they had at last found a successor to Trueman. In the second Test of that series, having been omitted from the first, he took 7-49 as West Indies were bowled out for 143 in a match which England would surely have won but for the intervention of a crowd riot. Snow went on to take 27 wickets in four Tests – the best haul by an England player in a series in the Caribbean before or since (Angus Fraser equalled it in six Tests in 1997/8). He was the key player in Illingworth's team which regained the Ashes in 1970/1, when he took 31 wickets in six Tests – the best since Larwood in 1932/3.

Snow's career was a chequered one, however. Unlike Trueman and Statham before him, but like Willis and Botham after him, Snow did not produce his best in county cricket. Only once in his career did he appear among the top 15 England qualified players in the first-class bowling averages – even Willis and Botham achieved this on three occasions. In 1971, he was omitted by Sussex. The county said

> 'the selection committee have decided to drop John Snow as a result of his poor performance in Championship matches. His bowling performances, and more especially his fielding, have been so lacking in effort that the selection committee had no alternative. While recognising the great physical strain of bowling fast, they felt that John Snow's indifferent attitude, if left unchecked, would jeopardise the morale of the rest of the side.'

Dropped by Sussex, Snow was inevitably omitted by England for the first three Tests of the 1971 series against Pakistan, despite these following his triumphs in Australia. Returning to the side for the first Test against India in the second half of the summer, he was involved in an incident in which he appeared deliberately to knock to the ground the Indian batsman Sunil Gavaskar. Snow was dropped for the next Test for disciplinary reasons as a consequence.

The 1972 Ashes series was notable for the emergence of the great Australian fast bowler Dennis Lillee, who took 31 England wickets. Snow was a touch overshadowed, but he remained England's top bowler with an impressive 24 wickets. The following season, Snow, now 31, for once was not England's leading wicket-taker in the early season series against New Zealand. Geoff Arnold, with 16 wickets at 22, slightly out-performed Snow, with 13 at 25 though their strike rates were similar. In the third Test, *Wisden* reported Snow as having bowled 'superbly well'. Yet after one more Test, he was dropped from the England team. England had lost to the West Indies by 158 runs, and Snow had a return of 3-133 from 49 overs. It was a harsh decision. Even harsher was the decision not to select him as one of four fast bowlers for the return winter tour to the West Indies. The opening bowlers chosen were Arnold, Bob Willis, Chris Old and Mike Hendrick. Arnold, who was England's most successful bowler in the two 1973 series, was an expected choice. Willis had made a

Unnatural Selection

reasonably successful return to the England side for the final Test of the summer (4-118 in West Indies' only innings of 652-8). Old, however, had not distinguished himself when he replaced Snow for the second Test and Hendrick had not played Test cricket before. Commenting on the touring party, John Woodcock in The *Times* said 'it was Hendrick's age [25 by the time of the tour] which settled it, and the feeling that Snow [32] can no longer come back as he used to. When in doubt it is usually right to send the younger man, especially where the sun is hot and the grounds are hard.'

With hindsight, the decision was the wrong one. Willis, Old and Arnold between them took just 12 wickets in five Tests in the West Indies and Hendrick was not selected. Although the pitches were unhelpful, the West Indies opening bowlers still managed to take a total of 28 wickets. But even without hindsight, the decision seems hard to justify. There was little evidence that Snow was over the hill, only that he had had one below par Test match following on the back of three in which he had bowled more than respectably. His record overseas was outstanding and as one of four faster bowlers, England would have retained the option of playing two or three younger men if it had turned out that Snow could indeed no longer take the heat.

Given that he was not selected for the West Indies in 1973/4, it is perhaps not surprising that he was not picked for Australia in 1974/5 either. Instead, England chose the same four opening bowlers as they had the previous winter, plus Peter Lever. Lever was a year older than Snow, and before then had last played for England in 1972. If England had wanted to take an experienced opening bowler to Australia, it is difficult to understand on what cricketing grounds Lever could have been preferred to Snow. Their Test records did not compare, nor even their record in county games in 1974 – not normally Snow's strong suit. That season Snow had taken 76 wickets at an average of just under 20 and a strike rate of a wicket every 45 balls: Lever had taken 57 at an average of 24 and a strike rate of 59.

The decision to omit Snow was certainly not that of his captain, Denness:

> 'I did not get my own way as far as John Snow was concerned. I wanted Snow in the party – he was always my choice – for the West Indies and later for the tour of Australia. He was number

one on my list for the West Indies but I got no support at that meeting [to select the squad for the Caribbean] or a year later when the party to tour Australia was chosen'.

Snow himself saw in his exclusion the hand of the chairman of selectors, Alec Bedser:

> '...Bedser and I have not seen eye to eye on many matters over the years. He is of a different generation, brought up in an era when the professionals were still work-horses accepting orders and not questioning their masters... I think it still amazes Alec that younger people today are prepared to get up and challenge some of the things they are asked to do.'

When Snow was finally recalled to the England side in 1975 he reassumed his place as England's premier bowler, the leading wicket taker in the Ashes series that summer, and taking 15 wickets in the three Tests for which he was fit in 1976 against West Indies.

In his 49 Tests for England, Snow had 12 different opening-bowler partners. The boldest choice was that of Willis. He joined the 1970/1 touring party in Australia after Alan Ward – widely regarded as the fastest bowler in England in the late '60s – was forced to return home injured. Willis was only 21, and had played just 16 County Championship matches for Surrey, for whom he was not yet a regular. There was little statistical evidence to support his selection – he had taken just 40 wickets at an average of 28 in 1970. But the selectors were shrewd in recognising his potential, for he made a useful contribution in the five Tests he played against Australia and New Zealand that winter. His county, Surrey, were less shrewd, for they failed to offer him a regular first-team place the following summer. Not surprisingly, Willis left and joined Warwickshire, for whom he did not qualify until half way through 1972. All this set back his England career, and it was not until the final Test of 1973 that he gained his sixth cap. During the subsequent three seasons, Willis spent long periods injured. As a consequence, despite their Test careers overlapping by six years, Snow and Willis, the best England opening bowlers to be born in the period 1931 (Trueman) to at least 1955 (Ian Botham), opened together on only two occasions.

Unnatural Selection

Feast then Famine

Snow's last Test in 1976 coincided with Willis's return from injury and the start of a run in which he played in 73 out of the next 85 Tests, opening the bowling in all but four. During this time, he had only 11 different opening partners and of these four bowlers accounted for 55 of the 69 Tests in which he opened: Botham (24), John Lever (11), Old (10) and Hendrick (10). From around 1976 until around 1984, England were blessed with greater depth in opening bowlers than they had been in the previous decade or were to be in the next decade – although it is probably also fair to say that the selectors were less fickle. Willis was at his peak from 1977 to 1983, and Botham from 1978 to 1986. From 1978 to 1983, England possessed in Willis and Botham a formidable and relatively settled pace attack, frequently supplemented by one of John Lever, Old and Hendrick until 1982 when all three were banned after going on the South African Breweries tour.

Old first played for England on the 1972/3 tour of India, and gradually established himself in the England side over the next four years. When fully fit, he ranked only behind Willis and Botham as an opening bowler, but his susceptibility to injury limited him to 46 Tests. Hendrick was an almost exact contemporary of Old, and made his England debut a year later in 1974. Although he opened the bowling for England in nearly half the 30 Tests he played, he was essentially a very effective defensive bowler. He never took five wickets in an innings, but his record of conceding just 2.17 runs per over in his Test career places him just a whisker behind Higgs in terms of economy rate among fast- or medium-pace bowlers who have taken 50 wickets for England since 1963. In addition he was, unusually for a bowler, an outstanding slip fielder. Lever was just a few months younger than Old and Hendrick, but made his debut rather later. He was first selected for the 1976/7 tour of India, where he was an instant success, taking 26 wickets in his first Test series, including 7-46 in his first Test innings. Although perhaps not inherently such a good bowler as Old, as a left-armer he added variety to seam attacks, and he had the important advantage of seldom being injured.

Finding the next generation of opening bowlers was to be more troublesome. Graham Dilley had appeared to be the most promising of the young bowlers in county cricket, and had the merit of being genuinely fast. He was selected for both the 1980/1 tour to the West Indies and the 1981/2 tour to India. He was conspicuously unsuccessful on the latter, and his form was not to return in 1982. Injury was to lay him low for most of 1983 and 1984, but he regained his England place in 1986 and was a fairly regular member of the England side until 1989 (when he joined Gatting's tour to South Africa), without quite fulfilling his potential.

For the 1982/3 tour to Australia, the selectors took a punt by selecting the 21-year-old fast bowler Norman Cowans of Middlesex, who had less than 50 first-class wickets behind him. It was a hunch redolent of that to send Willis to Australia in 1970/1 (albeit Willis replaced an injured player). Cowans took 6-77 in the second innings of the one Test which England won on that tour and played in 19 successive Tests finishing with the first Test of the 1985 season. He did not repeat his Melbourne heroics, finishing with 51 Test wickets at a disappointing average of 39. But he was still only 24. His record was comparable after 19 Tests to, in a subsequent era, James Anderson (60 wickets at 38, aged 25) and Stuart Broad (50 wickets at 40, aged 23). Although Cowans remained a successful player in county cricket for many years to come, he never again caught the selectors' eye at a time when competition among fast bowlers was weak.

Another 21-year-old identified by the selectors at this time was Neil Foster of Essex, who made his debut in 1983. His career was dogged by injury from the start and he made little initial impact. Included in the side for the fourth Test against India in 1984/5 after missing the previous seven, he bowled England to victory with 11-163 in the match. It was a performance which gave rise to ultimately unfulfilled hopes that England might have found a successor to Willis. Mainly because of injury, the only series in which he played all the Test matches was 1987, while his decision to join the rebel tour to South Africa in 1989 all but ended his Test career at a time when, while fit, he was at his peak. He returned – 'a self-confessed old crock' as Alan Lee described him in *The Times* – for a solitary Test in 1993. Another who had spectacular short-term success was Richard Ellison of Kent who, in the last two Tests against Australia in 1985, returned the remarkable figures of 17-185, which was critical to the return of the Ashes to England that summer. But again because of injury he played only three more Tests for England.

With Cowans discarded from 1985, and Dilley and Foster – the

Unnatural Selection

generally preferred pairing – having periods of injury, it was a tough time for the selectors from the mid-80s in selecting quicker bowlers. Often they had to take a gamble – none more so than when Greg Thomas of Glamorgan was selected for the 1985/6 tour to the West Indies. He was thought to be as fast a bowler as any in England (or indeed Wales) at the time, but although 25, had yet to win his county cap, and in a 1985 season affected by injury had taken just 39 wickets at an average of 31. His Test career was undistinguished, and he played only once more after the Caribbean tour. Other selections, perforce, were from the form county players, even where their long-term potential was likely to be limited. In this period Neil Radford of Worcestershire, Arnie Sidebottom of Yorkshire and Les Taylor of Leicestershire made their debuts at 29, 31 and 31 respectively, but played just six Tests between them.

With such volatility in the opening attack, it was easier for the selectors to pick 'Headingley specialists'. From the 1980s, Leeds developed a reputation – one it has not entirely lost – for conditions conducive to swing bowling, and on four occasions the selectors picked medium pacers with no expectation of their having a prolonged run at international level. Thus John Lever was recalled for the second Test against India in 1986 at the age of 37 – England's oldest opening bowler since Shackleton. He took 6-166 in the match so arguably justified his selection – though England lost. Lever was not picked again. Steve Watkin of Glamorgan made his debut against West Indies in 1991 and had a match return of 5-93 as England won (he played only twice more for his country). The following year, Neil Mallender of Somerset took 8-122 – a significant contribution to England's victory over Pakistan. He was picked for the next Test, the last of the series, but his skills were not deemed likely to be effective in India, and so he was not selected for the winter tour which followed, and was never picked again. The unfortunate Mike Smith of Gloucestershire was chosen for the Headingley Test of 1997 against Australia (he had been in the 12 for the previous Test), failed to take a wicket, and was never asked again. Had Thorpe held a fairly straightforward catch offered by Matthew Elliott, who went on to make 199, early in his innings, it might have been a different story. By such threads do some players' careers hang.

Two young players who emerged in the second half of the 80s were Gladstone Small and Phillip DeFreitas. Small, then 24, was selected for the fifth Test of the summer against New Zealand in 1986. Foster had been dropped after a poor run, and Small was the leading England-qualified wicket taker in county cricket. Five wickets in an innings in each of the last two Tests against Australia in 1986/7 suggested that England had uncovered a significant talent, but as with so many of England's quicker bowlers in the 80s, he then succumbed to injury which prevented him from having an extended run in the Test side until the final Test of 1989. But, perhaps because of his injuries, he was no longer the bowler he had promised to be, and while he played 12 more matches over the next 18 months, he took just 35 wickets at an average of 40.

DeFreitas was first picked for England's Ashes tour of Australia in 1986/7 at the age of 20. Like all selections of players at an early age, it gave rise to much excitement – not least because he had batting potential as well. But while always in the frame for selection over the next eight years (he went on every overseas tour from 1986/7 to 1994/5 except 1993/4), he was never quite consistent enough, and only in two seasons at home or overseas did he play in all the Tests. He played his last Test in 1995 at the age of 29, the young Dominic Cork effectively eclipsing him thereafter.

England used 12 seamers, including 10 different opening bowlers, against Australia in 1989, with conspicuous lack of success. Three (Dilley, Foster and Paul Jarvis) signed up for the Gatting tour during the season and were suspended from Test cricket. Of the others, Botham appeared to be past his best, and Phil Newport and Alan Igglesden failed to impress on their solitary appearances. For the subsequent tour of the West Indies, the selectors picked five of the rest – Small, DeFreitas, Capel (who effectively was competing with Pringle, who had also played in 1989), Fraser and Devon Malcolm, plus Ricardo Ellcock (who did not make the tour due to injury, and was replaced by Chris Lewis).

The 90s

There had been many misfiring selections but at least Fraser and Malcolm were both successful choices. They played significant roles in the first two Tests played in the Caribbean that winter in which England exceeded all expectations. In the first, in Jamaica, Fraser took 6-59 and Malcolm 5-128 as England won by 9 wickets – their first Test victory over the West Indies for 24 matches. The second Test was abandoned without

Unnatural Selection

a ball being bowled. In the third, Malcolm took 10-137, and Fraser 5-102, as England were denied victory by a combination of losing Gooch to a fractured left hand, rain, bad light and a cynically slow West Indian over rate. Chasing 151 to win, England finished at 121-5.

It seemed, at last, as if England had found a pair of Test-class opening bowlers, even though Small, not Fraser, had taken the new ball with Malcolm in these two Tests. They seemed perfect foils – Malcolm, undoubtedly the fastest bowler in England, albeit not very controlled; Fraser, a model of accuracy and with the ability to use his height to extract disconcerting bounce. Both had wonderful starts to their Test careers. Fraser took 47 wickets at an average of 27 in his first 11 Tests before suffering a serious hip injury half way through the 1990/1 Ashes series. This was to limit his first-class appearances in 1991 to two matches and delay his return to the England side until the final Test of the 1993 series. Here he played a crucial part in securing a consolation win for England over Australia. He followed this up with 16 wickets in four Tests in the Caribbean in 1993/4, including 8-75 in the first innings of the Barbados Test which England won. But for the Oval Test of 1994, Fraser was dropped; and, even more controversially, he was left out of the party to tour Australia in 1994/5.

Fraser had, it is true, had a moderate five Tests in 1994 – 14 wickets at 39. The chairman of selectors, Ray Illingworth, thought that he 'had lost his nip'. His replacement for the Oval Test was Joey Benjamin, then 33, who was having a good season for Surrey, and was a horse for a course without ever having previously been considered Test class. In fact, Benjamin took 4-42 in South Africa's first innings, and England won the match, so it was difficult not to include him in the squad for the winter tour to Australia. Three of the five pace bowlers selected themselves: Malcolm, Darren Gough, and DeFreitas had all distinguished themselves in the final Test against South Africa. The fifth opening bowler chosen was Martin McCague of Kent.

The decision was pretty dubious at the time. Fraser had played in 21 Tests and taken 85 wickets at 27. It was a better record than both DeFreitas and Malcolm. He had a good record in Australia and the West Indies. At 29, he was at his peak. 'Fraser deserves sympathy and will get it', wrote Alan Lee in *The Times*.

'Professionals, no less than spectators, like him as a man and respect him as a cricketer for his bravery, skill and honesty. But throughout the summer, the feeling grew that Fraser had lost the 'zip' that had made him such an accomplished medium-fast bowler.'

As for McCague, his selection was something of a punt, though he had been on the 'A' tour to South Africa in 1993/4. As with the selection of Thomas in 1985/6, there was a keen desire to confront Australia with real pace, and McCague was reckoned to be fast. He had also finished highest in the first-class bowling averages in 1994 among England qualified players. There was a case for taking him to Australia – but surely ahead of Benjamin rather than Fraser. Atherton certainly wanted Fraser in the party not least, and prophetically, because he regarded McCague as an injury risk, as did the coach, Keith Fletcher. But they were overruled.

As things turned out, it clearly was the wrong decision. McCague bowled disastrously in the first Test, and flew home soon afterwards with a stress fracture of the shin. Fraser was called in to replace him, and played in the last three Tests ahead of Benjamin, taking 14 wickets. Chris Lewis, summoned to replace Gough after he had broken his foot, also played ahead of Benjamin in the last two Tests. Benjamin's only Test was to be that Oval game against South Africa.

In Illingworth's defence, however, Fraser did show signs of decline after 1994/5 – a modest summer in 1995, followed by a poor tour of South Africa in 1995/6 during which he was dropped. It seemed that this might be the end of his career. He did not contend for a place in 1996 or 1997, and it was a surprise when he was recalled for the 1997/8 West Indies tour. Fraser had not had an exceptional season for Middlesex in 1997 – 47 wickets at 31 – and he was now 32. David Graveney, the chairman of selectors, explained the decision by saying 'one thing we have learnt this summer [another Ashes defeat] is the need for accurate seam bowling'. As it turned out, it was the right choice, for in the next 12 Tests, Fraser took 54 wickets at 20. A further tour to Australia in 1998/9, however, proved one too many.

Malcolm played in all 17 of England's Tests from his debut in 1989 until the second Test against the West Indies in 1991 – the longest unbroken run for an England opening bowler since the days of Willis. He took 35 wickets in his first eight Tests, including three five-wicket hauls. He did not, however, sustain his early successes. In his next 19, his record was 53 wickets at 43. On a fast, helpful, pitch, he could be a handful, but his often poor control frequently led to his being expensive in less sympathetic conditions; among England bowlers of the past 50 years who have taken 50 wickets, only Simon Jones and Craig White have inferior economy rates. For the selectors, he represented a classic dilemma, someone who could be a real match winner – as he demonstrated with his famous 9-57 in the second innings of the Oval Test against South Africa in 1994 which revived a career which looked to have blown itself out. But he could be a match loser too. In the Cape Town Test of 1995/6, he was brought back into the attack with South Africa 171-9 in response to England's 153, and the 18-year old Paul Adams, who had not scored a run in Test cricket, at the crease. According to the 1998 *Wisden*, Malcolm 'performed ineptly and appeared to bowl himself out of Test cricket' as the tenth-wicket pair added 73, and England went on to lose the match and the series. After this, and against the background of a public row with team manager Ray Illingworth, it was little surprise that Malcolm was not selected in 1996, nor for the 1996/7 tour. But the new selection team in 1997 were impressed with Malcolm's early-season county form, and allowed themselves to be persuaded that, at the age of 34, he could still make a difference. He played in the first two matches of the series, against Australia, and, as a result of an injury to Gough, the last two, but six wickets hardly justified his recall, and it was not repeated.

Andrew Caddick was selected for the first Test of the 1993 Ashes series against the background of a successful 'A' Team tour to Australia in 1992/3 and a good start to the 1993 season. He made no immediate impression, and while he bowled with reasonable success against the West Indies the following winter, it was not until 1997 that he was able to secure a regular place in the England attack, by which time he was 28 – an age at which the Test careers of the likes of Brown and Cowans were over. He was England's leading wicket-taker in that Ashes series, but fell behind a rejuvenated Fraser on the 1997/8 tour to the West Indies, and with Gough fit again and Dominic Cork for the time being well established in the side, he failed to find a place in the side for the 1998 Tests. But it was surprising that each of Alan Mullally, Alex Tudor and Dean Headley should have been chosen, alongside Gough, Fraser and Cork, ahead of Caddick for the 1998/9 tour to Australia. Caddick was the only England-qualified player to take 100 wickets in the summer of 1998. Headley, it is true, had bowled better than Caddick in the West Indies the previous winter, and Tudor was the young raw fast bowler upon whose development many hopes now focussed. But Mullally had done little in his nine previous Tests for England to push ahead of Caddick. Caddick's personality and temperament were not to everyone's taste, and maybe that counted against him. The turning point for Caddick was the appointment of Hussain as England captain in 1999. He rated Caddick in a way his predecessor, Stewart, seems not to have done – significantly, he played in none of the 11 Tests Stewart captained. In addition, with Gough injured again, and Fraser discarded, there was less competition. Caddick's 20 wickets in four Tests was one of the few positives for England to come out of the 1999 series against New Zealand, and he established himself in the side for the next three years.

Like McCague, Gough had been on the 'A' tour to South Africa in 1993/4, from which he had received good reports, and was selected for the Texaco series against New Zealand at the start of the 1994 season. Injury sustained then delayed his Test debut until the South Africa series in the second half of the summer. He had a tremendous start to the Australia tour of 1994/5, taking 20 wickets in the first three Tests, including 6-49 as Australia were dismissed for 116 in the first innings at Sydney, a match in which he also scored his maiden Test fifty. But at his moment of triumph, he suffered a broken foot, terminating his role on that tour. Although he played in three Tests in 1995, it seems that his foot was not fully healed; and in South Africa in 1995/6 he could not recover his form of the previous winter. Only towards the end of the summer of 1996 did he begin to reproduce the bowling which had troubled the Australians, and he won back a place in the England party for the following winter tour. In England's next nine Tests, in all of which he played, Gough took 42 wickets, and seemed to have re-established himself as England's premier opening bowler, only to become *hors de combat* once again with a knee injury. Fit once more in 1998, he had the misfortune to break a finger while batting in his recall Test against South Africa, and was unable to bowl. Recovered for the third Test, he went on to play a crucial role in the victory over South Africa in the last Test of the series, only to be sidelined through injury again for much of 1999. Only from the 1999/2000 tour of South Africa did Gough enjoy an extended run of 25 Tests, during which he was a formidable opening bowler for

Unnatural Selection

England, taking 103 wickets at 26. Caddick played in the same 25 Tests (87 wickets at 30), and this period represented the most stable opening-bowling partnership since Trueman and Statham. It was no coincidence that it was a period of significant progress in England's fortunes, with a series win over the West Indies in England in 2000, the first since 1969, and landmark series wins in both Pakistan and Sri Lanka in 2000/1. Gough and Caddick made significant contributions to all of these.

At the end of the 2001 season, Caddick was 32 and Gough 31. How much longer could they endure? Gough decided to make himself available only for the one-day internationals in the winter of 2001/2, and injured his knee in New Zealand in the second half of the winter causing him to miss much of the 2002 season, though he did play in England's one-day series with Sri Lanka and India. Nasser Hussain has written that during that series, Gough was 'not the bowler of old', nevertheless, he was desperate to take him to Australia in 2002/3: 'We knew Darren Gough wouldn't be fit for the start of the tour, but, as far as I was concerned, having Goughy out there for any part of the tour would be worthwhile and it was worth picking him'. In fact, his knee failed to recover in time, and he returned from Australia before the Test series had started. Whether it really made sense, against the background of his injuries and the emergence of a new generation of England opening bowlers, to recall him for the South Africa series in 2003 is perhaps doubtful: his figures of 1-215 in two Tests suggest it was the wrong call, and Gough retired from Test cricket after the second of these games. Caddick had fewer injuries to contend with, but his performances began to deteriorate after 2001. He did, however, leave the Test scene on an unusual high – taking 7-94 in Australia's second innings as England won the last Test of the 2002/3 series. He missed most of the 2003 season due to injury.

The third outstanding opening bowler of this generation was Cork. His potential had been recognised early, and he was picked for four successive 'A' team tours, and – not least in recognition of his useful and aggressive batting – for a number of home one-day internationals from the age of 20 before breaking into the Test side against West Indies in 1995. He made an extraordinary impact, with 7-43 in West Indies' second innings (the best-ever figures for an England bowler on debut) and followed it up two Tests later with the first hat-trick by an England player since 1957. Unsurprisingly, he became a fixture in the England side for the next three years, missing only the 1996/7 tour to Zimbabwe for personal reasons. Often he opened the bowling; at other times he was first change. But he was unable to maintain his early successes. After 10 Tests he enjoyed a strike rate of a wicket every 50 balls, but in his next 25 his strike rate was 69. He was dropped – for Headley – for the first time after two indifferent Tests in Australia in 1998/9, at an age when he might have been expected to be at his peak. *Wisden's* report of the tour in its 2000 almanack said 'the familiar concerns about Dominic Cork – irritating personality, on-field histrionics and questionable attitude – appeared again, and he did not swing the kookaburra ball either'. Cork was not to play another overseas Test match, but where it seemed that conditions were likely to be conducive to conventional swing, his skills remained in demand. Thus he was recalled with notable success for the Lord's Test against West Indies in 2000, where his match figures of 7-52, and 33 not out in a tight run chase, were key factors in England's victory. His 20 wickets at 12 in the series forced his way onto the tour to Pakistan that winter, but by now Gough and Caddick were established as the opening pair, and Craig White was enjoying his unexpected spell as an England all-rounder. Although Cork played in six more Tests over the course of the next two home seasons, he was unable to repeat his triumphs of 2000.

When injury or other reasons required the selectors to look beyond Gough, Caddick, Cork and Fraser in the second half of the 90s, their principal ports of call were Mullally (19 Tests) and Headley (15). Mullally was a successful containing bowler, but only once did he take five wickets in an innings. He was also a genuine number 11 at a time when England's premier spinner, Phil Tufnell, was the go-to last man. While Gough and Caddick had some batting talent, they were not number eights, where one or other of them had frequently to bat. With Duncan Fletcher as England coach from 1999 placing more emphasis on lower-order runs, Mullally was at a disadvantage, and he played just one more Test under the new regime. Headley had his triumphs – notably his 6-60 in the second innings of the Melbourne Test of 1998/9 which England won by just 12 runs. A serious back injury ended his career prematurely after the 1999 season.

Unnatural Selection

The Class of 2005

The selection of Matthew Hoggard for the Lord's Test of 2000 was an interesting one. He had not been on an 'A' team tour, and had not received his Yorkshire county cap. He was not even having an exceptional season in county cricket. Hussain had not actually met him when he was selected. It seems his hostility in a televised Benson and Hedges Cup quarter-final with Surrey counted in his favour. Required to bowl only 13 overs, and with Gough, Caddick, Cork and White ahead of him, he was dropped after one Test. But he had his foot in the door. He was the reserve quick bowler on the 2000/1 tours, and his opportunity came with Gough's unavailability for the winter tours of 2001/2, and Cork's demise. A poor tour of Australia in 2002/3, during which he was dropped, proved a setback, and as late as 2003/4 in Sri Lanka, James Kirtley was preferred to him for a couple of Tests. Only from the West Indies tour later that winter did he become an automatic selection – alongside Stephen Harmison.

Harmison had long been in the frame, representing England at Under-19 level, touring with England 'A' as a 20-year-old in 1998/9, selected again to tour in 1999/2000 (he withdrew due to injury) and joining the senior England squad in 2000. Duncan Fletcher would have picked him ahead of Ed Giddins for the Tests against Zimbabwe that summer, but allowed himself to be swayed by Hussain. Giddins, a swing bowler, was a classic horse for a course at Lord's, where around that time swing bowlers had been prospering; Cork was recalled for the second Lord's Test that summer for precisely the same reason. With Gough and Caddick continuing to lead the England attack, supported by Cork and then the emerging Hoggard, it was not until 2002 that Harmison's chance came when both Gough and Caddick were injured. He played just one Test as Caddick returned, and it was the 2002/3 tour of Australia, and then only after injury to Simon Jones, before he was able to cement a place in the England side.

Starting from the first Test of the West Indies tour of 2003/4, Hoggard and Harmison opened the bowling in the next 24 Tests. In all, they opened for England in 33 Tests, and played together in a further 12 in which Harmison bowled first change. It was a classic combination of essentially a swing bowler with one of raw pace and bounce. The consistency of selection was in some ways the more remarkable for the fact that for most of this period Flintoff was in the England side with James Anderson and Jones also competing for places – though, other than in the Indian sub-continent, when Flintoff was in the England side, four pace bowlers were picked. Both Harmison and Hoggard were major players in England's great Ashes triumph of 2005.

At the end of that Ashes series, Hoggard was 28, had played 45 Tests, taken 173 wickets at an average of 29.6 and a strike rate of 53. Harmison was 26, had played in 35 Tests, taken 138 wickets at an average of 28.5 and a strike rate of 55. But both, while still far short of fast-bowling dotage, had peaked. After that summer, Hoggard played in 22 Tests, and took 75 wickets at an average of 32.5 and a strike rate of 62. Harmison played in 27 Tests and took 84 wickets at a strike rate of 67 and an average of 37.6. These post-2005 returns are unexceptional by any standards, and it is perhaps unlikely that bowlers of lesser heritage would have been picked so regularly on the back of them. The deterioration, especially in Harmison's figures, raises the question of the extent to which they continued to be selected on reputation. Of course, as we have seen, there has been a whole raft of examples of impulsive selectors prematurely discarding class players such as Trueman, Snow and Fraser for lesser players on the basis of short-term blips in performance. But in the case of Harmison, and perhaps Hoggard, it may be that the selectors erred in the other direction.

Generally, Harmison and Hoggard remained automatic selections for England throughout 2006 and 2007 when fit, though injury prevented both from appearing in the series against India in the second half of the summer of 2007, which enabled the pairing of Ryan Sidebottom and Anderson to emerge. *Wisden* reported that against a strong Indian batting line up, and in the absence of Hoggard and Harmison (and Flintoff) 'James Anderson, Ryan Sidebottom and Chris Tremlett amazed everyone with the way they bowled, and did their captain proud'. Hoggard and Harmison were back for the tour to Sri Lanka in 2007/8, along with Anderson, Sidebottom and Stuart Broad. Hoggard was, in fact, the pick of those bowlers who played in the Tests, and Harmison emerged ahead of Anderson. For the first Test against New Zealand in the second tour of the winter, the seam-bowling attack was Hoggard, Sidebottom and Harmison. New Zealand won by 189 runs. Sidebottom returned match figures of 10-139; Hoggard's and

Harmison's were 1-151 and 1-121 respectively. Both were dropped for the next Test – Hoggard never to return. Anderson and Broad replaced them, and England won the next two Tests, with Anderson playing a big part in the first of them.

The dropping of Hoggard and Harmison was a pivotal moment in England drawing a line under the fairy story of 2005. It was all very well to lose series to Pakistan, Australia, India and Sri Lanka, as England had since 2005, but losing to New Zealand was a humiliation. There had been a significant diminution in confidence in Harmison ever since his disastrous first ball in the Ashes series of 2006/7,which ended at first slip, and his record was not such as to sustain his case for a place in the side. Hoggard, however, injured for much of 2007, had bowled better than anyone in the recent series against Sri Lanka. The decision to omit him was certainly supported, and maybe initiated, by the England captain, Michael Vaughan. But it is likely that the relatively new England coach, Peter Moores, saw it as an opportunity to stamp his authority on the side, and signal that England needed to move on from 2005, and the Duncan Fletcher era. In his autobiography, Vaughan writes 'when I mentioned to Peter that I thought we should drop Harmy his eyes physically lit up, no doubt seeing it as progress towards getting a new set of players in'. Whatever the reasoning, in initiating the era of Anderson and Broad, Moores and Vaughan were surely justified in dispensing with Hoggard and Harmison at an earlier age than might have been expected in a way that their predecessors had not been in regard to Trueman and Snow.

It was not, in fact, the end for Harmison. He was recalled for the Oval Test of 2008 against South Africa at the expense of the injured Sidebottom. Partly, this reflected the impulse of England's new captain, Kevin Pietersen, and partly Harmison's success in county cricket that season. But he was also a horse for a course – the fast Oval pitch generated the steep bounce which was Harmison's most potent weapon. Rejuvenated by Pietersen's confidence, he ended his retirement from one-day cricket, playing a significant part in England's victory over South Africa in the internationals at the end of the 2008 season, and was picked for the winter tours to India and the West Indies. In the second innings of the first Test against India, the home side chasing an unlikely 387 for victory, Harmison's first four overs went for 33, providing India with the foundation for a dramatic win. Dropped for the next Test, he played a couple more against West Indies, but was recalled for the fourth Test at Headingley against Australia in 2009. Flintoff was injured, and England decided to replace him with a bowler.

Harmison had been bowling well in county cricket, and to some extent represented the closest England could get to a like-for-like replacement for Flintoff as a bowler who could rattle the Australians with pace – even though Headingley traditionally was not a pitch which was conducive to fast bowling. In fact, Harmison bowled too short, and England lost. But when Flintoff returned for the Oval, he was retained ahead of Graham Onions, who had done little wrong in the previous three Tests. Doubtless the venue once again played its part in the decision. Harmison took three lower-order wickets in Australia's second innings, but was not central to England's victory, and unlike in 2008, he was not selected for the winter tours (to South Africa and Bangladesh) which followed.

Harmison was one of the selectors' biggest headaches of the last decade. In the four 'seasons' from 2003/4 to 2005, he played in 24 Tests and took 106 wickets, and was as formidable a fast bowler as any in the world. Thereafter, he continued to display sparks of brilliance, particularly in home Tests, amongst generally flaccid performances abroad – in part reflecting his deep lack of enthusiasm for touring. It is easy to see why the selectors continued to revert to someone who had the potential to be a game changer, though in retrospect they would have been better served by not recalling him after 2007.

The principal challengers to – or, in a four-seam bowling attack including Flintoff, accomplices to – Hoggard and Harmison were Jones and Anderson. Jones's rise was spectacular. In 2001, he finished 139th in the first-class averages, but impressed observers with his pace sufficiently to be selected to join the academy in Australia the following winter. He was judged to have performed well there, and with improved control in county cricket in 2002, was picked for the first Test against India in the second half of the summer. Alas, he sustained an injury which limited him to one appearance that summer, and then suffered a terrible knee injury on the first day of the Ashes series of 2002/3, and missed the whole of the 2003 season. Attached to the academy to rehabilitate the following winter, he demonstrated his fitness and was able to join the England team in the West Indies. Preferred to Anderson in conditions which did not encourage conventional swing, he took five wickets in the second innings of the second Test. Injured for two Tests in 2004, he returned in the second half of the summer only to bowl indifferently in the first Test against the West Indies. He was dropped for Anderson, but in three Tests Anderson failed to seize his opportunity. Both were chosen for the tour to South Africa in 2004/5, but they were competing for one place alongside Hoggard, Harmison and Flintoff. Jones was preferred at the start of the tour, but after three Tests had not done enough to cement his place, and Anderson replaced him for the fourth. But Anderson bowled poorly in that match, and Jones was back for the fifth. And so Jones was the man in possession at the start of the 2005 summer, and in four Tests against Australia took 18 wickets at 21 and a strike rate of 34, making a crucial contribution to England's Ashes victory through his pace and reverse swing. Sadly, the injury which kept him out of the last Test of the summer was to end his career prematurely. His last match, in which he took 5-44 in Australia's first innings, was played at the age of only 26.

The rise of Anderson was also spectacular. Although he had represented England at Under-19 level in 2001, it was only in 2002 that he forced his way into the Lancashire first team. He was chosen for the academy in Australia the following winter. England were also in Australia, the pace attack gradually disintegrating with injuries as the tour progressed. Gough and Jones were replaced by Tudor and Chris Silverwood, then Flintoff by White, and when Caddick was for a time indisposed, Anderson was called in as cover. He was only 20, and reports from the academy said that he was not ready for elevation. But in the one-day series in which he appeared he was England's joint leading wicket taker, including figures of 1-12 in 10 overs in one of the matches against Australia. As a consequence, despite having played only three one-day games for Lancashire, he found himself in the World Cup squad for 2003, and won the man of the match award in England's victory over Pakistan in the qualifying round. Unsurprisingly, he found himself in the Test side for the 2003 summer. He played in all seven games, and was England's leading wicket taker with 26. A star seemed to have been born.

 At that point, however, the wickets started to dry up. Injury kept him out of the series in Bangladesh in late 2003, and he played a single, undistinguished Test against Sri Lanka in the series that followed. By 2004 he was in direct competition with Jones, and Jones came to be generally preferred when he was fit. Anderson himself missed the summer of 2006 because of injury, and with an action remodelled to its detriment by the England coaching staff, he made little impact in those Tests for which he was selected subsequently. At the end of the series against Sri Lanka in late 2007, he had played 20 times for England, taken 62 wickets at an average of 39 and an economy rate of 3.7 an over. Among England opening bowlers over the last 50 years, only DeFreitas, Lewis and Broad have played more than 20 Tests for England with a worse record after 20 matches. And while Anderson was still only 25 at this point, he had shown deterioration, rather than improvement, over the previous four years.

Who knows how history might have been different had England not lost to New Zealand in the first Test of the 2007/8 series? Hoggard and Harmison would probably have retained their places in the side at least until the end of the series, and England might have looked elsewhere than Anderson to replace them in due course. If so, England would have been deprived of the services of their best opening bowler since Botham and Willis. As it was, it was Anderson and Broad who were in the squad in New Zealand and who played in the next Test. Anderson took 5-73 in the first innings, England won, and he has never looked back, becoming England's most prolific Test bowler in history. It is a quite phenomenal record of sustained high performance, and, for a fast bowler, of sustained fitness.

The other bowling star of the 2007/8 series in New Zealand was Sidebottom. He looked as if he might end up a one-Test wonder, like his father, Arnie, after failing to take a wicket when called in as one of four seamers for the Lord's Test of 2001. He was not recalled until the Headingley Test of 2007 against the West Indies. Hoggard was injured, while Anderson, for the time being, was out of favour following his poor tour to Australia the previous winter. It was a surprising selection, for Sidebottom was 29, and generally it has not been England policy over the last decade or so to select county stalwarts as opening bowlers. James Kirtley, picked against South Africa in 2003 at the age of 28, and Martin Saggers, picked at 30 against Bangladesh in 2003/4, are really the only other examples. Sidebottom was not having an exceptional season in county cricket, but the choice was inspired, for he took eight wickets in the match, and played in the next 15. In these 16 Tests he took 73 wickets at 24, before injury reduced his availability and his effectiveness waned.

Unnatural Selection

That injury led to one of the most extraordinary selections of the last 50 years. For the Lord's Test of 2008, England's attack had been Sidebottom, Anderson, Broad and Panesar. For the second Test at Headingley, Flintoff returned from injury and England decided to strengthen the bowling by his replacing Collingwood, while Chris Tremlett was added to the squad as the reserve opening bowler. Tremlett had not played Test cricket for a year, and Vaughan would have preferred Harmison in the squad. 'I now wanted Harmison back', Vaughan has written,

> 'as our Durham Ashes winner was looking so potent in the County Championship. Again it seemed to me that there was a concerted attempt to make us look as if we were going forward for the sake of it by persisting with Chris [Tremlett] when in my view Harmy was ready for a recall. I always thought a fit and firing Harmison – admittedly not always adjectives which applied to him – was worth a place.'

There were doubts about the fitness of Sidebottom and Anderson, and both Vaughan and Peter Moores seemed to judge Tremlett to have limited utility in conditions in which swing, rather than bounce, was likely to be key. It is puzzling why the selectors, looking for swing-bowler cover for what was probably going to be a one-off outing, did not recall Hoggard, who was taking plenty of wickets for Yorkshire, had represented England Lions earlier in the summer, was still only 31 and would be playing on his home ground. Instead, they called up Darren Pattinson, a Grimsby-born but Australian-raised Nottinghamshire player, and when Sidebottom declared himself unfit, he was selected ahead of Tremlett. Vaughan had not even previously met Pattinson. Aged 29, yet with just 11 first-class matches for Nottinghamshire and Victoria behind him, it remains a mystery why the selectors should have settled on Pattinson. Not only was he dropped for the third Test, never to return, he was not selected for either the senior or Lions' squads for the overseas tours of 2008/9. It is therefore difficult to conclude that his selection for the Headingley Test was anything other than an aberration.

Taking the Wickets - The Quicks

Trueman and Statham Redux

Stuart Broad's journey to the Test team was the classic path for a 21st-century England player. An Under-19 international in 2005, the summer he broke into the Leicestershire side, he was considered sufficiently promising to be selected for the academy the following winter, when he made his 'A' team debut in the West Indies. A successful county season in 2006 led to his being picked for England's one-day internationals at the end of the summer, and the 'A' team tour to Bangladesh in the winter, from which he received good reports. From the start of 2007, he was a regular in the limited-overs teams and began to deliver on his potential as a batsman – not least in scoring 45 not out in an unbroken partnership of 99 with Ravi Bopara which enabled England to beat India after having been 114-7. The question was when he would be ready for Test cricket. He was still only 21 and it was not all plain sailing with his bowling in limited-overs matches. In the T20 World Cup in South Africa, in September 2007, he was hit for six sixes in one over by Yuvraj Singh. Harmison, Hoggard, Sidebottom and Anderson were all ahead of him in the competition for opening bowling places. He was, however, picked for the winter tours of 2007/8, and made his debut in Sri Lanka when Hoggard was injured. But, as with Anderson, it was the decision to drop Hoggard and Harmison in New Zealand later in the winter which gave Broad his opportunity, and he has played in 73 of the next 84 Tests.

The selectors showed great faith in Broad's bowling potential, and were understandably influenced by his ability to contribute with the bat and thus shorten the tail. But he was quite slow to repay that faith. After 20 Tests, he had taken just 52 wickets at an average of 40 and a strike rate of 73. But this was the tipping point: he took five wickets in an innings in each of the next two Tests, against Australia in 2009 – his 5-37 at the Oval setting up England's victory which retained the Ashes. In his last 32 Tests he has taken 120 wickets at an average of 28 and a strike rate of 58. Was he picked too young? Or were those fairly unsuccessful first 20 Tests a necessary apprenticeship for the triumphs which followed? Either way, the selectors' perseverance had been well and truly justified.

Anderson and Broad have been regulars in the England pace attack for over six years. They have partnered each other with the new ball in a record number of 45 Tests and played in the same team on another 27 occasions. It has been an unprecedented pairing of fast bowlers.

In recent years, therefore, the selectors have generally only needed to consider whom to pick as a third seamer alongside Anderson and Broad, or, in 2008 and 2009, a fourth seamer alongside Anderson, Broad and Flintoff. To begin with, Harmison and Sidebottom were in the frame. Then in 2009, England selected Graham Onions. He had been on the fringe of the England side for a while – called up to the one-day squad in 2006 (though he didn't make the final elevens), and touring with the 'A' team in 2006/7 and 2007/8. But he was dropped by Durham in 2008, and did not get an 'A' team tour the following winter. Now 26, his moment seemed to have passed. But he was the form bowler of the early part of the 2009 season, and was selected for the first Test of the summer against the West Indies at Lord's where, in conditions assisting his swing bowling, he took 5-38 in the first innings. He continued to bowl well in the Tests which followed. In the winter series against South Africa, he was more notable for his batting – holding out for draws with nine wickets down in the first and third Tests – than for his bowling. Most observers considered that his figures of 8-336 in the first three Tests did not do him justice, and there was no obvious reason for his replacement by Sidebottom for the final Test – and nor did Sidebottom's subsequent performance suggest it was the right decision.

Onions and Sidebottom were both injured for the tour to Bangladesh which followed the South Africa trip, and England chose as one replacement Steven Finn, who made his debut at just 20. He had been playing for Middlesex since the age of 18, and was picked for the 'Lions' tour of 2009/10 which immediately preceded Bangladesh. It was another example of the selectors taking a gamble with raw pace – or at any rate raw bounce from the 6' 7" Finn. By chance or design, it was perhaps fortunate that Finn was able to settle in with four Tests against Bangladesh and he certainly took his opportunity. In an uninterrupted run of 11 Tests, he took 46 wickets at 26 and an unprecedented – in the last half century – strike rate of 40. After three Ashes Tests in 2010/11, in which he had taken 14 wickets, he was dropped. It was a harsh decision, but not an irrational one, and in retrospect the right one. The problem with Finn was not his strike rate, but his economy rate, and against Australia he had been going at 4.3 runs per over. In England's preferred post-Flintoff configuration of just four specialist bowlers, this degree of profligacy risked loss of control, and lifting of the unremitting pressure on the Australian batsmen which was judged crucial to the strategy. Tim Bresnan, who replaced Finn, took 11 wickets in the next two Tests at an economy rate of 2.6. Bresnan was an established member of England's one-day squad, having made his international debut as long ago as 2006, where his hard hitting batting complemented his tight bowling. At that time, however, he had played just four Tests – two against the West Indies in 2009 when England had chosen to play five specialist bowlers even though Flintoff was unfit; and in Bangladesh in 2009/10, in the absence of Anderson, Sidebottom and Onions.

The 2010/1 series saw another England fast bowler emerge in the form of Chris Tremlett. First picked for three Tests in 2007, subsequent injuries appeared to have ended his Test prospects, and his selection for the Australia tour of 2010/1, at the age of 29, was something of a surprise. His opportunity came in the third Test when Broad was injured. As the 2011 *Wisden* reported 'so beautifully did he bowl for the remainder of the series that no difference was noticed. Outrageously tall and strong, he was the find of the tour, a finished product at last with the ability to swing the ball through long accurate high-bounce spells that made the Australians play at more deliveries than was good for them.' With Broad returning at the start of the 2011 summer, there was initially no room for either Bresnan or Finn. But when Tremlett became injured in the second half of the summer, it was Bresnan, whose batting was of a standard that enabled him to be regarded as a genuine all-rounder, who was preferred to Finn.

An indifferent match for Bresnan in the first Test against the West Indies in 2012 rallied the supporters of Finn, but the selectors stuck with Bresnan and he bounced back with match figures of 8-141 and an important 39 not out in the second. The Bresnan v Finn debate continued to rage and led to the 'shoot out' experiment in which, with England already 2-0 up in the three-match series, both, along with a rejuvenated Onions, played ahead of Anderson and Broad in the final Test. The results were inconclusive. After South Africa had scored 637-2 against England in the first Test of the series which followed, the selectors felt compelled to change the bowling attack, and Finn came in replacing not Bresnan, but Swann. While he did not bowl obviously better than Bresnan in the second Test, with Bresnan's batting form having deserted him, when England reverted to their traditional bowling mix for the third Test, Finn was chosen ahead of Bresnan. With a match return of 8-149, albeit in a losing cause, Finn once again edged ahead of Bresnan, an advantage he would retain, partly assisted by injuries to Bresnan, until the second Test of the 2013 Ashes.

The dropping of Finn followed a first Test at Trent Bridge in which he returned figures of 2-117 off 25 overs, and was dealt with harshly by both Brad Haddin, and Australia's number-11 debutant, Ashton Agar. Finn seemed to have lost his rhythm and Alastair Cook seemed to have lost confidence in him. While he was selected to tour Australia the following winter, his bowling deteriorated to such a point that he lost all control and was sent home early to rebuild his action from scratch.

So Bresnan had his chance once more, and played in five of the next eight Tests in the back-to-back series against Australia in two stints punctuated by injury. While he bowled respectably enough in his three Tests in England, he appeared to have lost pace on his return from injury in Australia, and he was no longer making contributions with the bat which had been such an important second string to his bow just a year or two before.

The selectors had made two controversial inclusions, and one controversial omission, in the bowlers chosen to tour Australia in 2013/4. The former were Tremlett and Boyd Rankin. In picking Tremlett, then 32, and away from Test cricket with various injuries for much of the previous two years, the selectors were perhaps guilty of nostalgia, of looking to employ weapons that had proved effective in past battles when times had moved on. Tremlett had played a key role in England's victory over Australia in 2010/1, but his form with Surrey in 2013 was unspectacular. He could no longer bowl as fast as he managed in his prime – a fact the selectors might reasonably have been expected to have had intelligence of before they picked him. He was dropped after just one Test in Australia. Rankin appealed to the selectors because, like Broad, Finn and Tremlett, he was tall, and might be expected to unsettle the Australian batsmen with his bounce. Unlike Tremlett, he had had a successful season with Warwickshire in 2013 and he had impressed in the three one-day internationals in which he had bowled at the end of the season. He was picked for the fifth Test in Australia after Tremlett, Finn and Bresnan had fallen by the wayside. It was, alas, a somewhat shambolic debut, as he pulled up with cramp twice after the first balls of new spells and was forced to leave the field.

There was an alternative to Tremlett and Rankin in Onions. Injury, Finn and Bresnan had kept him out of the side since 2009/10, but he was the leading wicket taker in England in 2013 (10 more than Tremlett and Rankin combined). Although 31 by the end of the season, he was younger than Tremlett and only a little older than Rankin. A swing bowler rather than a 'hit the pitch' bowler, he offered a different style to the four taller bowlers who were in the event selected. It is difficult to understand why the selectors in this regard put all their eggs in one basket, and did not allow for the possibility that their initial bowling strategy might need amendment.

At the start of 2014, therefore, the selectors, needing to choose four seam bowlers because of the absence of a credible specialist spinner, had only Anderson and Broad inked in. Finn, Bresnan, Tremlett and Rankin were, in the light of their unhappy winter, at least for the moment out of the frame, while Ben Stokes, who had bowled well in Australia, was injured. During the course of the summer, England were to call on four bowlers in an attempt to find effective support for Anderson and Broad – Chris Jordan, Chris Woakes, Liam Plunkett, and a recovered Stokes. Jordan was picked on the back of successful one-day performances at the end of the Australia tour early in 2014, and again against Sri Lanka in the series which preceded the Test matches. Dropped after two unconvincing performances against Sri Lanka when Stokes was fit again at the start of the India Test, he found himself replacing Stokes two Tests later. He ended the season in the England side, but not securely so. Woakes had been around the one-day side for longer than Jordan – some three years – without cementing a place, and enjoying a solitary Test in unusual circumstances in 2013. He replaced the injured Plunkett for the third Test against India, but like Jordan failed to produce a totally convincing case for inclusion in the long run.

Plunkett's selection was much the most interesting of the four, for he had been out of Test cricket for seven years, and had made only two, one-off, one-day appearances since. He had done sufficiently well with Yorkshire in 2013 to win a place on the Lions tour to Sri Lanka and in that sense was on the selectors' radar at the start of the 2014 season. But essentially, he was a rare example in the 21st century of a player being picked on early season county form – in particular in relation to pace. After four Tests, including a five-for in the second, he succumbed to injury.

Stokes had been the one light in the darkness of England's disaster in Australia in 2013/4. 'The emergence of Stokes promised much' wrote *Wisden's* correspondent on the tour, George Dobell, in the 2015 edition, 'and suggested England might have found an all-rounder who could balance the side for a decade; he turned out to be the quickest bowler.' After recovering from injury, and having a short rehabilitative spell in county cricket, he was quickly drafted in to the England for the first Test against India, only to be dropped after one more. True, he batted spectacularly badly, with three ducks in succession. But because of the selection of Moeen Ali, he was now batting at eight. It was his bowling which was crucial, and he had bowled, at least statistically, better in his two Tests than had Jordan, who replaced him, in his two.

At the end of the summer of 2014, therefore, no third or fourth seamer had emerged pre-eminent. With Woakes injured and Finn having regressed again in the 2015 World Cup, Plunkett, Jordan, and Stokes once more, along with the uncapped Mark Wood, picked after a promising Lions tour of South Africa, were selected for the 2015 tour to the West Indies. Here they will be competing for the positions of third and fourth seamer – and perhaps, as the selectors must steel themselves to begin to contemplate, the eventual succession to James Anderson.

CHAPTER SEVEN

TAKING THE WICKETS – TWEAKERS

A Glut of Off Spinners

As far as England slow bowlers are concerned, the 1960s was the age of the off spinner. Three toured Australia in 1962/3 – David Allen, Fred Titmus and Ray Illingworth. Allen was the junior in terms of age, but departed for the Antipodes the senior in terms of Test experience. It was Titmus, however, who became the first choice in Australia and New Zealand – a decision no doubt influenced initially by his superior batting in the state games preceding the first Test. But it was his bowling in the eight Tests which cemented his superiority over Allen and Illingworth, collecting, as he did, 34 wickets. He followed this up with a highly successful tour of India the next winter – M J K Smith's tour report describes Titmus's bowling as being 'in a class of its own' – and South Africa the following winter. From 1962/3 to the end of the 1965/6 Ashes series with Australia, he played in 38 of England's 39 Tests and took 127 wickets at 28.5. But in this last series, Titmus went off the boil. *Wisden's* reporter, E M Wellings, wrote in the 1967 edition that 'as the tour progressed, his bowling became more and more defensive, his trajectory flatter and flatter.'

During the next two summers, he had to share the off-spinner's duties with Illingworth, who had had a disastrous tour of Australia in 1962/3, following on from an unsuccessful tour of the West Indies in 1959/60. Not only had he managed just one wicket in two Tests, he had not endeared himself to either manager or captain. In his tour report, Ted Dexter wrote of him 'he is selfish to a fault off the field...gave his best at all times on the field. Not quite good enough a bowler in hard wicket conditions'. Illingworth was not selected for any further overseas tours in the 60s (he was unavailable for South Africa in 1968/9), but his record in county cricket was hard to ignore, and he was the leading England wicket taker in the summer of 1967 against India and Pakistan. But it was Titmus (and the 21-year-old Pat Pocock – another off spinner) who were selected for the West Indies tour of 1967/8, and it was only Titmus's boating accident in which he lost four toes, apparently bringing his Test career to an end, which gave Illingworth a new chance. With Pocock judged to need more experience in county cricket, Illingworth was able to secure an unchallenged role as England's leading off spinner in the last two Tests of 1968.

As for Allen, he bowled well enough in his one Test in Australia in 1962/3, but for home Tests England could generally only accommodate one off spinner. Rather surprisingly, the selectors turned to Allen's Gloucestershire county colleague, John Mortimore, as second off spinner for the India tour of 1963/4, though Allen was back for the next two winter tours, and played crucial roles in England's two victories on them at Durban and Sydney. He might have been a better bet than Pocock for the West Indies in 1967/8 – though the selectors were undoubtedly influenced by the latter's outstanding season for Surrey, and the attractions of grooming a young player. Allen's last Test was thus the first in 1966, when he was a mere 30. Titmus and Illingworth were to continue to play for England into their 40s.

The options for a spinner to turn the ball in the other direction were, however, much more limited. In the mid-fifties, Tony Lock was England's outstanding slow left-arm bowler, but following doubts about the legality of his action, which led to his remodelling it, he was not selected by England during 1959 and 1960. After that, he was not the same bowler. He played in the 1963 series against the West Indies and, now 38, he flew out to replace Titmus following his accident in the West Indies in 1968. By then, he wintered playing for Western Australia, and he offered the rare advantage of an English player not on an MCC tour who was in match practice. But he made no significant contribution in either series as a bowler, although his batting was twice crucial. His ninth-wicket partnership of 89 with Phil Sharpe in the second innings of the Edgbaston Test of 1963, in which he scored his first Test fifty, helped set up England's victory; while without his 89 in Georgetown in 1968, England would surely have lost.

Of others, Norman Gifford was given a couple of tries in 1964; and Robin Hobbs, the leg spinner, was given a run in 1967. In the last 50 years, England's selectors have been desperate for a decent leg spinner, and have thrown caps at any prospect. Hobbs played seven Tests in all for England taking 12 wickets at an average of 40; a generation later, Ian Salisbury played 15 Tests taking 20 wickets at an average of 77; while in 2000, Chris Schofield played two Tests without taking a wicket at all. As recently as 2013/4 England selected Scott Borthwick as a wild card for the Sydney Test against Australia, where he was entrusted with just 13 of the 137 overs England bowled, and went for six an over. In all these cases, one senses a high degree of delusional thinking on the part of the selectors, egged on by a media which wishes but cannot will the success of wrist spin.

Deadly Derek

England were to find the slow (in fact rather brisk) left-armer they were looking for when they selected Derek Underwood in 1966. Credit should go to the selectors for picking him at the age of just 21 – though he was already into his fourth season as a regular for Kent. In his third Test match, against Pakistan at Trent Bridge in 1967, he demonstrated his lethality on a wet pitch by taking 5-22 in the second innings. It was not to be enough to win him a place on the winter tour to the West Indies which followed: Hobbs, along with Titmus and Pocock, was preferred. But the following summer, he produced a spectacular performance in the second innings of the Oval Test against Australia, when, on another drying pitch, he took 7-50 as England won by 226 runs with only minutes remaining, thus squaring the rubber. Underwood's reputation was now firmly established. He went on to play more Tests than any other England slow bowler before or since, and to be the most successful since Laker and Lock in the 1950s.

With Illingworth guaranteed a place from 1969 by virtue of being captain, and favouring a five-bowler attack with two spinners, the most enduring slow-bowling combination of the last 50 years was in place. Illingworth and Underwood played in 24 Tests together in which they took 162 wickets at an average of 25. The curiosity is that it was only 24 games. In nine Tests under Illingworth's captaincy, and one under Lewis's, Gifford was preferred to Underwood. There was no question that when the wicket was to his advantage, Underwood was devastating. In the first Test against New Zealand in 1970/1, for example, on a pitch described by *Wisden* in 1972 as 'damp and sparsely-grassed', he returned the extraordinary first-innings analysis of 11.6- (these were eight-ball overs) 7-12-6, and followed it up in the second innings with 32.3-7-85-6. But he was disproportionately less effective on good tracks. *Wisden's* correspondent on the 1970/1 tour, E M Wellings, argued in the 1972 edition that 'Underwood did little to develop the guile necessary on true batsmen's pitches, except where conditions were reasonably favourable to his bowling in Sydney. Even then he did not make the most of them, for when wickets did not come readily he tended to bowl faster and faster and dig the ball in more and more'.

The preference for Gifford over Underwood was controversial. 'It defies understanding that England should go to Old Trafford in unsettled weather without Underwood' wrote John Woodcock in *The Times* of the team selected for the first Test in 1972. In 26 Tests played between 1971 and 1973, Underwood played in 14 and Gifford in 13. Underwood took 46 wickets at an average of 33 and a strike rate of a wicket every 90 balls, while Gifford took 28 wickets at an average of 32 and a strike rate of 92. Underwood's figures include his 10-82 on the famous Headingley pitch of 1972 which had been affected by fungus fuserium, and reinforced his reputation for being 'deadly' in exploiting favourable conditions. But the selectors appear to have been right in regarding Gifford as at least comparable in other circumstances. From the end of the 1973 season until the end of the 1977 season, however, Underwood missed only two Tests, and these were ones in which no slow left armer was picked. At least in the first couple of years of this period, he may have been aided by the accession to the England captaincy of his county captain.

With Illingworth unavailable for the India and Pakistan tour of 1972/3, and dropped from the captaincy, and the team, for the 1973/4 tour to the Caribbean, the number-one off spinner role reverted to the now more mature Pocock. But his success was limited. The 1974 *Wisden* correspondent, Clive Taylor, wrote of his performance in the subcontinent that 'maybe because he tries to do too much with each delivery, his bowling often lacks steadiness'. For the 1974/5 tour, the selectors discarded Pocock and made the remarkable choice of the 41-year-old Titmus, after an absence from Test cricket of seven years. The decision was based on his county form in 1974 – he was fourth leading wicket taker – and the reputation he had gained on his first tour to Australia in 1962/3. As John Woodcock wrote in *The Times*, 'he will take to Australia

Unnatural Selection

a greater knowledge of spin bowling than anyone else playing the game today...and the Australians are never at their best against flighted off-spin'. The selectors, however, seemed to have ignored how limited Titmus's success was on his second tour of Australia in 1965/6, when his flight was less evident, and that he was already declining as a Test player even before his accident in 1968: in the 12 Tests leading up to then, he had taken just 24 wickets at 42. In his four Tests in Australia in 1974/5, he made little contribution, and his recall must be regarded as misjudged.

In 1975, the selectors reverted to youth ahead of experience by picking the young Philippe Edmonds at the age of 24. It was an instant success, as he took five Australian wickets in his first innings. But there was seldom a call for two slow left-armers in English conditions, and Underwood remained the undisputed first choice; by the time England toured again, to India in 1976/7, Edmonds' star had waned sufficiently for him to be passed over. The spinners picked for this tour were Underwood, Geoff Miller and Geoff Cope, the Yorkshire off spinner. Cope and Edmonds had both had similarly successful seasons in county cricket in 1976, and it is perhaps strange that Cope was preferred to the man who had had such a successful England debut. As it turned out, the decision was academic, as England – unusually in India – played just one specialist spinner, Underwood, throughout the series, with Tony Greig continuing the experiment begun in the West Indies in 1973/4 of abandoning his fast medium to bowl off breaks. Wisden's correspondent on that tour, Dicky Rutnagur, reported in the 1978 almanack that

> 'no longer could it be said of Underwood that he was principally a bowler for English conditions and that he had to be taken abroad "like an umbrella in case it rained". He exploited the conditions even more than India's own celebrated spinners. Accurate as always, he bowled with immense craft and wit – slower than before and with greater variation. That the Indians never mastered him is borne out by the fact that he claimed as many as nine wickets in the last Test.'

Underwood played a key role in England's victory over Australia in the second Test of the 1977 Ashes series, and his defection to Packer thereafter at his peak – he was 32 – was the greatest individual loss which England suffered as a result of World Series Cricket. It was hardly a surprise that he should be the first of the Packer players to return to the team after the ban ended in 1979, when alone among them he was recalled for the 1979/80 tour of Australia.

Coping with Rebel Tours

In the absence of Underwood, England's initial preferred spin attack comprised Edmonds and Miller. Edmonds re-established himself with 7-66 against Pakistan in Karachi on the 1977/8 tour, but his place was soon to come under pressure from his county colleague, John Emburey. Emburey joined Edmonds and Miller as the three spinners on the 1978/9 tour to Australia, and found a place in the Test side at the expense of Edmonds. It seems that Emburey's superior bowling to Edmonds against South Australia (6-115 against 1-146) in the game between the second and third Tests was the crucial moment. Edmonds was back for the summer of 1979 at Emburey's expense, but it was a lean one for him, and neither he nor Emburey were selected for the 1979/80 tour to Australia. No doubt, in Edmonds' case, his stormy relations with Mike Brearley contributed to the decision. But the main reason was Underwood's restored availability. Edmonds was not picked again for England until 1982, when Underwood – again – and Emburey left the frame, though he played only five more Tests until 1984/5.

As for Miller, he had an outstanding tour of Australia in 1978/9, but injury limited him to one Test on the 1979/80 tour. A strong county season in 1980 allowed Emburey to edge ahead of Miller, and indeed Underwood. In home Tests, and in the West Indies in 1980/1, Emburey was generally England's singleton spinner, supported, occasionally, by the part-time spin of Peter Willey. For India in 1981/2, his spin partner was Underwood.

When Underwood and Emburey chose to tour South Africa in 1982, England lost their first- and second-choice spin bowlers. But the damage was minimal. Underwood had been a less effective bowler from 1979/80 and in 1980 he was dropped, having previously missed only two Tests for which he was available since 1973. He was recalled for the India tour of 1981/2 on the basis of his successes there in 1976/7 but he was not to repeat them. He took only 10 wickets in the six-Test series, though he did take eight in the following Test against Sri Lanka, his last. In all, he played in 12 Tests after his return from World Series Cricket, taking 32 wickets at an average of 34 and a strike rate of 90, compared with 265 at an average of 25 and a strike rate of 72 in his previous 74. Emburey had also failed to sustain his early promise, and by the end of the India/Sri Lanka series of 1981/2, his career-Test bowling record was inferior to that of both Miller and Edmonds, who had played similar numbers of matches.

In Underwood's and Emburey's absence, Edmonds and Miller had the opportunity to re-establish their places in the England side, but they did not manage to do so. Edmonds was dropped after just three Tests for the 33-year-old off spinner, Eddie Hemmings who went on to be selected along with Miller, and a third off spinner, Vic Marks, for the tour of Australia in 1982/3. Edmonds was picked only twice more until the India tour of 1984/5. In county cricket in 1982 and 1983, he had been by some way the most successful slow bowler eligible to play for England, but it seems that Bob Willis was unable, any more than Brearley, to establish the necessary rapport with the iconoclastic Edmonds. It was left to the period of David Gower's captaincy for Edmonds to flourish in the England team.

 It is something of a mystery why Miller played only one more Test after 1982/3. He had had a more than reasonable tour of Australia, but Marks was preferred to him as the off spinner for the 1983/4 tours to New Zealand and Pakistan – despite having himself had a poor time the previous winter. Peter May, the chairman of selectors, in announcing the 1983/4 party, referred to the need for a number seven, and of Miller's not having quite filled the role in Australia. The inference is that Marks was preferred because of his superior batting, but it was far from clear that his batting was indeed superior. In four first-class games in Australia, Marks' top score had been 13, and in first-class cricket in 1983, Marks averaged 22 to Miller's 30. As it turned out, Marks scored three fifties in the Test series against Pakistan, so maybe May had seen something in him beyond the crude statistics. But Marks's bowling did not pass muster, and he was not picked for the Test side again. For the 1984/5 tour to India, Pocock was chosen instead of Miller. In 1984, Miller had been recalled to the Test team against the powerful West Indies. In two Tests, he contributed little, and was dropped. Pocock came back for the last two Tests against West Indies, and that against Sri Lanka which followed. He was by now 37, a veteran of 17 Tests in which he had taken just 43 wickets at an average of 43. True, he had an excellent season in county cricket in 1984, but less so than Miller, and he played a useful containing role in the three Tests – though 7-298 (off 123 overs) was unspectacular. It is difficult not to conclude that a man six years younger with a superior Test record and a vastly more capable batsman would have been the better choice. As it was, Pocock's 13 wickets in India came at 50 apiece.

Edmonds, recalled for the India tour where he bowled well (the 1986 *Wisden* described his Test bowling average of 42 as 'a travesty of justice') was now unchallenged as England's premier slow left-armer and played in 28 of England's 32 Tests from the start of that series. Emburey, available for selection once more from the start of the 1985 series, was at once recalled, and played in 38 of England's next 44 Tests. It was the first period of real stability in England's selection of slow bowlers since Underwood and Illingworth. But it was not a particularly successful pairing. In Edmonds' last 28 Tests, he took 66 wickets at 38; in his 38 Tests between his two South Africa bans (itself a singular record) Emburey took 82 wickets at 42.

That the selectors persevered with Edmonds and Emburey was largely because there was no other spinner challenging them. They were the stand-out spinners in county cricket until Edmonds' retirement in 1987. Underwood and Pocock were too old to be seriously considered after 1985. Nick Cook and Marks, who had had brief appearances earlier in the decade, did not develop. Hemmings had some good seasons, but failed to catch the selectors' eye. And while they had modest strike rates, Edmonds and Emburey were consistently tight – a factor which contributed significantly to both the Ashes victories of 1985 and 1986/7. Emburey's position as England's vice-captain from 1986/7 probably helped his cause – particularly when it came to the 1987/8 tour-party selection, after he had gone four Tests the previous summer without taking a wicket.

With Edmonds' retirement at the end of 1987, and Emburey's unavailability from the end of 1989, England were desperate for a new generation of spinners. Initially, however, they looked to the past. Cook and Hemmings were recalled – the former for three Tests over the period 1987/8 to 1989, the latter for 11 Tests between 1987/8 and 1990/1. John

Childs, the Essex left-arm spinner, played two Tests in 1988 – at 36 the oldest debutant in the last 50 years. But it was not until 1990/1 that England selected a young spinner.

The Tufnell Era

Phil Tufnell was chosen to tour Australia at the age of 24 and made his Test debut in Melbourne. *Wisden's* correspondent, John Thicknesse, reported in the 1992 edition that he 'provided the brightest hope for the future with his left arm spin...he looked in four Tests to be England's slowest spinner since Fred Titmus, at his best when tossing the ball up with a man out straight'. But this was an unhappy tour for Tufnell. He fielded badly, and the Australian crowds barracked him mercilessly. He also failed to establish a rapport with his captain, and was reprimanded by him in one of the Tests when he got involved in a spat with the umpire after an appeal had been turned down. Along with Gower, Tufnell was no doubt one of those with whose attitude Gooch was outspokenly unhappy at his press conference after the Perth Test. Richard Illingworth was preferred in those two of the first four Tests of the 1991 series in which England did not choose an all-seam attack. It was not a selection which was widely approved. In *The Times*, Alan Lee wrote that 'for the time being, Tufnell remains the best option – maverick, certainly, but a bowler of imagination to challenge the batsman rather than bore him'. Of Tufnell's recall for the final Test of the series, Lee wrote:

> 'Tufnell's comeback was inevitable on form...it could only be vetoed if the corrective isolation theory, employed after his eccentric behaviour on tour, had been taken to vindictive and self-defeating extremes. A chain smoker with stubble, a rebel with insolent eyes and barrow boy banter, Tufnell is, most relevantly, a highly gifted spin bowler whom John Emburey now believes to be the best in the country. If his confidence and variety is encouraged he could trouble the West Indian batsmen sorely.'

He did. In the final Test against West Indies in 1991, he bowled England to victory with 6-25 in the first innings, and embarked on a remarkable spell of five Tests in which he took 28 wickets. Appendicitis kept him out of the early Tests in 1992, and when he returned, the magic seemed to have gone. Dropped after the second Test of 1993, he played only 13 times between then and his recall for the Oval Test of 1997. Personal problems kept him out of county cricket for the first half of 1994, but he was selected for the 1994/5 tour to Australia. But although he played in four out of five Tests, he met with little success, and once again his behaviour gave cause for concern. Commenting on his bowling in Melbourne, Ray Illingworth wrote that he had become too defensive:

> 'even when a new batsman came in, Tufnell bowled over the wicket to him, and that is a tactic which should be used only sparingly, and when things are not working. I thought Tufnell had a disappointing game, because he did not spin it a lot on a surface on which Hick showed it would turn.'

Of his tour generally, Illingworth commented that he 'did a reasonable job and the captain thinks a lot of him, but he still has a lot of work to do on his general attitude. He worked hard at his fielding, but I sense that he has gone back a bit as a Test bowler, mainly because he does not spin it a great deal.'

Tufnell did not play for England again until the 1996/7 tours to Zimbabwe and New Zealand, and while he played in all five Tests with reasonable success, Robert Croft was deemed to have performed the better of the two, and filled the one spinner's place for the first five Tests of 1997. Tufnell's recall for the Oval Test (again) in 1997 was, however, a selectorial triumph. His 11-93 in England's nail-biting victory over Australia won him the man of the match award and a place in the touring party to the Caribbean the following winter. It was not, however, the breakthrough which England supporters had been willing. He did not take another five-for, and in 14 more Tests spread over four years, took just 28 more wickets at 49. That he played as many as this was down to the confidence which Nasser Hussain, as England captain from 1999, had in him. Hussain persuaded the selectors to pick Tufnell for the tour to South Africa in 1999/2000, against the judgement of the coach, Duncan Fletcher, who considered that Ashley Giles represented a better 'all-round package'. Tufnell's failure to take any wickets on a fifth-day pitch at Durban as South Africa held out for a draw seems to have been a defining moment. Fletcher was keen for bowlers to contribute

Unnatural Selection

significantly with the bat or in the field as well as with the ball: if Tufnell was not going to do this his bowling needed to be a head in front of any challenger – and by 1999 it was not.

A measure of the extent of the selectors' concern about Tufnell's confidence and attitude, his batting and fielding, and his underlying talent as a spinner, was who they were willing to pick ahead of him. For the 1992/3 tour to India and Sri Lanka, John Emburey was recalled. Even more than the recall of Gatting, also made available by the lifting of the ban on those who had toured South Africa in 1989/90, it reflected a failure to recognise his deteriorating Test performances in the period leading up to 1989. He was now 40, and as the experience of Illingworth, Titmus and Pocock had all shown, he was unlikely to be as good a bowler as he had been a decade earlier despite a very strong performance for Middlesex in 1992. After an undistinguished series, he was dropped, only to be recalled for the fifth Test against Australia in 1993. This was to be his last. He ended his career with the second-highest bowling average (38) (Ashley Giles averaged over 40) and lowest strike rate (105) of any specialist bowler to have represented England in more than 25 Tests in the last half-century.

Also on the 1992/3 tour was the leg spinner Salisbury – but as a net bowler, not a full member of the party. Bizarrely, his performance in the nets led to his being selected for the first Test ahead of Tufnell and Emburey. In a career of just 15 Tests, Salisbury was selected and then dropped on eight separate occasions. In the era of Shane Warne, England were desperate to have a match-winning leg spinner of their own, even though the repeated evidence of Salisbury was that he could not deliver at Test level. Each time he was recalled he demonstrated his limitations, but then the selectors' memories faded, and he was briefly back again.

England might have been better off to have persevered with the less exciting but more reliable off spinner Peter Such or slow left-armer Richard Illingworth. Starting his career with six wickets in an innings against Australia, Such played in five Tests in the summer of 1993 as England's first choice spinner, only to lose out to Tufnell and Salisbury for the 1993/4 tour to the West Indies. Atherton himself has written that this was a 'glaring error' on his part:

'Peter Such...had been our best spinner throughout the summer against Australia. My thinking was fine – I viewed spin as an attacking option and felt Tufnell and Salisbury would have a better chance of winning matches. But I did not envisage the phalanx of left handers who would play against us and I soon regretted Such's omission.'

Such was back for the first half of the summer of 1994, but was dropped after three Tests – for Salisbury. Raymond Illingworth, it seemed, wanted a more attacking spinner than Such was proving to be. Despite consistent performances in county cricket, and the continuing failures of the alternatives, it was to be 1998/9, and then only briefly, before Such was back in the England frame.

Richard Illingworth, who played nine Tests in 1991 and 1995/6, also suffered from being characterised as a defensive bowler, but had a better career average and indeed strike rate than Tufnell and Salisbury ended up with. After a very respectable tour of South Africa in 1995/6, he was dropped for slow left-armer Min Patel at the start of 1996. Ray Illingworth concedes that his namesake 'was probably unlucky to miss out', but says 'it was decided to have a look at Min Patel'. Richard Illingworth was never picked for England again, while Patel was dropped after a couple of Tests, also never to return.

The debutant at the end of the 1996 series was Croft, the Glamorgan off spinner. He was given a more extended run by the selectors, playing in 14 of England's next 19 Tests, being temporarily supplanted by Tufnell after his dramatic contribution to England's victory against Australia after his recall at the end of 1997. Like so many England spin bowlers chosen in the 80s and 90s, he could not sustain a good start to his international career, and after failing to take a wicket in the first three Tests against South Africa in 1998, he was replaced by Salisbury, who failed to take a wicket in the last two! The selectors reverted to Such for the Australia tour of 1998/9, and he took 11 wickets in two Tests. But with the appointment of Hussain as captain, Tufnell reverted, for a period, to being England's number-one spinner, and Such did not even make it to South Africa the following winter as second spinner. Instead the selectors skipped a generation, and picked the 20-year-old Graeme Swann. Not least of the reasons for preferring Swann was his potential as a batsman. The selectors could not contemplate two such undisputed number 11s as Tufnell and Such batting in the same side, especially as it would have required Darren Gough, Andrew Caddick or, heaven forbid, Alan Mullally batting at eight or nine.

But Swann notoriously made a bad impression in the changing room on that tour; and as we have seen, Hussain and Fletcher all but gave up on Tufnell. Logically enough, the selectors next point of call was the spinners on the 'A' team tour to Bangladesh and New Zealand in 1999/2000, Mike Davies and Chris Schofield, the latter of whom had been the leading wicket-taker on the tour. *Wisden's* Ralph Dellor was impressed: 'he started taking [wickets] on turning pitches in Bangladesh and continued on seamers' pitches in New Zealand ....he did more than enough to warrant his subsequent inclusion among the 12 players awarded ECB central contracts, and could develop into a formidable player'. Fletcher has written:

> Gatting [the 'A' team tour manager] was certain about leg spinner Chris Schofield – whom I had pushed to be included on that A tour because we needed to have a look at him in our desperate search for a spinner. Gatting said he was the future of England cricket. As a result we offered him a central contract; it was the gravest of errors.'

Picked for two Tests against Zimbabwe, in only one of which he was required to bowl, he impressed Hussain neither as a leg spinner nor an individual, and he was not selected again.

From Giles to Swann

The selectors were now really struggling. In the two Tests against West Indies in 2000 in which a spinner was played, the choice fell on Croft, but for the winter tour, England looked back to Salisbury again and forward to Giles. Giles had played in one Test in the 1998 series, where he was the only England spinner that summer to take a Test wicket – but it was only one. He had also been around the England one-day squad since 1997, though had only played in five internationals. Now 27, he had had a good county season in 2000 as a bowler, but what distinguished him from his competitors – notably Tufnell – was his batting: he averaged 40 in first-class cricket in 2000, and if he was not going to excel as a bowler, at least he could contribute with the bat. Giles was to go on six successive tours for England, and was from 2000/1 usually England's first-choice spinner when fit. But there were exceptions: for example, for the Oval Test of 2001, Tufnell was recalled to repeat his heroics of 1991 and 1997: he took 1-174!

Fletcher was a great fan of Giles, 'the most professional cricketer anyone could wish to have in their side', and kept faith with him even when he was not taking wickets. By the middle of the summer of 2004, after 36 Tests, he was averaging 40 with the ball, mitigated a little by a batting average of 20. Twenty-two wickets in the series against West Indies in the second half of the summer cemented his place, and he was a key member of the Ashes winning side of 2005. Here, however, it was his batting which made the impact – steering England to victory at Trent Bridge by three wickets after coming in at 111-6 needing 129; and scoring 59 as England secured a draw at the Oval.

Giles left the 2005/6 tour to Pakistan prematurely with an injury which was to keep him out of cricket for the duration of the following summer. His replacement for the tour to India which followed was the 23-year-old Monty Panesar. His talent had been recognised as early as 2002/3, when he toured Sri Lanka with the England Academy, though he had not been on any 'A' tours since, and he had had a good county season in 2005. Fletcher would have preferred the off spinner Alex Loudon, who was thought to have a doosra, and felt that Panesar's selection was driven by media pressure. He played in all three Tests alongside either Ian Blackwell or Shaun Udal. In the third, which England won, Udal had out-bowled Panesar, and Fletcher wanted Udal to play ahead of Panesar in 2006. But he was outvoted, and in that summer Panesar took 27 wickets at 27, and was an automatic choice for the winter tour to Australia which followed. What was less obvious was that Giles should accompany him. He had played no first-class cricket since November 2005, and in his last 12 Tests prior to his injury had taken just 24 wickets at 53. But nobody else was demanding selection. Of those who had been in India, Udal was now 37 and had had a modest season in county cricket, while Blackwell too had been injured for most of 2006.

The shock was that Giles should be preferred ahead of Panesar for the first Test of the Ashes series. It was the most contentious selection of Fletcher's time as England coach. He had been less impressed than others with Panesar's summer in 2006. He did not think that Panesar had an arm ball and – in a familiar reprise of the debates over Tufnell

– was intolerant of Panesar's limitations as a batsman and fielder. He was insistent that none of Mathew Hoggard, Steve Harmison or Jimmy Anderson – England's three faster bowlers alongside Andrew Flintoff – could credibly bat at 8, as one would have to if Panesar were included. He also felt that Giles had bowled better than Panesar in the warm-up games. In addition, Fletcher saw in Giles a more aggressive character than Panesar, which he judged important. The captain and, it seems, the other selectors, Graveney and Miller (when consulted before the tour) had also favoured Giles. And Fletcher has written that when he argued for Panesar to come in for the second Test at Adelaide, as a second spinner alongside Giles, he had no support from the tour management committee. Most of the media were outraged by the preference for Giles ahead of Panesar, a decision which of course accompanied the only slightly less controversial reinstatement of Geraint Jones for Chris Read as wicket-keeper (see Chapter 3). *Wisden's* correspondent, Simon Briggs, wrote in 2008 derisively of Fletcher's 'pathological distrust of spinners who cannot also knit, juggle and tap dance'.

Fletcher's arguments were perfectly logical. Unfortunately, however, events turned out not to support his logic. In the first two Tests, Giles's figures were 3-262, he dropped a vital catch in the second when his fielding had been an important discriminator between him and his rival, and while he scored some runs in his first three innings, he failed to score in the second innings of the second Test as Warne bowled Australia to victory on the final day. He was unsurprisingly dropped for the third Test, just before his wife's illness forced him to return home early anyway. He did not play Test cricket again. Panesar came back into the side, and immediately took 5-92 in the first innings of the third Test.

Panesar now embarked on a remarkable unbroken run of 27 Tests as England's first-choice spinner during which he took 89 wickets and probably bowled more consistently than any other England spinner since Underwood. But there was a significant opportunity cost in terms of the strength of England's lower-order batting until Stuart Broad emerged in New Zealand in 2007/8. England's number eights were successively Sajid Mahmood, Liam Plunkett, Hoggard, Chris Tremlett and Ryan Sidebottom. None of England's scheduled bottom four in the post-Giles era, excluding instances when the batting order was distorted by a night-watchman, scored a fifty until Broad in 2008.

The new England second spinner who emerged to fill the vacuum created by the demise of Giles was Swann. It had appeared that he was consigned to county obscurity like three others who were part of the new-look England party of 1999/2000 – Chris Adams, Darren Maddy and Gavin Hamilton. Until 2007, he had done little in county cricket to suggest he was a contender for a Test place, and even in 2007 his first-class bowling performance had been solid rather than spectacular. He was picked for the Sri Lanka tour of 2007/8 principally for the one-day internationals, where his aggressive batting enabled him to bring something to the party which Panesar, who had been a regular member of England's one-day side since the previous winter, could not. He played an important role in England's victory in the matches against Sri Lanka, and supplanted Panesar as England's first-choice limited-overs spinner. His Test debut, however, had to wait until England decided to play two spinners, which was not until the India tour in 2008/9. Swann's figures in two Tests were marginally superior to Panesar's, but Panesar remained first choice for the first two Tests against West Indies in 2008/9.

The decision to replace Panesar with Swann for the third Test of that series was by no means obvious. It could hardly have been on the basis of Panesar's performance in the previous Test, as that had lasted a mere 1.4 overs before being abandoned due to the dangerous condition of the pitch and outfield. It is true that Panesar's bowling over the previous year had deteriorated and he had made little impact in the first Test of the series. It was, however, a highly-successful decision. Swann took five wickets in the first innings of the third Test, and another five in West Indies only innings, of 749, of the fourth. He subsequently played in every England Test side, apart from the second Test against South Africa in 2012, and three others for which he was injured, until his abrupt retirement at the end of 2013. His strike rate of 60 was unmatched by any England slow bowler of the past 50 years, and his average of 29 bettered only by Underwood; in addition, he enjoyed a batting average higher than any other front-line spin bowler since Illingworth.

Panesar now became England's second-choice spinner. But the post-Fletcher regime has remained sensitive to the impact on the lower-order batting of including Panesar in the side, and for the second Test in Sri Lanka in 2011/2 was willing to rely on Patel as a second spinner. There was some speculation as to whether Panesar would be selected for the touring party to India in 2012/3 at all, and that England would

Unnatural Selection

prefer James Tredwell, who played as England's specialist spinner in the one-day internationals when Swann was injured. But his first-class bowling performance in 2012 could not compare with Panesar, and his superior batting (and fielding) was insufficient to overcome this deficit. Bowling alongside Swann in three of the four Tests in India, Panesar was one of the great success stories in England's first series win in that country since 1984/5.

Alas, disaster was to follow this triumph. First, in Swann's absence injured, Panesar had a distinctly ordinary tour of New Zealand early in 2013. Then, in the summer of 2013 he was dropped and then sacked by Sussex following a drunken and unsavoury incident in Brighton. The 2014 Wisden reported that it was clear even before then that Ed Joyce, Sussex's captain, had lost confidence in Panesar. 'It was suggested by those closest to the dressing room that missing out on the Ashes Tests was the main source of Panesar's unhappiness, which manifested itself in petulance on the field and a discordant attitude off it'. Panesar moved on to Essex and, unsurprisingly, England looked elsewhere when seeking a second spinner for the final Test of the 2013 summer. Thus they picked the young slow left-armer Simon Kerrigan. But Kerrigan proved unable to bowl at Test level with the control he exhibited in county games; his eight overs went for 53 runs, and England reverted to Panesar for the winter tour down under.

The selectors might have regarded the choice of second spinner for Australia to be a matter of largely academic importance. Swann's place in the side was not in doubt, and England had not played two spinners in a side for a Test in Australia since 1990/1. Not only did England choose to do precisely this for the second Test of the series, but following the third game Swann announced his retirement.

To the outside world, at least, this thunderbolt came from a pretty clear blue sky. Swann had been England's leading wicket-taker in the 2013 series against Australia. In the first three Tests of the following series, however, Swann was treated with dismissive disrespect by the Australian batsmen, as a result of which he achieved neither penetration nor control. It is for debate as to whether the decision was precipitate – any bowler can have three bad Tests, and Swann's decline was at least in part due to the failure of England's batsmen to impose any sort of scoreboard pressure on their opponents in the way that they had managed in previous years. Swann himself, however, was clear that his elbow, which had been subject to two operations, prevented him from imparting the spin which he needed to achieve the success to which he had become accustomed. There was also debate as to whether it was appropriate for a player to retire in mid-series. Some saw his decision as that of a rat leaving a sinking ship. Certainly it was unprecedented. And it added to the woes of England as they struggled to avoid a 5-0 whitewash.

It was far from clear that Panesar would be a superior option to a diminished Swann. He had been equally unsuccessful when playing alongside Swann in the second Test, and was no more so when, inevitably, he replaced Swann for the fourth Test Puzzlingly, Cook was reluctant to use him in the fourth innings of the match until Australia were well set for victory chasing 230. But it remains extraordinary that the selectors looked outside the touring party for a spinner for the fifth Test, and one can only assume – not least against the background of Panesar's earlier difficulties with Sussex, and subsequent ones with Essex – that perceived problems in attitudes off the field played a significant part in his demise.

Thus it was that Tredwell, an accomplished off spinner in England's one-day squad, and Scott Borthwick, a young leg spinning all-rounder playing grade cricket in Australia, were called up into the Test squad. While Tredwell might have been a relatively safe selection for the fifth Test, it was Borthwick who was chosen. It was the strangest decision since Darren Pattinson in 2008. Borthwick had successfully worked his way up Durham's batting order from eight to three during 2013 but he had made little progress as a leg spinner and finished bottom of Durham's bowling averages with just 34 wickets. Throwing a young bowler with such limited credentials into an England side reeling 4-0 down for what could well be a singleton Test, especially after the Kerrigan experience, is very hard to understand. It was, perhaps, emblematic of the extent to which the wheels were coming off the wagon towards the end of that disastrous tour.

The selectors had no more difficult problem than that of picking one or more spinners for most of the last 50 years. England have only produced two world-class slow bowlers in this period – Underwood and Swann. Between them, the selectors struggled to find any spinner who was consistently effective. Frustratingly for them, those that showed early promise almost always failed to develop. There were 11 spinners who represented England between 1979 – when Underwood was lost to Packer – and 2008 – when Swann made his debut, and who played in more than 10 Tests: Cook, Edmonds, Emburey, Giles, Hemmings, Miller, Panesar, Pocock, Salisbury, Such, and Tufnell. Of these, only Hemmings and Giles were more successful in the second halves of their careers. In the cases of Miller, Such and Tufnell, the difference between the halves is marginal. In the other six cases, the first half was significantly better than the second. In the instances of Pocock and Emburey, this in part reflected the selectors' decision to recall them in the autumn of their careers, but in all cases it was evidence of the failure of potential to be realized in the cricketing trade in which increasing experience at Test level might have been expected to deliver the greatest returns. Faced with the absence of an outstanding spinner, it is perhaps understandable that they settled in many instances for someone economical like Emburey or Giles, at least keeping reasonable control while the faster bowlers were rotated, and making a contribution with the bat. And it was, of course, this latter consideration which determined England's choice of Moeen Ali for the 2014 summer.

England Test Series 1962/3-2014

Year	Opponents	Won	Lost	Drawn	Captain
1962/3	Australia	1	1	3	Dexter
	New Zealand	3	0	0	Dexter
1963	West Indies	1	3	1	Dexter
1963/4	India	0	0	5	Smith
1964	Australia	0	1	3	Dexter
1964/5	South Africa	1	0	4	Smith
1965	New Zealand	3	0	0	Smith
	South Africa	0	1	2	Smith
1965/6	Australia	1	1	3	Smith
	New Zealand	0	0	3	Smith
1966	West Indies	1	3	1	Smith/Cowdrey/Close
1967	India	3	0	0	Close
	Pakistan	2	0	1	Close
1967/8	West Indies	1	0	4	Cowdrey
1968	Australia	1	1	3	Cowdrey/Graveney
1968/9	Pakistan	0	0	3	Cowdrey
1969	West Indies	2	0	1	Illingworth
	New Zealand	2	0	1	Illingworth
1970/1	Australia	2	0	4	Illingworth
	New Zealand	1	0	1	Illingworth
1971	Pakistan	1	0	2	Illingworth
	India	0	1	2	Illingworth
1972	Australia	2	2	1	Illingworth
1972/3	India	1	2	2	Lewis
	Pakistan	0	0	3	Lewis
1973	New Zealand	2	0	1	Illingworth
	West Indies	0	2	1	Illingworth
1973/4	West Indies	1	1	3	Denness
1974	India	3	0	0	Denness
	Pakistan	0	0	3	Denness
1974/5	Australia	1	4	1	Denness/Edrich
	New Zealand	1	0	1	Denness
1975	Australia	0	1	3	Denness/Greig
1976	West Indies	0	3	2	Greig
1976/7	India	3	1	1	Greig
	Australia	0	1	0	Greig
1977	Australia	3	0	2	Brearley

England Test Series 1962/3-2014

Year	Opponents	Won	Lost	Drawn	Lost
1977/8	Pakistan	0	0	3	Brearley/Boycott
	New Zealand	1	1	1	Boycott
1978	Pakistan	2	0	1	Brearley
	New Zealand	3	0	0	Brearley
1978/9	Australia	5	1	0	Brearley
1979	India	1	0	3	Brearley
1979/0	Australia	0	3	0	Brearley
	India	1	0	0	Brearley
1980	West Indies	0	1	4	Botham
	Australia	0	0	1	Botham
1980/1	West Indies	0	2	2	Botham
1981	Australia	3	1	2	Botham/Brearley
1981/2	India	0	1	5	Fletcher
	Sri Lanka	1	0	0	Fletcher
1982	India	1	0	2	Willis
	Pakistan	2	1	0	Willis/Gower
1982/3	Australia	1	2	2	Willis
1983	New Zealand	3	1	0	Willis
1983/4	New Zealand	0	1	2	Willis
	Pakistan	0	1	2	Gower
1984	West Indies	0	5	0	Gower
	Sri Lanka	0	0	1	Gower
1984/5	India	2	1	2	Gower
1985	Australia	3	1	2	Gower
1985/6	West Indies	0	5	0	Gower
1986	India	0	2	1	Gower/Gatting
	New Zealand	0	1	2	Gatting
1986/7	Australia	2	1	2	Gatting
1987	Pakistan	0	1	4	Gatting
1987/8	Pakistan	0	1	2	Gatting
	Australia	0	0	1	Gatting
	New Zealand	0	0	3	Gatting
1988	West Indies	0	4	1	Gatting/Emburey/Cowdrey/Gooch
	Sri Lanka	1	0	0	Gooch
1989	Australia	0	4	2	Gower
1989/0	West Indies	1	2	1	Gooch/Lamb
1990	New Zealand	1	0	2	Gooch

England Test Series 1962/3-2014

Year	Opponents	Won	Lost	Drawn	Captain
	India	1	0	2	Gooch
1990/1	Australia	0	3	2	Gooch/Lamb
1991	West Indies	2	2	1	Gooch
	Sri Lanka	1	0	0	Gooch
1991/2	New Zealand	2	0	1	Gooch
1992	Pakistan	1	2	2	Gooch
1992/3	India	0	3	0	Gooch/Stewart
	Sri Lanka	0	1	0	Stewart
1993	Australia	1	4	1	Gooch/Atherton
1993/4	West Indies	1	3	1	Atherton
1994	New Zealand	1	0	2	Atherton
	South Africa	1	1	1	Atherton
1994/5	Australia	1	3	1	Atherton
1995	West Indies	2	2	2	Atherton
1995/6	South Africa	0	1	4	Atherton
1996	India	1	0	2	Atherton
	Pakistan	0	2	1	Atherton
1996/7	Zimbabwe	0	0	2	Atherton
	New Zealand	2	0	1	Atherton
1997	Australia	2	3	1	Atherton
1997/8	West Indies	1	3	2	Atherton
1998	South Africa	2	1	2	Stewart
	Sri Lanka	0	1	0	Stewart
1998/9	Australia	1	3	1	Stewart
1999	New Zealand	1	2	1	Hussain/Butcher
1999/0	South Africa	1	2	2	Hussain
2000	Zimbabwe	1	0	1	Hussain
	West Indies	3	1	1	Hussain/Stewart
2000/1	Pakistan	1	0	2	Hussain
	Sri Lanka	2	1	0	Hussain
2001	Pakistan	1	1	0	Hussain/Stewart
	Australia	1	4	0	Hussain/Atherton
2001/2	India	0	1	2	Hussain
	New Zealand	1	1	1	Hussain
2002	Sri Lanka	2	0	1	Hussain
	India	1	1	2	Hussain
2002/3	Australia	1	4	0	Hussain

England Test Series 1962/3-2014

Year	Opponents	Won	Lost	Drawn	Lost
2003	Zimbabwe	2	0	0	Hussain
	South Africa	2	2	1	Hussain/Vaughan
2003/4	Bangladesh	2	0	0	Vaughan
	Sri Lanka	0	1	2	Vaughan
	West Indies	3	0	1	Vaughan
2004	New Zealand	3	0	0	Vaughan/Trescothick
	West Indies	4	0	0	Vaughan
2004/5	South Africa	2	1	2	Vaughan
2005	Bangladesh	2	0	0	Vaughan
	Australia	2	1	2	Vaughan
2005/6	Pakistan	0	2	1	Vaughan/Trescothick
	India	1	1	1	Flintoff
2006	Sri Lanka	1	1	1	Flintoff
	Pakistan	3	0	1	Strauss
2006/7	Australia	0	5	0	Flintoff
2007	West Indies	3	0	1	Vaughan/Strauss
	India	0	1	2	Vaughan
2007/8	Sri Lanka	0	1	2	Vaughan
	New Zealand	2	1	0	Vaughan
2008	New Zealand	2	0	1	Vaughan
	South Africa	1	2	1	Vaughan/Pietersen
2008/9	India	0	1	1	Pietersen
	West Indies	0	1	4	Strauss
2009	West Indies	2	0	0	Strauss
	Australia	2	1	2	Strauss
2009/0	South Africa	1	1	2	Strauss
	Bangladesh	2	0	0	Cook
2010	Bangladesh	2	0	0	Strauss
	Pakistan	3	1	0	Strauss
2010/1	Australia	3	1	1	Strauss
2011	Sri Lanka	1	0	2	Strauss
	India	4	0	0	Strauss
2011/2	Pakistan	0	3	0	Strauss
	Sri Lanka	1	1	0	Strauss
2012	West Indies	2	0	1	Strauss
	South Africa	0	2	1	Strauss
2012/3	India	2	1	1	Cook

England Test Series 1962/3-2014

Year	Opponents	Won	Lost	Drawn	Captain
	New Zealand	0	0	3	Cook
2013	New Zealand	2	0	0	Cook
	Australia	3	0	2	Cook
2013/14	Australia	0	5	0	Cook
2014	Sri Lanka	0	1	1	Cook
	India	3	1	1	Cook

England Test Batting Averages 1962/3-2014

Player	Span	Mat	Inns	NO	Runs	HS	Ave	100	50	0
CJ Adams	1999-2000	5	8	0	104	31	13.00	0	0	0
U Afzaal	2001-2001	3	6	1	83	54	16.60	0	1	0
JP Agnew	1984-1985	3	4	3	10	5	10.00	0	0	0
Kabir Ali	2003-2003	1	2	0	10	9	5.00	0	0	0
MM Ali	2014-2014	7	10	1	286	108*	31.77	1	0	0
DA Allen	1960-1966	39	51	15	918	88	25.50	0	5	4
PJW Allott	1981-1985	13	18	3	213	52*	14.20	0	1	2
TR Ambrose	2008-2009	11	16	1	447	102	29.80	1	3	2
DL Amiss	1966-1977	50	88	10	3612	262*	46.30	11	11	10
JM Anderson	2003-2014	99	135	48	949	81	10.90	0	1	15
KV Andrew	1954-1963	2	4	1	29	15	9.66	0	0	0
GG Arnold	1967-1975	34	46	11	421	59	12.02	0	1	5
MA Atherton	1989-2001	115	212	7	7728	185*	37.69	16	46	20
CWJ Athey	1980-1988	23	41	1	919	123	22.97	1	4	2
RJ Bailey	1988-1990	4	8	0	119	43	14.87	0	0	2
DL Bairstow	1979-1981	4	7	1	125	59	20.83	0	1	1
JM Bairstow	2012-2014	14	24	2	593	95	26.95	0	4	1
JC Balderstone	1976-1976	2	4	0	39	35	9.75	0	0	2
GS Ballance	2014-2014	8	13	1	729	156	60.75	3	3	1
RW Barber	1960-1968	28	45	3	1495	185	35.59	1	9	1
GD Barlow	1976-1977	3	5	1	17	7*	4.25	0	0	1
KJ Barnett	1988-1989	4	7	0	207	80	29.57	0	2	1
KF Barrington	1955-1968	82	131	15	6806	256	58.67	20	35	5
GJ Batty	2003-2005	7	8	1	144	38	20.57	0	0	1
IR Bell	2004-2014	105	181	22	7156	235	45.00	21	42	11
JE Benjamin	1994-1994	1	1	0	0	0	0.00	0	0	1
MR Benson	1986-1986	1	2	0	51	30	25.50	0	0	0
MP Bicknell	1993-2003	4	7	0	45	15	6.42	0	0	3
JG Binks	1964-1964	2	4	0	91	55	22.75	0	1	0
J Birkenshaw	1973-1974	5	7	0	148	64	21.14	0	1	1
ID Blackwell	2006-2006	1	1	0	4	4	4.00	0	0	0
RJ Blakey	1993-1993	2	4	0	7	6	1.75	0	0	2
JB Bolus	1963-1964	7	12	0	496	88	41.33	0	4	0
RS Bopara	2007-2012	13	19	1	575	143	31.94	3	0	5
SG Borthwick	2014-2014	1	2	0	5	4	2.50	0	0	0
IT Botham	1977-1992	102	161	6	5200	208	33.54	14	22	14
G Boycott	1964-1982	108	193	23	8114	246*	47.72	22	42	10

England Test Batting Averages 1962/3-2014

Player	Span	Mat	Inns	NO	Runs	HS	Ave	100	50	0
JM Brearley	1976-1981	39	66	3	1442	91	22.88	0	9	6
TT Bresnan	2009-2013	23	26	4	575	91	26.13	0	3	3
BC Broad	1984-1989	25	44	2	1661	162	39.54	6	6	3
SCJ Broad	2007-2014	74	104	13	2193	169	24.09	1	10	14
DJ Brown	1965-1969	26	34	5	342	44*	11.79	0	0	6
SJE Brown	1996-1996	1	2	1	11	10*	11.00	0	0	0
AR Butcher	1979-1979	1	2	0	34	20	17.00	0	0	0
MA Butcher	1997-2004	71	131	7	4288	173*	34.58	8	23	10
RO Butcher	1981-1981	3	5	0	71	32	14.20	0	0	1
JC Buttler	2014-2014	3	3	0	200	85	66.66	0	2	0
AR Caddick	1993-2003	62	95	12	861	49*	10.37	0	0	19
DJ Capel	1987-1990	15	25	1	374	98	15.58	0	2	4
MA Carberry	2010-2014	6	12	0	345	60	28.75	0	1	2
TW Cartwright	1964-1965	5	7	2	26	9	5.20	0	0	2
JH Childs	1988-1988	2	4	4	2	2*	-	0	0	0
R Clarke	2003-2003	2	3	0	96	55	32.00	0	1	0
DB Close	1949-1976	22	37	2	887	70	25.34	0	4	3
LJ Coldwell	1962-1964	7	7	5	9	6*	4.50	0	0	1
PD Collingwood	2003-2011	68	115	10	4259	206	40.56	10	20	6
NRD Compton	2012-2013	9	17	2	479	117	31.93	2	1	1
AN Cook	2006-2014	109	194	11	8423	294	46.02	25	38	7
G Cook	1982-1983	7	13	0	203	66	15.61	0	2	1
NGB Cook	1983-1989	15	25	4	179	31	8.52	0	0	2
GA Cope	1977-1978	3	3	0	40	22	13.33	0	0	1
DG Cork	1995-2002	37	56	8	864	59	18.00	0	3	5
RMH Cottam	1969-1973	4	5	1	27	13	6.75	0	0	0
NG Cowans	1982-1985	19	29	7	175	36	7.95	0	0	5
CS Cowdrey	1984-1988	6	8	1	101	38	14.42	0	0	1
MC Cowdrey	1954-1975	114	188	15	7624	182	44.06	22	38	9
JP Crawley	1994-2003	37	61	9	1800	156*	34.61	4	9	4
RDB Croft	1996-2001	21	34	8	421	37*	16.19	0	0	2
TS Curtis	1988-1989	5	9	0	140	41	15.55	0	0	1
RKJ Dawson	2001-2003	7	13	3	114	19*	11.40	0	0	0
PAJ DeFreitas	1986-1995	44	68	5	934	88	14.82	0	4	10
MH Denness	1969-1975	28	45	3	1667	188	39.69	4	7	2
ER Dexter	1958-1968	62	102	8	4502	205	47.89	9	27	6
GR Dilley	1979-1989	41	58	19	521	56	13.35	0	2	10

England Test Batting Averages 1962/3-2014

Player	Span	Mat	Inns	NO	Runs	HS	Ave	100	50	0
BL D'Oliveira	1966-1972	44	70	8	2484	158	40.06	5	15	4
PR Downton	1981-1988	30	48	8	785	74	19.62	0	4	4
MA Ealham	1996-1998	8	13	3	210	53*	21.00	0	2	0
PH Edmonds	1975-1987	51	65	15	875	64	17.50	0	2	5
JH Edrich	1963-1976	77	127	9	5138	310*	43.54	12	24	6
RM Ellison	1984-1986	11	16	1	202	41	13.46	0	0	1
JE Emburey	1978-1995	64	96	20	1713	75	22.53	0	10	16
NH Fairbrother	1987-1993	10	15	1	219	83	15.64	0	1	1
ST Finn	2010-2013	23	29	14	169	56	11.26	0	1	6
JA Flavell	1961-1964	4	6	2	31	14	7.75	0	0	0
KWR Fletcher	1968-1982	59	96	14	3272	216	39.90	7	19	6
A Flintoff	1998-2009	78	128	9	3795	167	31.89	5	26	17
JS Foster	2001-2002	7	12	3	226	48	25.11	0	0	1
NA Foster	1983-1993	29	45	7	446	39	11.73	0	0	9
G Fowler	1982-1985	21	37	0	1307	201	35.32	3	8	3
ARC Fraser	1989-1998	46	67	15	388	32	7.46	0	0	9
BN French	1986-1988	16	21	4	308	59	18.11	0	1	2
JER Gallian	1995-1995	3	6	0	74	28	12.33	0	0	2
MW Gatting	1978-1995	79	138	14	4409	207	35.55	10	21	16
ESH Giddins	1999-2000	4	7	3	10	7	2.50	0	0	3
N Gifford	1964-1973	15	20	9	179	25*	16.27	0	0	1
AF Giles	1998-2006	54	81	13	1421	59	20.89	0	4	9
GA Gooch	1975-1995	118	215	6	8900	333	42.58	20	46	13
D Gough	1994-2003	58	86	18	855	65	12.57	0	2	14
DI Gower	1978-1992	117	204	18	8231	215	44.25	18	39	7
TW Graveney	1951-1969	79	123	13	4882	258	44.38	11	20	8
AW Greig	1972-1977	58	93	4	3599	148	40.43	8	20	5
IA Greig	1982-1982	2	4	0	26	14	6.50	0	0	0
A Habib	1999-1999	2	3	0	26	19	8.66	0	0	0
GM Hamilton	1999-1999	1	2	0	0	0	0.00	0	0	2
JH Hampshire	1969-1975	8	16	1	403	107	26.86	1	2	2
SJ Harmison	2002-2009	62	84	23	742	49*	12.16	0	0	20
FC Hayes	1973-1976	9	17	1	244	106*	15.25	1	0	6
DW Headley	1997-1999	15	26	4	186	31	8.45	0	0	3
WK Hegg	1998-1999	2	4	0	30	15	7.50	0	0	0
EE Hemmings	1982-1991	16	21	4	383	95	22.52	0	2	5
M Hendrick	1974-1981	30	35	15	128	15	6.40	0	0	8

England Test Batting Averages 1962/3-2014

Player	Span	Mat	Inns	NO	Runs	HS	Ave	100	50	0
GA Hick	1991-2001	65	114	6	3383	178	31.32	6	18	11
K Higgs	1965-1968	15	19	3	185	63	11.56	0	1	2
RNS Hobbs	1967-1971	7	8	3	34	15*	6.80	0	0	1
MJ Hoggard	2000-2008	67	92	27	473	38	7.27	0	0	19
AJ Hollioake	1997-1998	4	6	0	65	45	10.83	0	0	1
BC Hollioake	1997-1998	2	4	0	44	28	11.00	0	0	1
N Hussain	1990-2004	96	171	16	5764	207	37.18	14	33	14
RA Hutton	1971-1971	5	8	2	219	81	36.50	0	2	1
AP Igglesden	1989-1994	3	5	3	6	3*	3.00	0	0	2
R Illingworth	1958-1973	61	90	11	1836	113	23.24	2	5	7
RK Illingworth	1991-1995	9	14	7	128	28	18.28	0	0	3
MC Ilott	1993-1995	5	6	2	28	15	7.00	0	0	0
RC Irani	1996-1999	3	5	0	86	41	17.20	0	0	0
RD Jackman	1981-1982	4	6	0	42	17	7.00	0	0	2
SP James	1998-1998	2	4	0	71	36	17.75	0	0	1
JA Jameson	1971-1974	4	8	0	214	82	26.75	0	1	0
PW Jarvis	1988-1993	9	15	2	132	29*	10.15	0	0	1
RL Johnson	2003-2003	3	4	0	59	26	14.75	0	0	0
GO Jones	2004-2006	34	53	4	1172	100	23.91	1	6	2
IJ Jones	1964-1968	15	17	9	38	16	4.75	0	0	2
SP Jones	2002-2005	18	18	5	205	44	15.76	0	0	3
CJ Jordan	2014-2014	5	6	0	125	35	20.83	0	0	0
SC Kerrigan	2013-2013	1	1	1	1	1*	-	0	0	0
RWT Key	2002-2005	15	26	1	775	221	31.00	1	3	2
A Khan	2009-2009	1	-	-	-	-	-	-	-	-
RJ Kirtley	2003-2003	4	7	1	32	12	5.33	0	0	0
BR Knight	1961-1969	29	38	7	812	127	26.19	2	0	2
NV Knight	1995-2001	17	30	0	719	113	23.96	1	4	1
APE Knott	1967-1981	95	149	15	4389	135	32.75	5	30	8
AJ Lamb	1982-1992	79	139	10	4656	142	36.09	14	18	9
W Larkins	1980-1991	13	25	1	493	64	20.54	0	3	6
JDF Larter	1962-1965	10	7	2	16	10	3.20	0	0	2
MN Lathwell	1993-1993	2	4	0	78	33	19.50	0	0	1
DV Lawrence	1988-1992	5	6	0	60	34	10.00	0	0	0
JK Lever	1976-1986	21	31	5	306	53	11.76	0	1	2
P Lever	1970-1975	17	18	2	350	88*	21.87	0	2	1
AR Lewis	1972-1973	9	16	2	457	125	32.64	1	3	2

England Test Batting Averages 1962/3-2014

Player	Span	Mat	Inns	NO	Runs	HS	Ave	100	50	0
CC Lewis	1990-1996	32	51	3	1105	117	23.02	1	4	6
J Lewis	2006-2006	1	2	0	27	20	13.50	0	0	0
D Lloyd	1974-1975	9	15	2	552	214*	42.46	1	0	0
TA Lloyd	1984-1984	1	1	1	10	10*	-	0	0	0
GAR Lock	1952-1968	49	63	9	742	89	13.74	0	3	8
BW Luckhurst	1970-1974	21	41	5	1298	131	36.05	4	5	4
MJ McCague	1993-1994	3	5	0	21	11	4.20	0	0	2
A McGrath	2003-2003	4	5	0	201	81	40.20	0	2	0
DL Maddy	1999-2000	3	4	0	46	24	11.50	0	0	0
SI Mahmood	2006-2007	8	11	1	81	34	8.10	0	0	3
DE Malcolm	1989-1997	40	58	19	236	29	6.05	0	0	16
NA Mallender	1992-1992	2	3	0	8	4	2.66	0	0	0
VJ Marks	1982-1984	6	10	1	249	83	27.66	0	3	0
PJ Martin	1995-1997	8	13	0	115	29	8.84	0	0	2
MP Maynard	1988-1994	4	8	0	87	35	10.87	0	0	2
C Milburn	1966-1969	9	16	2	654	139	46.71	2	2	1
G Miller	1976-1984	34	51	4	1213	98*	25.80	0	7	5
EJG Morgan	2010-2012	16	24	1	700	130	30.43	2	3	4
H Morris	1991-1991	3	6	0	115	44	19.16	0	0	0
JE Morris	1990-1990	3	5	2	71	32	23.66	0	0	0
JB Mortimore	1959-1964	9	12	2	243	73*	24.30	0	1	1
MD Moxon	1986-1989	10	17	1	455	99	28.43	0	3	2
AD Mullally	1996-2001	19	27	4	127	24	5.52	0	0	12
TA Munton	1992-1992	2	2	1	25	25*	25.00	0	0	1
JT Murray	1961-1967	21	28	5	506	112	22.00	1	2	3
PJ Newport	1988-1991	3	5	1	110	40*	27.50	0	0	1
CM Old	1972-1981	46	66	9	845	65	14.82	0	2	10
G Onions	2009-2012	9	10	7	30	17*	10.00	0	0	3
J Ormond	2001-2001	2	4	1	38	18	12.66	0	0	1
KE Palmer	1965-1965	1	1	0	10	10	10.00	0	0	0
MS Panesar	2006-2013	50	68	23	220	26	4.88	0	0	20
PH Parfitt	1961-1972	37	52	6	1882	131*	40.91	7	6	5
PWG Parker	1981-1981	1	2	0	13	13	6.50	0	0	1
JM Parks	1954-1968	46	68	7	1962	108*	32.16	2	9	3
MM Patel	1996-1996	2	2	0	45	27	22.50	0	0	0
SR Patel	2012-2012	5	7	0	109	33	15.57	0	0	1
DJ Pattinson	2008-2008	1	2	0	21	13	10.50	0	0	0

England Test Batting Averages 1962/3-2014

Player	Span	Mat	Inns	NO	Runs	HS	Ave	100	50	0
KP Pietersen	2005-2014	104	181	8	8181	227	47.28	23	35	10
ACS Pigott	1984-1984	1	2	1	12	8*	12.00	0	0	0
LE Plunkett	2005-2014	13	20	5	238	55*	15.86	0	1	7
PI Pocock	1968-1985	25	37	4	206	33	6.24	0	0	10
JSE Price	1964-1972	15	15	6	66	32	7.33	0	0	5
RM Prideaux	1968-1969	3	6	1	102	64	20.40	0	1	0
DR Pringle	1982-1992	30	50	4	695	63	15.10	0	1	6
MJ Prior	2007-2014	79	123	21	4099	131*	40.18	7	28	13
G Pullar	1959-1963	28	49	4	1974	175	43.86	4	12	3
NV Radford	1986-1988	3	4	1	21	12*	7.00	0	0	1
CT Radley	1978-1978	8	10	0	481	158	48.10	2	2	1
MR Ramprakash	1991-2002	52	92	6	2350	154	27.32	2	12	12
DW Randall	1977-1984	47	79	5	2470	174	33.37	7	12	14
WB Rankin	2014-2014	1	2	0	13	13	6.50	0	0	1
CMW Read	1999-2007	15	23	4	360	55	18.94	0	1	5
DA Reeve	1992-1992	3	5	0	124	59	24.80	0	1	1
SJ Rhodes	1994-1995	11	17	5	294	65*	24.50	0	1	1
CJ Richards	1986-1988	8	13	0	285	133	21.92	1	0	2
PE Richardson	1956-1963	34	56	1	2061	126	37.47	5	9	1
RT Robinson	1984-1989	29	49	5	1601	175	36.38	4	6	5
SD Robson	2014-2014	7	11	0	336	127	30.54	1	1	0
GRJ Roope	1973-1978	21	32	4	860	77	30.71	0	7	3
JE Root	2012-2014	22	40	6	1732	200*	50.94	5	7	1
BC Rose	1977-1981	9	16	2	358	70	25.57	0	2	0
FE Rumsey	1964-1965	5	5	3	30	21*	15.00	0	0	0
RC Russell	1988-1998	54	86	16	1897	128*	27.10	2	6	8
WE Russell	1961-1967	10	18	1	362	70	21.29	0	2	2
MJ Saggers	2003-2004	3	3	0	1	1	0.33	0	0	2
IDK Salisbury	1992-2000	15	25	3	368	50	16.72	0	1	4
CP Schofield	2000-2000	2	3	0	67	57	22.33	0	1	1
MWW Selvey	1976-1977	3	5	3	15	5*	7.50	0	0	1
D Shackleton	1950-1963	7	13	7	113	42	18.83	0	0	0
OA Shah	2006-2009	6	10	0	269	88	26.90	0	2	0
A Shahzad	2010-2010	1	1	0	5	5	5.00	0	0	0
PJ Sharpe	1963-1969	12	21	4	786	111	46.23	1	4	1
Rev.DS Sheppard	1950-1963	22	33	2	1172	119	37.80	3	6	2
K Shuttleworth	1970-1971	5	6	0	46	21	7.66	0	0	1

England Test Batting Averages 1962/3-2014

Player	Span	Mat	Inns	NO	Runs	HS	Ave	100	50	0
A Sidebottom	1985-1985	1	1	0	2	2	2.00	0	0	0
RJ Sidebottom	2001-2010	22	31	11	313	31	15.65	0	0	3
CEW Silverwood	1996-2002	6	7	3	29	10	7.25	0	0	2
WN Slack	1986-1986	3	6	0	81	52	13.50	0	1	2
GC Small	1986-1991	17	24	7	263	59	15.47	0	1	4
AC Smith	1962-1963	6	7	3	118	69*	29.50	0	1	0
AM Smith	1997-1997	1	2	1	4	4*	4.00	0	0	1
CL Smith	1983-1986	8	14	1	392	91	30.15	0	2	1
DM Smith	1986-1986	2	4	0	80	47	20.00	0	0	1
MJK Smith	1958-1972	50	78	6	2278	121	31.63	3	11	11
RA Smith	1988-1996	62	112	15	4236	175	43.67	9	28	8
JA Snow	1965-1976	49	71	14	772	73	13.54	0	2	17
JB Statham	1951-1965	70	87	28	675	38	11.44	0	0	13
DS Steele	1975-1976	8	16	0	673	106	42.06	1	5	1
JP Stephenson	1989-1989	1	2	0	36	25	18.00	0	0	0
GB Stevenson	1980-1981	2	2	1	28	27*	28.00	0	0	0
AJ Stewart	1990-2003	133	235	21	8463	190	39.54	15	45	14
MJ Stewart	1962-1964	8	12	1	385	87	35.00	0	2	1
BA Stokes	2013-2014	6	11	0	279	120	25.36	1	0	3
AJ Strauss	2004-2012	100	178	6	7037	177	40.91	21	27	15
PM Such	1993-1999	11	16	5	67	14*	6.09	0	0	3
GP Swann	2008-2013	60	76	14	1370	85	22.09	0	5	5
CJ Tavare	1980-1989	31	56	2	1755	149	32.50	2	12	5
JP Taylor	1993-1994	2	4	2	34	17*	17.00	0	0	1
K Taylor	1959-1964	3	5	0	57	24	11.40	0	0	0
LB Taylor	1985-1985	2	1	1	1	1*	-	0	0	0
RW Taylor	1971-1984	57	83	12	1156	97	16.28	0	3	10
JWA Taylor	2012-2012	2	3	0	48	34	16.00	0	0	0
VP Terry	1984-1984	2	3	0	16	8	5.33	0	0	0
NI Thomson	1964-1965	5	4	1	69	39	23.00	0	0	1
GP Thorpe	1993-2005	100	179	28	6744	200*	44.66	16	39	12
FJ Titmus	1955-1975	53	76	11	1449	84*	22.29	0	10	4
RW Tolchard	1977-1977	4	7	2	129	67	25.80	0	1	1
JC Tredwell	2010-2010	1	1	0	37	37	37.00	0	0	0
CT Tremlett	2007-2013	12	15	4	113	25*	10.27	0	0	3
ME Trescothick	2000-2006	76	143	10	5825	219	43.79	14	29	12
IJL Trott	2009-2013	49	87	6	3763	226	46.45	9	18	5

England Test Batting Averages 1962/3-2014

Player	Span	Mat	Inns	NO	Runs	HS	Ave	100	50	0
FS Trueman	1952-1965	67	85	14	981	39*	13.81	0	0	11
AJ Tudor	1998-2002	10	16	4	229	99*	19.08	0	1	2
PCR Tufnell	1990-2001	42	59	29	153	22*	5.10	0	0	15
SD Udal	2005-2006	4	7	1	109	33*	18.16	0	0	1
DL Underwood	1966-1982	86	116	35	937	45*	11.56	0	0	19
MP Vaughan	1999-2008	82	147	9	5719	197	41.44	18	18	9
A Ward	1969-1976	5	6	1	40	21	8.00	0	0	4
IJ Ward	2001-2001	5	9	1	129	39	16.12	0	0	1
SL Watkin	1991-1993	3	5	0	25	13	5.00	0	0	1
M Watkinson	1995-1996	4	6	1	167	82*	33.40	0	1	1
AP Wells	1995-1995	1	2	1	3	3*	3.00	0	0	1
JJ Whitaker	1986-1986	1	1	0	11	11	11.00	0	0	0
C White	1994-2002	30	50	7	1052	121	24.46	1	5	8
P Willey	1976-1986	26	50	6	1184	102*	26.90	2	5	2
NF Williams	1990-1990	1	1	0	38	38	38.00	0	0	0
RGD Willis	1971-1984	90	128	55	840	28*	11.50	0	0	12
D Wilson	1964-1971	6	7	1	75	42	12.50	0	0	0
CR Woakes	2013-2014	4	5	3	75	26*	37.50	0	0	1
B Wood	1972-1978	12	21	0	454	90	21.61	0	2	1
RA Woolmer	1975-1981	19	34	2	1059	149	33.09	3	2	4

England Test Bowling Averages 1962/3-2014

Player	Span	Mat	Balls	Runs	Wkts	BBI	BBM	Ave	Econ	SR	5	10
CJ Adams	1999-2000	5	120	59	1	1/42	1/42	59.00	2.95	120.0	0	0
U Afzaal	2001-2001	3	54	49	1	1/49	1/49	49.00	5.44	54.0	0	0
JP Agnew	1984-1985	3	552	373	4	2/51	2/97	93.25	4.05	138.0	0	0
Kabir Ali	2003-2003	1	216	136	5	3/80	5/136	27.20	3.77	43.2	0	0
MM Ali	2014-2014	7	1054	618	22	6/67	8/129	28.09	3.51	47.9	1	0
DA Allen	1960-1966	39	11297	3779	122	5/30	9/162	30.97	2.00	92.5	4	0
PJW Allott	1981-1985	13	2225	1084	26	6/61	6/85	41.69	2.92	85.5	1	0
JM Anderson	2003-2014	99	22114	11295	380	7/43	11/71	29.72	3.06	58.1	16	2
GG Arnold	1967-1975	34	7650	3254	115	6/45	9/91	28.29	2.55	66.5	6	0
MA Atherton	1989-2001	115	408	302	2	1/20	1/20	151.00	4.44	204.0	0	0
JC Balderstone	1976-1976	2	96	80	1	1/80	1/80	80.00	5.00	96.0	0	0
GS Ballance	2014-2014	8	12	5	0	-	-	-	2.50	-	0	0
RW Barber	1960-1968	28	3426	1806	42	4/132	6/139	43.00	3.16	81.5	0	0
KJ Barnett	1988-1989	4	36	32	0	-	-	-	5.33	-	0	0
KF Barrington	1955-1968	82	2715	1300	29	3/4	5/111	44.82	2.87	93.6	0	0
GJ Batty	2003-2005	7	1394	733	11	3/55	5/153	66.63	3.15	126.7	0	0
IR Bell	2004-2014	105	108	76	1	1/33	1/33	76.00	4.22	108.0	0	0
JE Benjamin	1994-1994	1	168	80	4	4/42	4/80	20.00	2.85	42.0	0	0
MP Bicknell	1993-2003	4	1080	543	14	4/84	6/155	38.78	3.01	77.1	0	0
J Birkenshaw	1973-1974	5	1017	469	13	5/57	6/146	36.07	2.76	78.2	1	0
ID Blackwell	2006-2006	1	114	71	0	-	-	-	3.73	-	0	0
JB Bolus	1963-1964	7	18	16	0	-	-	-	5.33	-	0	0
RS Bopara	2007-2012	13	434	290	1	1/39	1/39	290.00	4.00	434.0	0	0
SG Borthwick	2014-2014	1	78	82	4	3/33	4/82	20.50	6.30	19.5	0	0
IT Botham	1977-1992	102	21815	10878	383	8/34	13/106	28.40	2.99	56.9	27	4
G Boycott	1964-1982	108	944	382	7	3/47	3/47	54.57	2.42	134.8	0	0
TT Bresnan	2009-2013	23	4674	2357	72	5/48	8/141	32.73	3.02	64.9	1	0
BC Broad	1984-1989	25	6	4	0	-	-	-	4.00	-	0	0
SCJ Broad	2007-2014	74	15515	7894	264	7/44	11/121	29.90	3.05	58.7	12	2
DJ Brown	1965-1969	26	5098	2237	79	5/42	7/98	28.31	2.63	64.5	2	0
SJE Brown	1996-1996	1	198	138	2	1/60	2/138	69.00	4.18	99.0	0	0
AR Butcher	1979-1979	1	12	9	0	-	-	-	4.50	-	0	0
MA Butcher	1997-2004	71	901	541	15	4/42	5/68	36.06	3.60	60.0	0	0
AR Caddick	1993-2003	62	13558	6999	234	7/46	10/215	29.91	3.09	57.9	13	1
DJ Capel	1987-1990	15	2000	1064	21	3/88	4/154	50.66	3.19	95.2	0	0
TW Cartwright	1964-1965	5	1611	544	15	6/94	6/94	36.26	2.02	107.4	1	0
JH Childs	1988-1988	2	516	183	3	1/13	2/92	61.00	2.12	172.0	0	0

England Test Bowling Averages 1962/3-2014

Player	Span	Mat	Balls	Runs	Wkts	BBI	BBM	Ave	Econ	SR	5	10
R Clarke	2003-2003	2	174	60	4	2/7	3/11	15.00	2.06	43.5	0	0
DB Close	1949-1976	22	1212	532	18	4/35	5/53	29.55	2.63	67.3	0	0
LJ Coldwell	1962-1964	7	1668	610	22	6/85	9/110	27.72	2.19	75.8	1	0
PD Collingwood	2003-2011	68	1905	1018	17	3/23	3/35	59.88	3.20	112.0	0	0
AN Cook	2006-2014	109	18	7	1	1/6	1/6	7.00	2.33	18.0	0	0
G Cook	1982-1983	7	42	27	0	-	-	-	3.85	-	0	0
NGB Cook	1983-1989	15	4174	1689	52	6/65	11/83	32.48	2.42	80.2	4	1
GA Cope	1977-1978	3	864	277	8	3/102	4/91	34.62	1.92	108.0	0	0
DG Cork	1995-2002	37	7678	3906	131	7/43	9/162	29.81	3.05	58.6	5	0
RMH Cottam	1969-1973	4	903	327	14	4/50	6/85	23.35	2.17	64.5	0	0
NG Cowans	1982-1985	19	3452	2003	51	6/77	8/146	39.27	3.48	67.6	2	0
CS Cowdrey	1984-1988	6	399	309	4	2/65	2/91	77.25	4.64	99.7	0	0
MC Cowdrey	1954-1975	114	119	104	0	-	-	-	5.24	-	0	0
RDB Croft	1996-2001	21	4619	1825	49	5/95	7/143	37.24	2.37	94.2	1	0
TS Curtis	1988-1989	5	18	7	0	-	-	-	2.33	-	0	0
RKJ Dawson	2001-2003	7	1116	677	11	4/134	4/134	61.54	3.63	101.4	0	0
PAJ DeFreitas	1986-1995	44	9838	4700	140	7/70	9/165	33.57	2.86	70.2	4	0
ER Dexter	1958-1968	62	5317	2306	66	4/10	6/77	34.93	2.60	80.5	0	0
GR Dilley	1979-1989	41	8192	4107	138	6/38	9/128	29.76	3.00	59.3	6	0
BL D'Oliveira	1966-1972	44	5706	1859	47	3/46	5/62	39.55	1.95	121.4	0	0
MA Ealham	1996-1998	8	1060	488	17	4/21	6/111	28.70	2.76	62.3	0	0
PH Edmonds	1975-1987	51	12028	4273	125	7/66	7/66	34.18	2.13	96.2	2	0
JH Edrich	1963-1976	77	30	23	0	-	-	-	4.60	-	0	0
RM Ellison	1984-1986	11	2264	1048	35	6/77	10/104	29.94	2.77	64.6	3	1
JE Emburey	1978-1995	64	15391	5646	147	7/78	7/105	38.40	2.20	104.7	6	0
JA Flavell	1961-1964	4	792	367	7	2/65	3/126	52.42	2.78	113.1	0	0
KWR Fletcher	1968-1982	59	285	193	2	1/6	1/6	96.50	4.06	142.5	0	0
JS Foster	2001-2002	7	-	-	-	-	-	-	-	-	-	-
NA Foster	1983-1993	29	6261	2891	88	8/107	11/163	32.85	2.77	71.1	5	1
G Fowler	1982-1985	21	18	11	0	-	-	-	3.66	-	0	0
ARC Fraser	1989-1998	46	10876	4836	177	8/53	11/110	27.32	2.66	61.4	13	2
JER Gallian	1995-1995	3	84	62	0	-	-	-	4.42	-	0	0
MW Gatting	1978-1995	79	752	317	4	1/14	1/14	79.25	2.52	188.0	0	0
ESH Giddins	1999-2000	4	444	240	12	5/15	7/42	20.00	3.24	37.0	1	0
N Gifford	1964-1973	15	3084	1026	33	5/55	8/127	31.09	1.99	93.4	1	0
AF Giles	1998-2006	54	12180	5806	143	5/57	9/122	40.60	2.86	85.1	5	0
GA Gooch	1975-1995	118	2655	1069	23	3/39	5/69	46.47	2.41	115.4	0	0

England Test Bowling Averages 1962/3-2014

Player	Span	Mat	Balls	Runs	Wkts	BBI	BBM	Ave	Econ	SR	5	10
D Gough	1994-2003	58	11821	6503	229	6/42	9/92	28.39	3.30	51.6	9	0
DI Gower	1978-1992	117	36	20	1	1/1	1/1	20.00	3.33	36.0	0	0
TW Graveney	1951-1969	79	260	167	1	1/34	1/34	167.00	3.85	260.0	0	0
AW Greig	1972-1977	58	9802	4541	141	8/86	13/156	32.20	2.77	69.5	6	2
IA Greig	1982-1982	2	188	114	4	4/53	4/72	28.50	3.63	47.0	0	0
GM Hamilton	1999-1999	1	90	63	0	-	-	-	4.20	-	0	0
SJ Harmison	2002-2009	62	13192	7091	222	7/12	11/76	31.94	3.22	59.4	8	1
DW Headley	1997-1999	15	3026	1671	60	6/60	8/102	27.85	3.31	50.4	1	0
EE Hemmings	1982-1991	16	4437	1825	43	6/58	7/101	42.44	2.46	103.1	1	0
M Hendrick	1974-1981	30	6208	2248	87	4/28	8/95	25.83	2.17	71.3	0	0
GA Hick	1991-2001	65	3057	1306	23	4/126	5/28	56.78	2.56	132.9	0	0
K Higgs	1965-1968	15	4112	1473	71	6/91	8/119	20.74	2.14	57.9	2	0
RNS Hobbs	1967-1971	7	1291	481	12	3/25	5/98	40.08	2.23	107.5	0	0
MJ Hoggard	2000-2008	67	13909	7564	248	7/61	12/205	30.50	3.26	56.0	7	1
AJ Hollioake	1997-1998	4	144	67	2	2/31	2/55	33.50	2.79	72.0	0	0
N Hussain	1990-2004	96	30	15	0	-	-	-	3.00	-	0	0
RA Hutton	1971-1971	5	738	257	9	3/72	3/90	28.55	2.08	82.0	0	0
AP Igglesden	1989-1994	3	555	329	6	2/91	3/146	54.83	3.55	92.5	0	0
R Illingworth	1958-1973	61	11934	3807	122	6/29	7/29	31.20	1.91	97.8	3	0
RK Illingworth	1991-1995	9	1485	615	19	4/96	6/150	32.36	2.48	78.1	0	0
MC Ilott	1993-1995	5	1042	542	12	3/48	4/152	45.16	3.12	86.8	0	0
RC Irani	1996-1999	3	192	112	3	1/22	1/31	37.33	3.50	64.0	0	0
RD Jackman	1981-1982	4	1070	445	14	4/110	5/141	31.78	2.49	76.4	0	0
JA Jameson	1971-1974	4	42	17	1	1/17	1/17	17.00	2.42	42.0	0	0
PW Jarvis	1988-1993	9	1912	965	21	4/107	4/154	45.95	3.02	91.0	0	0
RL Johnson	2003-2003	3	547	275	16	6/33	9/93	17.18	3.01	34.1	2	0
IJ Jones	1964-1968	15	3546	1769	44	6/118	6/118	40.20	2.99	80.5	1	0
SP Jones	2002-2005	18	2821	1666	59	6/53	7/110	28.23	3.54	47.8	3	0
CJ Jordan	2014-2014	5	906	496	15	4/18	7/50	33.06	3.28	60.4	0	0
SC Kerrigan	2013-2013	1	48	53	0	-	-	-	6.62	-	0	0
A Khan	2009-2009	1	174	122	1	1/111	1/122	122.00	4.20	174.0	0	0
RJ Kirtley	2003-2003	4	1079	561	19	6/34	8/114	29.52	3.11	56.7	1	0
BR Knight	1961-1969	29	5377	2223	70	4/38	6/110	31.75	2.48	76.8	0	0
AJ Lamb	1982-1992	79	30	23	1	1/6	1/6	23.00	4.60	30.0	0	0
JDF Larter	1962-1965	10	2172	941	37	5/57	9/145	25.43	2.59	58.7	2	0
DV Lawrence	1988-1992	5	1089	676	18	5/106	7/173	37.55	3.72	60.5	1	0
JK Lever	1976-1986	21	4433	1951	73	7/46	10/70	26.72	2.64	60.7	3	1

England Test Bowling Averages 1962/3-2014

Player	Span	Mat	Balls	Runs	Wkts	BBI	BBM	Ave	Econ	SR	5	10
P Lever	1970-1975	17	3571	1509	41	6/38	9/103	36.80	2.53	87.0	2	0
CC Lewis	1990-1996	32	6852	3490	93	6/111	7/114	37.52	3.05	73.6	3	0
J Lewis	2006-2006	1	246	122	3	3/68	3/122	40.66	2.97	82.0	0	0
D Lloyd	1974-1975	9	24	17	0	-	-	-	4.25	-	0	0
BW Luckhurst	1970-1974	21	57	32	1	1/9	1/9	32.00	3.36	57.0	0	0
MJ McCague	1993-1994	3	593	390	6	4/121	4/179	65.00	3.94	98.8	0	0
A McGrath	2003-2003	4	102	56	4	3/16	3/16	14.00	3.29	25.5	0	0
DL Maddy	1999-2000	3	84	40	0	-	-	-	2.85	-	0	0
SI Mahmood	2006-2007	8	1130	762	20	4/22	6/130	38.10	4.04	56.5	0	0
DE Malcolm	1989-1997	40	8480	4748	128	9/57	10/137	37.09	3.35	66.2	5	2
NA Mallender	1992-1992	2	449	215	10	5/50	8/122	21.50	2.87	44.9	1	0
VJ Marks	1982-1984	6	1082	484	11	3/78	3/78	44.00	2.68	98.3	0	0
PJ Martin	1995-1997	8	1452	580	17	4/60	4/60	34.11	2.39	85.4	0	0
G Miller	1976-1984	34	5149	1859	60	5/44	6/57	30.98	2.16	85.8	1	0
JB Mortimore	1959-1964	9	2162	733	13	3/36	3/60	56.38	2.03	166.3	0	0
MD Moxon	1986-1989	10	48	30	0	-	-	-	3.75	-	0	0
AD Mullally	1996-2001	19	4525	1812	58	5/105	5/84	31.24	2.40	78.0	1	0
TA Munton	1992-1992	2	405	200	4	2/22	3/62	50.00	2.96	101.2	0	0
PJ Newport	1988-1991	3	669	417	10	4/87	7/164	41.70	3.73	66.9	0	0
CM Old	1972-1981	46	8858	4020	143	7/50	9/88	28.11	2.72	61.9	4	0
G Onions	2009-2012	9	1606	957	32	5/38	7/102	29.90	3.57	50.1	1	0
J Ormond	2001-2001	2	372	185	2	1/70	1/70	92.50	2.98	186.0	0	0
KE Palmer	1965-1965	1	378	189	1	1/113	1/189	189.00	3.00	378.0	0	0
MS Panesar	2006-2013	50	12475	5797	167	6/37	11/210	34.71	2.78	74.7	12	2
PH Parfitt	1961-1972	37	1326	574	12	2/5	2/19	47.83	2.59	110.5	0	0
JM Parks	1954-1968	46	54	51	1	1/43	1/43	51.00	5.66	54.0	0	0
MM Patel	1996-1996	2	276	180	1	1/101	1/148	180.00	3.91	276.0	0	0
SR Patel	2012-2012	5	606	257	4	2/27	2/36	64.25	2.54	151.5	0	0
DJ Pattinson	2008-2008	1	181	96	2	2/95	2/96	48.00	3.18	90.5	0	0
KP Pietersen	2005-2014	104	1311	886	10	3/52	4/78	88.60	4.05	131.1	0	0
ACS Pigott	1984-1984	1	102	75	2	2/75	2/75	37.50	4.41	51.0	0	0
LE Plunkett	2005-2014	13	2659	1536	41	5/64	9/176	37.46	3.46	64.8	1	0
PI Pocock	1968-1985	25	6650	2976	67	6/79	8/142	44.41	2.68	99.2	3	0
JSE Price	1964-1972	15	2724	1401	40	5/73	5/104	35.02	3.08	68.1	1	0
RM Prideaux	1968-1969	3	12	0	0	-	-	-	0.00	-	0	0
DR Pringle	1982-1992	30	5287	2518	70	5/95	7/120	35.97	2.85	75.5	3	0
G Pullar	1959-1963	28	66	37	1	1/1	1/1	37.00	3.36	66.0	0	0

England Test Bowling Averages 1962/3-2014

Player	Span	Mat	Balls	Runs	Wkts	BBI	BBM	Ave	Econ	SR	5	10
NV Radford	1986-1988	3	678	351	4	2/131	2/148	87.75	3.10	169.5	0	0
MR Ramprakash	1991-2002	52	895	477	4	1/2	1/2	119.25	3.19	223.7	0	0
DW Randall	1977-1984	47	16	3	0	-	-	-	1.12	-	0	0
WB Rankin	2014-2014	1	125	81	1	1/47	1/81	81.00	3.88	125.0	0	0
DA Reeve	1992-1992	3	149	60	2	1/4	1/15	30.00	2.41	74.5	0	0
RT Robinson	1984-1989	29	6	0	0	-	-	-	0.00	-	0	0
GRJ Roope	1973-1978	21	172	76	0	-	-	-	2.65	-	0	0
JE Root	2012-2014	22	510	225	4	2/9	2/9	56.25	2.64	127.5	0	0
FE Rumsey	1964-1965	5	1145	461	17	4/25	6/133	27.11	2.41	67.3	0	0
WE Russell	1961-1967	10	144	44	0	-	-	-	1.83	-	0	0
MJ Saggers	2003-2004	3	493	247	7	2/29	3/62	35.28	3.00	70.4	0	0
IDK Salisbury	1992-2000	15	2492	1539	20	4/163	5/122	76.95	3.70	124.6	0	0
CP Schofield	2000-2000	2	108	73	0	-	-	-	4.05	-	0	0
MWW Selvey	1976-1977	3	492	343	6	4/41	6/152	57.16	4.18	82.0	0	0
D Shackleton	1950-1963	7	2078	768	18	4/72	7/165	42.66	2.21	115.4	0	0
OA Shah	2006-2009	6	30	31	0	-	-	-	6.20	-	0	0
A Shahzad	2010-2010	1	102	63	4	3/45	4/63	15.75	3.70	25.5	0	0
PJ Sharpe	1963-1969	12	-	-	-	-	-	-	-	-	-	-
K Shuttleworth	1970-1971	5	1071	427	12	5/47	5/41	35.58	2.39	89.2	1	0
A Sidebottom	1985-1985	1	112	65	1	1/65	1/65	65.00	3.48	112.0	0	0
RJ Sidebottom	2001-2010	22	4812	2231	79	7/47	10/139	28.24	2.78	60.9	5	1
CEW Silverwood	1996-2002	6	828	444	11	5/91	5/91	40.36	3.21	75.2	1	0
GC Small	1986-1991	17	3927	1871	55	5/48	8/183	34.01	2.85	71.4	2	0
CL Smith	1983-1986	8	102	39	3	2/31	2/31	13.00	2.29	34.0	0	0
MJK Smith	1958-1972	50	214	128	1	1/10	1/10	128.00	3.58	214.0	0	0
RA Smith	1988-1996	62	24	6	0	-	-	-	1.50	-	0	0
JA Snow	1965-1976	49	12021	5387	202	7/40	10/142	26.66	2.68	59.5	8	1
JB Statham	1951-1965	70	16056	6261	252	7/39	11/97	24.84	2.33	63.7	9	1
DS Steele	1975-1976	8	88	39	2	1/1	2/20	19.50	2.65	44.0	0	0
GB Stevenson	1980-1981	2	312	183	5	3/111	3/111	36.60	3.51	62.4	0	0
AJ Stewart	1990-2003	133	20	13	0	-	-	-	3.90	-	0	0
BA Stokes	2013-2014	6	1228	724	22	6/99	8/161	32.90	3.53	55.8	1	0
PM Such	1993-1999	11	3124	1242	37	6/67	8/145	33.56	2.38	84.4	2	0
GP Swann	2008-2013	60	15349	7642	255	6/65	10/132	29.96	2.98	60.1	17	3
JP Taylor	1993-1994	2	288	156	3	1/18	2/82	52.00	3.25	96.0	0	0
K Taylor	1959-1964	3	12	6	0	-	-	-	3.00	-	0	0
LB Taylor	1985-1985	2	381	178	4	2/34	3/73	44.50	2.80	95.2	0	0

England Test Bowling Averages 1962/3-2014

Player	Span	Mat	Balls	Runs	Wkts	BBI	BBM	Ave	Econ	SR	5	10
RW Taylor	1971-1984	57	12	6	0	-	-	-	3.00	-	0	0
JG Thomas	1986-1986	5	774	504	10	4/70	4/70	50.40	3.90	77.4	0	0
GP Thorpe	1993-2005	100	138	37	0	-	-	-	1.60	-	0	0
FJ Titmus	1955-1975	53	15118	4931	153	7/79	9/162	32.22	1.95	98.8	7	0
JC Tredwell	2010-2010	1	390	181	6	4/82	6/181	30.16	2.78	65.0	0	0
CT Tremlett	2007-2013	12	2902	1431	53	6/48	8/150	27.00	2.95	54.7	2	0
ME Trescothick	2000-2006	76	300	155	1	1/34	1/34	155.00	3.10	300.0	0	0
IJL Trott	2009-2013	49	702	398	5	1/5	1/5	79.60	3.40	140.4	0	0
FS Trueman	1952-1965	67	15178	6625	307	8/31	12/119	21.57	2.61	49.4	17	3
AJ Tudor	1998-2002	10	1512	963	28	5/44	7/109	34.39	3.82	54.0	1	0
PCR Tufnell	1990-2001	42	11288	4560	121	7/47	11/93	37.68	2.42	93.2	5	2
SD Udal	2005-2006	4	596	344	8	4/14	5/67	43.00	3.46	74.5	0	0
DL Underwood	1966-1982	86	21862	7674	297	8/51	13/71	25.83	2.10	73.6	17	6
MP Vaughan	1999-2008	82	978	561	6	2/71	2/71	93.50	3.44	163.0	0	0
A Ward	1969-1976	5	761	453	14	4/61	4/75	32.35	3.57	54.3	0	0
SL Watkin	1991-1993	3	534	305	11	4/65	6/152	27.72	3.42	48.5	0	0
M Watkinson	1995-1996	4	672	348	10	3/64	5/92	34.80	3.10	67.2	0	0
C White	1994-2002	30	3959	2220	59	5/32	5/57	37.62	3.36	67.1	3	0
P Willey	1976-1986	26	1091	456	7	2/73	2/73	65.14	2.50	155.8	0	0
NF Williams	1990-1990	1	246	148	2	2/148	2/148	74.00	3.60	123.0	0	0
RGD Willis	1971-1984	90	17357	8190	325	8/43	9/92	25.20	2.83	53.4	16	0
D Wilson	1964-1971	6	1472	466	11	2/17	3/72	42.36	1.89	133.8	0	0
CR Woakes	2013-2014	4	570	313	6	3/30	4/54	52.16	3.29	95.0	0	0
B Wood	1972-1978	12	98	50	0	-	-	-	3.06	-	0	0
RA Woolmer	1975-1981	19	546	299	4	1/8	1/8	74.75	3.28	136.5	0	0

England Players in ICC Top 20 1962-2014

Year (1st Sept)	Batsman 1-10	Batsman 11-20	Bowler 1-10	Bowler 11-20
1962	Dexter, Cowdrey, Barrington, Pullar	Graveney	Trueman, Staham, Allen, Lock	Dexter, Coldwell
1963	Barrington, Dexter, Cowdrey		Trueman, Allen, Statham, Lock	Titmus, Dexter, Knight
1964	Barrington, Cowdrey, Dexter		Trueman, Titmus, Allen	Statham, Lock, Dexter
1965	Barrington, Cowdrey, Dexter		Titmus, Allen	Statham, Lock
1966	Barrington, Cowdrey	Dexter	Higgs, Titmus	Lock, Knight
1967	Barrington, Cowdrey	Graveney, Dexter	Higgs	Titmus, Illingworth
1968	Edrich, Cowdrey	Boycott, Graveney, D'Oliveira	Snow, Illingworth	Titmus, Underwood, Brown
1969	Edrich	Cowdrey, D'Oliveira, Boycott	Underwood, Snow, Illingworth	Titmus
1970	Edrich, Cowdrey	D'Oliveira, Boycott	Underwood, Snow	Illingworth, Titmus
1971	Boycott, Edrich	D'Oliveira, Knott	Underwood, Snow, Illingworth	Titmus
1972	Boycott	D'Oliveira, Edrich, Knott	Underwood, Snow, Illingworth	
1973	Boycott	Greig, Fletcher	Arnold, Snow, Underwood	Illingworth
1974	Amiss, Fletcher	Greig, Boycott	Underwood, Arnold, Greig	Snow, Old
1975	Greig, Fletcher	Edrich, Amiss, Knott	Underwood, Greig	Snow, Old
1976		Greig, Fletcher, Amiss, Knott	Underwood	Greig, Old, Willis
1977	Greig, Boycott	Knott, Woolmer	Underwood. Willis	Greig, Old
1978	Boycott	Gower, Knott	Botham, Willis, Underwood	Edmonds, Old
1979	Gower, Boycott	Botham	Botham, Willis, Hendrick	Underwood, Old, Edmonds
1980	Boycott	Gower, Gooch	Botham, Willis	Hendrick, Underwood, Old
1981	Boycott	Gower, Botham, Gooch	Botham, Willis	Hendrick
1982	Botham, Gower	Gooch	Botham, Willis	Emburey, Lever
1983	Gower	Botham, Lamb, Tavare	Willis	Botham, Miller

England Players in ICC Top 20 1962-2014

Year (1st Sept)	Batsman 1-10	Batsman 11-20	Bowler 1-10	Bowler 11-20
1984	Gower	Botham, Lamb	Botham	Cook
1985	Gower, Gatting, Robinson	Lamb, Botham, Gooch	Botham	Emburey, Edmonds, Ellison
1986	Gower Gatting	Gooch	Botham	Emburey, Edmonds
1987	Gower Gatting		Dilley	Edmonds, Botham, Emburey
1988	Gooch, Gower	Broad, Gatting	Dilley, Foster	
1989		Gower, Smith		Foster
1990	Gooch, Smith	Atherton, Lamb		Fraser, Foster, Malcolm
1991	Gooch, Smith			DeFreitas, Fraser, Foster, Malcolm
1992	Gooch, Smith	Stewart	DeFreitas	Fraser, Malcolm, Tufnell, Foster
1993	Gooch, Smith	Atherton, Stewart		Fraser, DeFreitas Malcolm
1994	Stewart, Gooch, Atherton	Hick	Fraser	DeFreitas
1995	Thorpe, Atherton, Hick	Stewart, Smith		Fraser
1996	Atherton, Stewart	Thorpe		Cork, Fraser
1997	Thorpe	Stewart, Atherton		Gough
1998	Stewart	Atherton, Thorpe, Hussain	Fraser	Gough, Cork
1999	Stewart, Hussain			Gough, Caddick
2000	Stewart	Atherton	Caddick	Gough
2001		Thorpe, Stewart, Trescothick	Gough	Caddick
2002		Trescothick, Vaughan	Hoggard	Caddick, Gough
2003	Vaughan	Butcher		
2004		Thorpe, Trescothick	Harmison	Giles, Hoggard, Flintoff
2005	Trescothick	Strauss	Hoggard	Flintoff, Harmison, Jones, Giles
2006		Pietersen, Strauss, Trescothick	Flintoff, Hoggard	Harmison
2007	Pietersen	Collingwood, Cook	Hoggard	Flintoff, Panesar
2008	Pietersen	Cook	Sidebottom, Panesar	Anderson, Flintoff
2009		Strauss, Pietersen	Anderson, Swann	Broad, Sidebottom
2010		Trott	Swann, Anderson, Broad	
			Anderson, Swann, Broad	Tremlett, Finn

England Players in ICC Top 20 1962-2014

Year (1st Sept)	Batsman 1-10	Batsman 11-20	Bowler 1-10	Bowler 11-20
2011	Cook, Bell, Trott, Pietersen		Anderson, Swann, Broad, Bresnan	Tremlett, Finn
2012	Pietersen	Cook, Trott, Bell	Anderson, Broad	Swann, Finn
2013	Bell, Cook	Pietersen, Trott, Proir	Swann, Anderson, Broad	
2014	Root	Bell	Anderson, Broad	

Acknowledgements / Bibliography

Primary Sources

Interviews: the late Sir Alec Bedser; Mr Ted Dexter; Mr John Hampshire; Mr Doug Insole; Mr Micky Stewart

The MCC Archives, the Lord's library

Secondary Sources

Fred by John Arlott (Eyre and Spotiswoode, 1971)

Opening Up by Mike Atherton (Hodder and Stoughton, 2002)

Phil Edmonds: A Singular Man by Simon Barnes (Guild Publishing, 1986)

The Art of Captaincy by Mike Brearley (Hodder and Stoughton, 1985)

Micky Stewart and the Changing Face of Cricket by Stephen Chalke (Fairfield Books, 2012)

With England in Australia by John Clarke (Stanley Paul, 1966)

MCC: the Autobiography of a Cricketer by Colin Cowdrey (Hodder and Stoughton, 1976)

Driving Ambition by Andrew Strauss (Hodder and Stoughton, 2013)

I Declare by Mike Denness (Arthur Baker, 1977)

Ted Dexter Declares by Ted Dexter (Stanley Paul, 1966)

Behind the Shades by Duncan Fletcher (Simon and Shuster, 2007)

My Autobiography by Graham Gooch (Collins Willow, 1995)

Gower – the Autobiography by David Gower (Fontana, 1993)

Playing with Fire by Nasser Hussain (Michael Joseph, 2004)

Yorkshire and Back by Ray Illingworth (Queen Anne press, 1980)

One-Man Committee by Ray Illingworth and Jack Bannister (Headline Book Publishing, 1996)

Lord Ted by Alan Lee (Gollancz/Witherby, 1995)

Cricket Rebel by John Snow (Hamlyn, 1976)

David Gower by Rob Steen (Victor Gollancz, 1995)

Time to Declare by Michael Vaughan (Hodder and Stoughton, 2009)

Lasting the Pace by Bob Willis (Collins Willow, 1985)

Quotations and extracts from Wisden Cricketers' Almanack are reproduced by kind permission of John Wisden & Co Ltd

Daily Telegraph, Sunday Telegraph, The Times, The Sunday Times, The Independent, The Independent on Sunday, The Guardian, The Cricketer, Cricinfo.com and cricketarchive.com

Pictures

All pictures courtesy of Topfoto with exceptions of:

Illingworth and Bairstow – The David Frith Collection

Rear cover – Clare Skinner/MCC

Index

Adams, Chris 79
Adams, Paul 197
Agar, Ashton 211
Akram, Wasim 111
Alderman, Terry 143
Ali, Moeen 119-20, 213, 233
Allen, David 215-6
Allen, Sir George 'Gubby' 2, 48, 98
Alley, Bill 137
Ambrose, Tim 115
Ames, Les 44, 46, 98
Amiss, Dennis iii, 5, 19, 27, 43, 53-4, 56, 60, 94, 128, 131, 133-7, 140, 161
Anderson, James 8, 20-1, 26, 28, 30, 87, 117, 176, 202-10, 213, 229
Andrew, Keith 90
Arlott, John 183
Arnold, Geoff 53, 188-9
Atherton, Michael 4, 13-15, 21, 73-4, 76, 78-80, 83, 88, 125, 152, 155-7, 162, 164-9, 196
Athey, Bill 70, 135, 143, 144
Bailey, Jack 98-9
Bailey, Rob 72, 74, 145, 156-7
Bairstow, David 19, 101
Bairstow, Jonny 21, 25-6, 28, 115, 177-80
Balderstone, Chris 53
Ballance, Gary 35, 179-81
Bannister, Alex 91, 128
Barber, Bob iii, 3, 17, 22, 43-4, 93-4, 128-9
Barlow, Graham 133
Barnes, Simon 32, 87
Barnett, Kim 19, 70, 72, 76, 145, 155
Barrington, Ken iii, iv, 3, 5, 27, 40, 58, 93-7, 102, 121-2, 124-5, 129-30
Bell, Ian 26-7, 87, 171-2, 174-8, 181
Benjamin, Joey 14, 195-6
Bedser, Sir Alec 4, 11, 44, 46, 48, 60, 98, 101, 127, 190
Benson, Mark 156
Bicknell, Martin 19-20
Bishop, Ian 164
Blackwell, Ian 228
Blakey, Richard 106-8
Bligh, Hon Ivo 58
Blofeld, Henry 40
Bolus, Brian 6, 49
Bopara, Ravi 25-6, 84, 91, 173-5, 177-8, 203
Borthwick, Steve 119-20, 217, 232
Botham, Sir Ian v, 12, 15, 17, 28, 31-2, 38, 57-9, 61, 68, 71, 74, 76, 81, 90, 100, 102, 104-5, 110-1. 120, 132, 136, 146, 161, 188, 190-1, 194, 206
Boycott, Geoff iii, 3, 17, 19, 27, 31-2, 43-4, 48-9, 50, 56, 60, 96, 121, 126-8, 134-5, 137-8, 140-1
Brearley, Mike 17, 23, 29, 32, 49, 53, 56, 58-9, 68, 75, 85, 87, 101, 116-7, 123, 127, 133, 136, 220-1
Bresnan, Tim 20-1, 26, 116-7, 210-2
Briggs, Simon 229
Broad, Chris iv, 63, 70-2, 142-3, 155
Broad, Stuart 20-1, 25-6, 28, 30, 87, 202-3, 206-11, 229
Brown, David 95-6, 186-7, 197
Brown, Freddie 55
Brown, Simon 23-4
Burge, Peter 183
Butcher, Alan 19-20, 136, 140

Index

Butcher, Basil 183
Butcher, Mark 12, 21, 74, 166, 168-71
Butcher, Roland 17
Buttler, Joss 22, 115-6
Caddick, Andrew 197-201, 205, 227
Capel, David 105, 194
Carberry, Michael 25, 178-9
Carr, Donald 41, 45, 98, 151
Cartwright, Tom 95-9, 186
Chappell, Greg 57, 100
Childs, John 223
Clark, David 44, 46, 48
Clarke, Giles 34
Clarke, John 186
Clarke, Michael 86
Close, Brian 2, 12, 19, 22, 43-7, 49, 53, 68, 75, 93, 98, 123-5, 136-7, 176-7, 207
Collingwood, Paul v, 23, 25, 84-5, 170-1, 173-4, 176-7, 207
Compton, Denis 67, 122, 124
Compton, Nick 74, 222, 223
Coney, Jeremy 64
Constant, David 63
Cook, Alastair 15, 27-8, 30, 86-8, 115, 119, 161, 172, 176-7, 179, 181, 211, 232
Cook, Geoff 17, 19-20, 140-1
Cook, Nick 74, 222, 233
Cope, Geoff 219
Cork, Dominic iv, 194, 197, 199-201
Cottam, Bob 96, 98, 186
Cowans, Norman 30, 192, 197
Cowdrey, Christopher 18, 56, 68-70, 75, 105

Cowdrey, Colin iii, 2, 3, 11, 27, 38-44, 47-8, 51, 94-6, 98, 121-7, 129-30, 132, 134, 136, 146
Crawley, John 13, 24, 91, 153, 159, 164-6, 167, 170
Croft, Robert 224, 226-7
Curtis, Tim 71-2, 155
Davies, Mike 227
Dawson, Richard 24, 28
DeFreitas, Phillip 71, 99, 193-5, 206
Dellor, Ralph 169
Denly, Joe 22
Denness, Mike 2, 12, 31, 38, 49, 51-3, 75, 79, 127, 131, 134, 189
de Villiers, Abraham 90
Dexter, Ted 3, 5-6, 11-13, 17, 24, 38-41, 69-71, 73-4, 76, 79, 90-1, 93, 95-6, 121-2, 124-5, 129-130, 135-6, 145-6, 156, 215
Dilley, Graham 30, 64, 70, 191-2, 194
Dobell, George 213
D'Oliveira, Basil 3, 12-3, 29, 43-4, 93-5, 97-9, 102, 130
Donald, Allan 168
Downton, Paul 11, 35, 101-4, 149
Ealham, Mark 110
Edmonds, Philippe 32, 53, 103, 219-222, 233
Edrich, John 18, 27, 43-4, 49-50, 52, 74, 95-6, 124, 126-7, 132, 134-7
Elcock, Ricardo 74, 110, 194
Elliott, Matthew 193
Ellison, Richard iv, 70, 192
Emburey, John 19, 60, 67, 70, 72, 101-3, 149, 151, 220-2, 225, 233
Engel, Matthew 67, 150
Fairbrother, Neil 22, 149, 152

Index

Finn, Steven 21, 26, 30, 117, 209-13
Flavell, Jack 16-7, 183
Fletcher, Duncan 8-9, 14, 24, 30-1, 33-4, 79-83, 109, 112, 114, 160, 168-9, 171-2, 200-1, 203, 224, 227-9
Fletcher, Keith iii, 6, 8, 13, 17, 20, 50-1, 53, 59, 60, 75-6, 95-6, 107-8, 130-2, 149, 161, 163, 196
Flintoff, Andrew v, 8, 58, 79, 81-4, 90, 110-4, 116, 119-20, 132-5, 171, 173, 174, 202, 204-5, 207, 209-10, 229
Flower, Andy 10, 15, 33, 87, 112, 118
Foster, James 28, 31, 112-3, 115
Foster, Neil 70-1, 77, 158, 192, 194
Fowler, Graeme 19, 140-1
Fraser, Angus iv, 13, 71, 73, 106, 187, 194-8, 200, 202
French, Bruce 70, 103-4
Gallian, Jason 166
Gatting, Mike 4-5, 13-15, 20, 32, 37-8, 62-6, 68-70, 72, 76-7, 83, 143-4, 149-53, 155, 158, 160-2, 164-5, 192, 225, 227
Gavaskar, Sunni 188
Giddins, Ed 201
Gifford, Norman 5, 49, 216-8
Giles, Ashley 8, 10, 82, 225-226, 227-229, 233
Gilliat, Richard 136
Gilligan, Arthur 46, 98
Gooch, Graham 4, 12-14, 17-18, 28, 32, 53, 57, 60-1, 63, 67-70, 72-7, 78-9, 83, 105-110, 126, 135, 140-5, 147-9, 151-3, 155-7, 160-2, 166, 195, 223
Gough, Darren 79, 195-201, 205, 227
Gower, David 5, 12-13, 15, 20, 24, 27-8, 32-3, 38, 43-4, 61-2, 65, 68-71, 73-75, 77, 79, 83, 97, 103, 144-152, 155, 161-2, 167-8, 221, 223
Graveney, David 7-9, 11, 14, 28, 70, 77-8, 80, 82, 196, 229
Graveney, Tom 43-4, 47, 74, 95-6, 121, 124-5, 129-30, 135
Graves, Colin 35
Greig, Tony v, 12, 51, 53-6, 81, 90-1, 99-101, 120, 130, 181, 219
Griffith, Charlie 43, 185
Griffith, Billy 43, 45, 98
Habib, Aftab 24, 170
Haddin, Brad 211
Hadlee, Sir Richard 32
Hall, Wes 43, 185
Hamilton, Gavin 79, 230
Hampshire, John 131-2
Harmison, Stephen 8, 26, 30, 82, 201-4, 206-9, 229
Harris, Mike 136
Hayes, Frank 132
Headley, Dean 23-4, 197-8, 200
Hegg, Warren 109, 113
Hemmings, Eddie 221-2, 233
Hendrick, Mike 57, 60, 188-9, 191
Herath, Rangana 87
Hick, Graeme 15, 25, 110, 148-9, 152-3, 157-163, 165
Higgs, Ken 16, 28-9, 43-4, 95, 187, 191
Hobbs, Robin 3, 216-7
Hoggard, Matthew v, 8, 23, 26, 30, 201-4, 206, 208, 229

Index

Holder, Vanburn 136
Holding, Michael 135-7
Hollioake, Adam 110
Hollioake, Ben 22, 110
Hughes, Mervyn 148
Humpage, Geoff 22, 60
Hunte, Conrad 126, 183
Hussain, Nasser 4, 12, 14, 24, 50, 74, 77-80, 83, 88, 109, 145, 156-60, 162, 165, 167, 169-70, 173, 198-99, 201, 224, 226-227
Hutton, Sir Len 39, 43, 166
Igglesden, Alan 74, 194
Illingworth, Raymond 2, 6-8, 11, 13-4, 18, 28, 43, 47-9, 50, 74, 92, 95, 99, 101, 108, 110-1, 120, 131-2, 152, 159, 164, 167, 187, 195-7, 215-8, 222, 224-6, 230
Illingworth, Richard 223, 225-226
Insole, Doug 3, 11, 44, 46, 96, 98
Irani, Ronnie 110
Jackman, Robin 58
Jameson, John 136
Jarvis, Paul 70-1, 194
Johnson, Mitchell 86, 180
Jones, Geraint v, 25-6, 31, 113-5, 229
Jones, Jeff 28, 96, 186-7
Jones, Simon 30, 173, 197, 201-2, 204
Jordan, Chris 212-3
Joyce, Ed 221, 231
Kallis, Jacques 90
Kenyon, Don 44, 46, 98
Kerrigan, Simon 20-1, 118-9, 231
Key, Robert 170-1, 173
Khan, Imran 63, 90
Khan, Shakeel 63

Kieswetter, Craig 21, 115
Kirtley, James 201, 206
Knight, Barry 91-2, 94-5
Knight, Nick 22, 159, 166-9
Knott, Alan 28-9, 54, 60, 91, 96, 99-103
Laker, Jim 132, 217
Lamb, Allan 12, 29, 68, 72, 74, 143-7, 155, 157, 161-2
Larkins, Wayne 17, 19, 60, 74, 135, 156, 168
Larwood, Harold 187
Lathwell, Mark 24, 77, 158
Lawrence, David 19
Lawry, Bill 126
Lee, Alan 65, 77-8, 106, 108, 146, 163, 165, 192, 195, 223
Lever, Peter 19, 189
Lever, John 25, 29, 57, 60, 191, 193
Lewis, Chris 110-1, 158, 194, 196, 206
Lewis, Tony 18, 49, 50, 75
Lillee, Dennis 18, 51-2, 57, 130, 135, 188
Lloyd, Clive 137
Lloyd, David 7-8, 14, 135, 158
Lock, Tony 45, 216-7
Loudon, Alex 228
Loye, Mal 22
Luckhurst, Brian 29, 134-5
Lush, Peter 63, 147
Lynch, Monty 22
McCague, Martin 13, 195, 196, 198
McDermott, Craig 148
McGrath, Anthony 170
MacLaurin, Lord 78
Maddy, Darren 168, 230
Mahmood, Sajid 229

Index

Malcolm, Devon 7, 71, 73, 194-7
Mallender, Neil 193
Marks, Victor 19, 103, 221-2
Marsh, Rodney 8, 113
Martin-Jenkins, Christopher 69
Masood, Asif 124
Mathews, Angelo 87
May, Peter 3-4, 6, 11, 38, 45-7, 60, 66, 68-9, 79, 98, 124, 130, 221
Maynard, Matthew 70, 72, 145, 165
Medlycott, Keith 74
Miandad, Javed 64
Milburn, Colin 18, 43, 94-5, 98, 129
Miller, Geoff 9, 11, 15, 53, 82, 101-3, 219-222, 229, 233
Miller, Keith 67
Mohammed, Dave 113
Moores, Peter 10, 15, 83, 85, 203, 207
Morgan, Eoin 23, 25-6, 28, 117, 176-8
Morris, Hugh 76, 156, 170
Morris, John 147
Mortimore, John 216
Moxon, Martyn 71, 76, 143, 155, 167
Mullally, Alan 23-4, 197-8, 200, 227
Murray, John 18, 43-4, 90-1, 96
Newport, Philip 20, 71, 194
Norfolk, 16th Duke of 92, 184
Old, Chris 57, 60, 188-9, 191
Onions, Graham 21, 204, 209-10, 212
Packer, Kerry 54-5, 134-5, 137, 219-20, 233 Palmer, Ken 63
Panesar, Monty 14, 20, 117-9, 174, 207, 228-31
Parfitt, Peter 91, 124-5
Parker, Paul 19-20
Parks, Jim 43-4, 47, 90-2, 114
Patel, Min 226
Patel, Samit 26, 117-9, 178-9, 230
Pattinson, Darren 207, 232
Pietersen, Kevin v, 8, 10, 22, 26, 28-9, 33-5, 84-5, 97, 171-8, 180-1, 203
Plunkett, Liam 28, 30, 212-3, 229
Pocock, Pat 28, 96, 217-8, 221-2, 225, 233
Pollock, Shaun 168
Ponting, Ricky 82
Price, John 13, 16-17, 186
Prideaux, Roger 47, 95-6, 98
Pringle, Derek 69, 74, 78, 104-5, 194
Prior, Matt 21-2, 87, 114-7, 120, 176
Pullar, Geoff 123, 126
Radford, Neal 193
Radley, Clive 16, 19, 134
Ramprakash, Mark 15, 25, 31, 78, 148, 157, 160-2, 165-6, 175
Rana, Shakeel 64-5
Randall, Derek 27, 133, 136-8, 141
Rankin, Boyd 26, 28, 120, 211-2
Read, Chris 14, 25-6, 31, 109, 113-5, 229
Reeve, Dermot 110
Rhodes, Steve 108-9, 111
Richards, Jack 103-4
Richards, Sir Vivian vi
Roberts, Sir Andy 136
Robins, Walter 3, 11, 39
Robinson, Tim 70-2, 142-3, 155,

Index

166-7
Robson, Sam 24, 180
Roope, Graham 53, 56, 131, 136
Root, Joe 28, 30, 35, 87, 118, 178-81
Rose, Brian 135
Rumsey, Fred 183-4
Russell, Eric 127
Russell, Jack 20, 73, 106-9, 166-7
Rutnagur, Dicky 219
Saggers, Mike 206
Salisbury, Ian 217, 225-7, 233
Sangakarra, Kumar 90
Schofield, Chris 25, 28, 217, 227
Schofield, Ken 8-9, 15
Selvey, Mike iv, 53
Shackleton, Derek 15, 185, 193
Shah, Owais 26, 84, 174-5
Sharpe, Philip 96, 125-6, 216
Sheppard, Rev David 39, 123, 126
Shuttleworth, Ken 187
Sidebottom, Arnie 60, 193
Sidebottom, Ryan 202-3, 206-10, 229
Silverwood, Chris 24, 80, 205
Singh, Yuvraj 208
Slack, Wilf 140
Small, Gladstone 71, 193-5
Smith, Alan 49, 69, 76, 90
Smith, Chris 141, 155
Smith, Mike 6, 13, 18, 38, 40-42, 45, 75, 90, 123, 125, 135-6, 184, 193, 215
Smith, Robin iv, 73, 149, 155, 157-8, 162-7
Snow, John iii, 12, 15, 19, 27-8, 32, 43-4, 48, 54, 95-6, 187-91, 202

Sobers, Sir Garry 47, 67, 90, 183
Solanki, Vikram 21, 169
Statham, Brian 38, 183, 185-6, 188, 199
Steele, David 16, 29, 53, 132-4
Steen, Rob 147
Stephenson, John 71, 74, 155-6
Stewart, Alec 27, 74, 7-80, 90, 106-9, 111-3, 120, 145, 149, 153, 156-7, 162, 166-70, 198
Stewart, Micky 5-6, 8, 12-3, 33, 40, 63, 65, 69-70, 76, 146
Stokes, Ben 118-9, 212-3
Strauss, Andrew 8, 15, 21-2, 25, 29, 31, 39, 80, 82, 83-6, 88, 112, 161, 170, 173-80
Streeton, Richard 162
Strudwick, Herbert 102
Subba Row, Raman 5, 64-5, 69
Such, Peter iv, 225-226, 233
Swann, Graeme v, 20, 22, 24, 29, 79, 101, 116-20, 176, 210, 226-7, 230-3
Swanton, E W 51, 97
Tavare, Chris 20, 72, 140-1, 155
Taylor, Clive 218
Taylor, Les 60, 193
Taylor, Bob 29, 57, 101-3, 120
Taylor, James 24-6, 28, 177-8, 180
Taylor, Neil 156
Terry, Paul 140
Thicknesse, John 52, 103, 147, 223
Thomas, Greg 30, 193
Thomson Jeff 18, 51, 70, 130, 135
Thomson, Ian 186
Thorpe, Graham iv, 13, 27, 79, 158-9, 162-4, 167, 169-72, 193

Index

Titmus, Fred 6, 43-4, 47, 52, 92, 215-9, 223, 225
Tredwell, James 231-2
Tremlett, Chris 20-1, 26, 118, 202, 207, 210-12, 229
Trescothick, Marcus 21-2, 30, 79, 81-2, 126, 168-72, 175
Trott, Jonathan v, 24, 29, 161, 170, 174-8, 181
Trueman, Fred iii, iv, 16, 27, 38, 45, 183-8, 190, 199, 202
Tudor, Alex 30, 197-8, 205
Tufnell, Phil 15, 158, 200, 223-228, 233
Tyson, Frank 30
Udal, Shaun 23, 228
Underwood, Derek 18, 28, 43, 52, 54, 57, 60, 95-6, 100, 102, 217-23, 230, 232
Vaughan, Michael 4, 8, 21, 24, 30-1, 79-85, 88, 126, 168-75, 203, 207
Walker, Max 52
Ward, Alan 28, 30, 170, 190
Warne, Shane 116, 152-3, 172, 225, 229
Washbrook, Cyril 124, 168
Watkin, Steve 193
Watkinson, Mike 14
Waugh, Steve vi, 64
Wellings, E M 42, 131, 215, 218
Wells, Alan 14, 70, 175
Wheatley, Ossie 4, 69, 70, 76
Whitaker, James 9, 11, 15
White, Craig 110-2, 153, 197, 200-1, 205
Wilde, Simon 81
Willey, Peter 53, 60, 102, 220
Williams, Neil 19-20
Willis, Bob 15, 28, 30, 32, 57-61, 83, 188-92, 196, 206, 221
Woakes, Chris 21, 118, 212-3
Wood, Barry 53, 131, 136
Wood, Mark 213
Woodcock, John 31, 49, 51, 58-9, 61, 97, 102, 104, 127, 131-2, 156, 189, 218
Woolmer, Bob 53-4, 60, 133-4
Wright, Graeme 66
Wright, Luke 21